Jeffrey Peake usefully demonstrates an important but often overlooked consequence of partisan polarization in Congress: it has rendered the treaty process unworkable. Having no option, presidents rely almost entirely on unilateral tools to make international agreements. This dysfunctional practice has weakened the role of Congress, undermined the country's international commitments, and decreased America's influence on international law.

George C. Edwards III, Texas A&M University and University of Oxford

No one has more thoroughly documented the decline of the U.S. treaty process than Jeffrey Peake. In this important book, Peake integrates and extends his groundbreaking empirical work on increasing presidential unilateralism in the making of international agreements. And he shows how this trend undermines the democratic legitimacy of international law and adversely impacts U.S. foreign policy. Both political scientists and international law scholars will learn a great deal from *Dysfunctional Diplomacy*.

Jack Goldsmith, Harvard University Law School

This is one of the most comprehensive and engaging modern accounts of a "lost art"—the politics of treaty ratification—in an era of deep partisanship and polarization in American politics. The rich data analysis in this book, combined with fascinating case studies of the politics of contemporary treaty ratification and the rise of executive agreements, expose key ingredients in our dysfunctional diplomacy. But they also offer us a way out by exposing critical nodes of resistance and challenge in the process.

Jeffrey S. Lantis, The College of Wooster

DYSFUNCTIONAL DIPLOMACY

US diplomacy is broken. As a result, the United States sits on the sidelines as the remainder of the world writes international law dealing with a host of vexing problems. The source of the dysfunction is domestic politics. Partisan polarization has rendered the domestic treaty process unworkable. Instead, presidents rely entirely on unilateral tools to complete their agreements, making them far weaker and less legitimate. Using a mixed-methods approach, Peake assesses the politics surrounding treaty ratification and the use of unilateral authority since World War Two, with a particular focus on the twenty-first century. He employs original data from 1949 through 2020, including 1,000 treaties and more than 3,000 executive agreements. The analysis provides case studies of the domestic politics of several recent international agreements, including on climate change, Iranian nuclear weapons, security in Iraq and Afghanistan, human rights, and the law of the sea.

Jeffrey S. Peake is Professor of Political Science at Clemson University, in Clemson, South Carolina, where he teaches courses on US politics, Congress, and U.S. foreign policy.

DYSFUNCTIONAL DIPLOMACY

The Politics of International Agreements in an Era of Partisan Polarization

Jeffrey S. Peake

Routledge
Taylor & Francis Group
NEW YORK AND LONDON

Designed cover image: Shutterstock/Jean-Pierre Thimot

First published 2023
by Routledge
605 Third Avenue, New York, NY 10158

and by Routledge
4 Park Square, Milton Park, Abingdon, Oxon, OX14 4RN

Routledge is an imprint of the Taylor & Francis Group, an informa business

ISBN: 978-1-032-38912-7 (hbk)
ISBN: 978-0-367-42977-5 (pbk)
ISBN: 978-1-003-34742-2 (ebk)

DOI: 10.4324/9781003347422

Typeset in Bembo
by Newgen Publishing UK

CONTENTS

ILLUSTRATIONS

Figure

Tables

ACKNOWLEDGMENTS

This book was a long time coming. My first book on the topic, *Treaty Politics and the Rise of Executive Agreements*, co-authored with Glen Krutz, was published in 2009. We documented how the process evolved during the twentieth century. The period we assessed ended in 2000. Soon after, the domestic politics surrounding the treaty process began to change, and the changes were not well explained by the prior work. In 2012, I published an article with Glen Krutz and Tyler Hughes assessing the first few years of the Obama Administration, where we reported significant changes to the process. Obama was avoiding treaties and when he submitted treaties, they rarely were approved. As a result, I had to rethink treaty politics and set out to document how the process worked and why we were witnessing these significant changes. As I did so, the problem worsened, and the apparent cause seemed clear to me. The U.S. political system suffers from record-levels of partisan polarization, which has broken the Senate treaty process, emboldened opponents to U.S. participation in international law, and provided additional incentives for presidents to rely on unilateral tools to complete international agreements. As a result, international commitments made by recent presidents are far weaker and the U.S. often excludes itself when the world writes international law.

Documenting the process meant collecting a lot of data on treaties and executive agreements. For help with this, I relied on Clemson University's innovative undergraduate student research program, Creative Inquiry. The program provided modest funding for data collection, analysis, and dissemination of results. Most importantly, it provided outstanding undergraduate research assistants, who got to experience the research process first-hand, and several were able to travel to conferences to present papers stemming from the project. The Clemson undergraduate students who worked on the project over the years include Maeve Cuddy, Chase Forrester, Benjamin Goldstein, Courtney Hall, Clay Hamlett, Anna

Herd, Jade Killion, Ashley Lambert, Erica Lendl, Audrey McMakin, Reece Pelley, Danielle Preskitt, Sarah Quarles, Elizabeth Wilson, and Morgan Winkler. Without their help, it would have been impossible to code 1,000 treaties and over 3,000 executive agreements and write case studies on more than a dozen major international agreements. The most enjoyable part of working on this project was the discussions with these students, who are passionate about politics and making the world a better place. Academic colleagues were also helpful in providing encouragement and sharing ideas about data. I would especially like to thank Kiki Caruson, George Edwards, Jack Goldsmith, and Jeff Lantis.

I am also thankful for the support provided by the editors at Routledge, who gave me a great deal of freedom to work on this project at my own pace. Their patience as I worked through delays to add analysis of the completed Trump administration made for a better, more complete book. Finally, I thank my family. Lori Peake has been an incredibly supportive spouse and I am lucky to have her and the support of my two sons, Jacob, and Nathan.

Additional Resources

The data that support the findings of this book are openly available in The Harvard Dataverse, available at: https://dataverse.harvard.edu/dataverse/jeffreypeake/

1

INTRODUCTION

In the summer of 2015, the Obama administration was nearing completion of one of its most important international agreements, the Iran Nuclear Agreement. The multilateral agreement was designed to curtail Iran's nascent nuclear weapons program in exchange for the reduction of severe economic sanctions. It was the culmination of more than six years of diplomatic work on the part of the administration and the centerpiece of President Obama's foreign policy legacy. In the end, the administration signed the agreement, but largely cut Congress out of the process, something that frustrated Republicans who sought to scuttle the deal. During congressional testimony on the agreement in 2015, when asked why one of the most important agreements completed by Obama was not completed as a treaty, Secretary of State John Kerry responded, "I spent quite a few years ago trying to get a lot of treaties through the United States Senate, and frankly, it's become physically impossible. You can't pass a treaty anymore" (Roberts 2015).[1]

Indeed, President Obama's experience with the treaty process was unlike any of his predecessors in that it was fraught with partisanship and numerous failed efforts to push stalled treaties through the US Senate. Even bilateral treaties, which typically sailed through the process, were met with substantial delay, or even ignored by the Senate. The problem was highlighted most spectacularly in 2012 when the UN Convention on the Rights of the Disabled, a key human rights treaty based on US domestic law, failed in a disastrous floor vote in the Senate. Democrats controlled the Senate for the first six years of Obama's presidency yet were unable to move many treaties Obama supported through the chamber. As a result of the dysfunction in the treaty approval process, Obama grew to rely more on his unilateral executive authority than his predecessors to complete international agreements, pushing the envelope of executive power in this area (Goldsmith 2016), a trend that has been continued by his successors. Diplomacy without Congress, however,

DOI: 10.4324/9781003347422-1

leads to less resilient agreements, as evidenced by President Trump's withdrawal from the Iran Nuclear Agreement in 2018.

What caused the recent dysfunction in the treaty process and what are its implications for US foreign policy? These are the questions that I seek to answer in this book. Casual observers of US politics are likely to point to partisan polarization as the reason why the Senate process no longer works effectively, and they would be right. Partisan polarization occurs when "the preferences of legislators (or any policymaker) become bimodal" based on the two political parties, and the "two modes move farther apart" (Lee 2015, 263). Treaties require supermajority (two-thirds) votes in the Senate to pass, and mustering sizable bipartisan majorities has become more difficult as the two political parties have become more ideologically polarized. Partisan polarization is only part of the answer, however. Presidents have a great deal of freedom in how they choose to complete their international agreements. In fact, most international agreements are not treaties at all, but instead are completed using the president's unilateral authority over executive agreements. During the twentieth century, executive agreements overtook treaties as the primary diplomatic tool used by presidents to complete binding international agreements. Even so, presidents still used treaties to finalize many of the most significant agreements and to codify US efforts to lead in the making of international law (Krutz and Peake 2009). That no longer appears to be the case, as Obama and his successors have pretty much abandoned treaties altogether, opting instead for unilateral tools. And, for its part, Congress has been unable or unwilling to check presidential unilateralism.

The implications for treaty dysfunction are severe, as I describe throughout this book. In brief, the United States has a commitment problem. While the rest of the world writes international law, they can no longer count on the United States to fully participate, largely due to its domestic politics. Thus, weak deals are completed to address potentially devastating international problems like climate change and nuclear weapons proliferation. As David Kaye (2013) argues, treaty dysfunction has limited Americans' ability to shape international law. The dysfunction affects the negotiation stage, as US diplomats are unable to use the prospects for domestic ratification as an argument to help shape treaty provisions, as other states cannot count on the United States to fully ratify the agreement. Moreover, as a nonparty state to numerous multilateral conventions, the United States is unable to shape the rules governing how the world addresses key issues like the exploitation of seabed resources or freedom of the high seas.

In this chapter, I provide a base of knowledge on the treaty power, its historical development, and how it has changed since the Constitution was written. I also lay out the general theoretical perspective of the book, which emphasizes the importance of domestic politics in formulating foreign policy. As the history reveals, norms surrounding the treaty process developed during the Cold War, which allowed presidents to efficiently negotiate and execute diplomacy (Krutz and Peake 2009). In brief, presidents would complete most international agreements unilaterally as executive agreements, reserving the treaty power for certain types of agreements and agreements of special significance. The Senate, for its part, would give due consideration to the president's treaties. However, the norms that worked well for the latter half of the twentieth century have deteriorated during the twenty-first century due to the increase in partisan polarization and the politicization of a broader set of foreign policy issues governed by international agreements, including the environment, human rights, arms control, and security cooperation. Thus, the system, as designed by the framers and developed over two centuries, has weakened to such a degree that US leadership in the realm of international law is now compromised, and US diplomacy is dysfunctional.

Recent Trends in the Treaty Process

The history reveals that a deeply politicized process surrounding the treaty process emerged in the late nineteenth and early twentieth centuries: another period of heightened partisan polarization. World War Two, and the resulting consensus favoring executive authority in foreign policy, however, pushed international agreement making toward an approach that valued efficiency and the maintenance of US leadership abroad, resulting in the rise of executive agreements, the unilateral alternative to treaties. This is the argument that I made in my 2009 book on the topic with Glen Krutz, *Treaty Politics and the Rise of Executive Agreements*. During the second half of the twentieth century, while 94 percent of all international agreements were completed as executive agreements rather than as treaties, Congress participated in the most consequential agreements, as one would expect in a system that valued shared power. During the post–Cold War period, the process that developed during the twentieth century began to break down, setting the stage for the more recent period, which is the primary focus of this book.

The balance between executive unilateralism and shared power with Congress that developed during the twentieth century began to unravel during the George W. Bush administration, in the wake of 9/11 and during the war on terror. Its full unravelling culminated during the subsequent Obama administration. The use of treaties declined significantly during the Obama presidency, as Obama submitted far fewer treaties to the Senate for approval than his predecessors. Obama submitted just under five treaties per year, whereas his predecessors since Franklin Roosevelt submitted about 16 per year. President Obama's treaty record was abysmal—when he submitted treaties to the Senate, he succeeded at far lower rates than any of his predecessors. As I demonstrate in this book, partisan polarization was partly to blame. More than any president before him, Obama relied overwhelmingly on unilateral authority rather than treaties in forging international agreements, which resulted in much weaker and less resilient commitments. In 2017, Donald Trump entered office with a clearly hostile attitude toward international agreements; almost immediately he ordered a reassessment of all multilateral agreements. During his one term in office, President Trump submitted just five treaties, the fewest by a president in the modern era. In fact, Trump formally left as many treaties as he signed and submitted to the Senate. Through April 2022, President Biden had submitted just two treaties to the Senate, signaling a continuation of the trend. All the while, the Senate, for the most part, refused to play its part in the institutional process, withholding its advice and consent to major treaties.

In a sense, then, this book is an update to my previous book on the topic. However, the changes to the process recently require a reconsideration of the conclusions of that prior work. In the book, *Treaty Politics*, we argued that the rise of executive agreements does not represent a trampling over the separation of powers, which is a view expressed by some scholars, but rather was a rational response by separate institutions sharing power to the need for efficiency and predictability in completing international agreements in an uncertain world. While the desire for efficiency may have led to the rise in executive agreements, it is difficult to look at today's treaty politics and conclude that the process is efficient or working effectively. Moreover, the process has gotten to be politicized to the point that it has broken down and presidents now rely overwhelmingly on unilateral tools of diplomacy, to the detriment of US foreign policy. President Obama's disuse of treaties, the degree to which his treaties were ignored in the Senate, his reliance on unilateral methods of diplomacy, and Trump's behavior on international agreements, however, requires a reassessment of this earlier argument. The rise in executive agreements and other unilateral diplomatic tools during the twentieth century did not mean the near complete absence of treaties and participation by Congress, as twentieth-century presidents continued to submit many consequential treaties to the Senate, which approved a large share of submitted treaties.

Because the Obama administration so rarely used treaties, the basic "institutional bargain" described in *Treaty Politics* appears to have been set aside for a process that overwhelmingly favors executive unilateralism. As we saw play out during the Trump presidency, this has profound implications for US foreign policy. Not only has separation of powers broken down, but the credibility of US commitments is significantly diminished as a result. The United States is often unable to participate in making international law, which compromises its leadership of international institutions created to solve vexing transnational problems like climate change and arms proliferation (Kaye 2013). Moreover, President Trump's reversals of Obama's signature international agreements signals to potential agreement partners those commitments made by one president may not bind future presidents. This is an untenable position for US diplomacy.

Defining Concepts

This book is about the US domestic politics of international agreements. When we think of international agreements, we typically think of treaties. Other forms of international agreements exist, however, including executive agreements and the more nebulous political commitment, thus it is important at the outset to define what it is we are talking about. Treaty is a term that differs depending on whether one is considering international law or US domestic (i.e., constitutional) law. Under international law, treaty simply means a formal, legally binding agreement between two or more sovereign states establishing a legal commitment. Thus, the term is quite broad and encompasses all legally binding international agreements completed by the United States, including all forms of executive agreements. Under US domestic law, however, the term treaty has a narrower definition. Also referred to as "Article II treaties," the domestic law definition includes only those international agreements signed by the president or their agent and submitted to the Senate for advice and consent. Synonyms for treaty include convention, accord, agreement, compact, and protocol. Most of the historically significant international agreements completed by the United States, at least for most of its history, are Article II treaties.

Executive agreements are a form of international agreement holding the same legal authority as a treaty under international law, but they are not submitted to the Senate for advice and consent. Typically, executive agreements are completed upon signature by the president or their agent. In other words, executive agreements represent binding international law, and international law does not distinguish between the two types of agreements. However, executive agreements represent a different category under domestic law in terms of how they are completed. The Supreme Court has regularly upheld the use of executive agreements in place of treaties, indicating in *United States v. Pink* (315 US 203 [1942]) that "all international compacts and agreements" are to be treated "with similar dignity" as treaties. Some important distinctions do exist for the purposes of domestic law, however, placing duly ratified treaties as more significant than executive agreements.[2]

There are also important political differences, in that treaties are often given greater weight by international actors because they have the imprimatur of legislative approval, whereas executive agreements usually do not, and thus a treaty is seen as a more credible international commitment (Martin 2000). While most executive agreements involve technical matters and often lack much controversy, they have been used to complete significant international agreements ranging from important agreements on trade (e.g., NAFTA), arms control (e.g., the original Strategic Arms Limitation Talks agreement with the Soviet Union), US security commitments (e.g., to Iraq and Afghanistan during the Bush and Obama administrations), foreign aid commitments, and ending wars (e.g., including the Vietnam War in 1973 and hostilities between NATO and Serbia in 1999).

Political commitments are international agreements whereby the president or president's agent makes a commitment to another state or multiple states to undertake a particular action. Political commitments are neither a treaty nor an executive agreement under domestic law and are not considered a formal treaty under international law and are nonbinding under international law. "As a result, a successor President is not bound by a previous President's political commitment under either domestic or international law and can thus legally disregard it at will" (Bradley and Goldsmith 2018, 1201). Political commitments are part of the president's plenary foreign policy powers as chief diplomat. Presidents have completed political commitments on the entire range of diplomatic topics, including climate change (the 2008 Group of Eight Declaration on the Environment and Climate Change), the opening of formal relations with the People's Republic of China (the Shanghai Communiqué), and security assurances providing for the denuclearization of former Soviet states (the 1994 Budapest Memorandum on Security Assurances).

Each form of agreement uses a separate process to complete. The Article II treaty process is quite cumbersome and includes five basic steps, including: (1) the president or his agents negotiate and sign the treaty; (2) the president transmits the treaty to the Senate via a memorandum that requests advice and consent, laying out the president's reasons for seeking ratification of the treaty; (3) the treaty is referred to the Senate Foreign Relations Committee which writes the resolution of ratification and reports it to the full Senate; (4) the treaty is debated and voted on the Senate floor, requiring a two-thirds vote for approval; (5) the president ratifies the treaty by signing the instrument of ratification, which is then exchanged with treaty partners, having the effect of entering the treaty into force for domestic and international law. The president formally declares an agreement is a treaty, under domestic law, by transmitting it to the Senate for advice and consent. During the committee stage of the process, the committee may decide to attach conditions to the treaty, typically referred to as reservations, understandings, or declarations (RUDs), which will become part of the resolution considered on the floor. Additional RUDs can be added on the floor and can include significant policy riders altering the treaty or its interpretation or even addressing policies unrelated to the treaty (Auerswald and Maltzman 2003).

Executive agreements, on the other hand, are negotiated by the executive and then signed by the executive branch official, typically going into effect upon signature or once the other parties to the agreement complete their ratification process. Executive agreements are completed unilaterally by the executive branch, either based in some congressionally delegated authority, authority pursuant to a prior treaty, or the president's plenary foreign policy powers.[3] Thus, executive agreements provide the president with a unilateral tool, meaning without congressional involvement, to complete a legally binding international agreement. Executive agreements are a foreign policy tool that provides presidents with an efficient and expedient mechanism to complete international agreements. Of course, they also present presidents an avenue to avoid congressional checks on their diplomatic powers. Political commitments are also unilateral, but given their nonbinding nature are a much weaker form of international agreement in terms of being credible commitments.

Given these options available to presidents, why do presidents use treaties at all? Why has Congress seemingly acquiesced to the widespread use of executive agreements to complete important international commitments? I addressed these questions extensively in prior work, pointing to demands for efficiency and credibility in the international agreement process (Krutz and Peake 2009). While the questions remain relevant, the abandonment of treaties by recent presidents requires a fresh look at the treaty process in today's era of polarized politics.

International Agreements: A Brief Political History

Any discussion of the history of the treaty power must begin with the Constitution. Article II, §2 of the US Constitution states, "The President . . . shall have the Power, by and with the Advice and Consent of the Senate, to make Treaties, provided two thirds of the Senators present concur." Elsewhere, the Constitution clearly establishes the treaty power is exclusive to the federal government (in Article I, §10), the federal judiciary is tasked with interpreting treaties (Article III, §2), and that treaties are "supreme law" (Article VI). The framers intended for the executive and legislature to share the treaty power. Alexander Hamilton writes that treaties and "every other species of convention usual among nations" require joint action by the president and the Senate (*Federalist 69*). In *Federalist 64*, John Jay argues against delegating the treaty power to the president, laying out a strong case for the Senate's inclusion in the advice and consent stage of the treaty process, while excluding the House of Representatives. As Glennon has noted, James Madison "considered treaty making more of a legislative function" (1990, 181).

Although the framers' intent was clear, conflict over the treaty process emerged soon after the Constitution's ratification. Did advice and consent preclude Senate involvement in the treaty-making stage of the process, or did it require it? Two competing views emerged. The dominant view is that the treaty-negotiating process is a presidential monopoly, and the Senate merely approves treaties rather than providing advice along the way. In the words of Justice Sutherland, the president "alone negotiates" treaties (Corwin 1984, 488), which means they can present the Senate with faits accomplis, but the Senate is not obliged to approve (Corwin 1984, 210). The other view argues that the framers clearly intended for Senate involvement throughout the treaty process. Rather than possessing just a veto on the president's treaties, this line of reasoning suggests that Senate advice is appropriate throughout (Fisher 1985, 256–7). Following the Constitutional Convention, Pierce Butler of South Carolina remarked that treaties should "be gone over, clause by clause, by the president and the Senate together" (Franck and Weisband 1979, 136). Initially, President Washington appeared to share this perspective. In 1789, he brought an Indian treaty he was negotiating to the Senate floor for advice. The meeting did not go well, and Washington reportedly vowed that "he would be damned if he ever went there again" (Milkis and Nelson 1999,

75). Washington's successors soon ended the practice of seeking Senate advice on treaties undergoing negotiation.

This change proved costly for presidents of that era. Beginning in the early nineteenth century, the Senate began providing its advice through the amendment process during the ratification debate. Thus, presidents would negotiate a treaty and submit it to the Senate, only to have the Senate change the treaty, which endangered the agreement because treaty partners might balk at the changes. The dominant view among Senators during the nineteenth and early twentieth centuries is reflected in the remark by Senator Henry Cabot Lodge (R-MA), "that a treaty sent to the Senate is not properly a treaty but merely a project" (Holt 1933, 179). Examples of important treaties that failed final ratification due to changes in the Senate include the King–Hawkesbury Convention of 1803 and the Hay–Pauncefote Treaty of 1900 (Franck and Weisband 1979, 136).

The Senate of Lodge's time was considered a graveyard for treaties, as not a single significant treaty received Senate consent between 1869 and 1898 (Lindsay 1994). Of the 22 outright Senate rejections of proposed treaties in the scope of US history, 14 occurred between 1860 and 1935 (Krutz and Peake 2009, 33). This was highly problematic for US diplomacy. President Teddy Roosevelt once remarked, "Individual Senators evidently consider the prerogatives of the Senate as far more important than the welfare of the country" (Holt 1933, 178). President Woodrow Wilson had his own frustrations with the Senate over the Treaty of Versailles, the peace treaty that ended World War One. The treaty failed on the Senate floor in a defeat engineered by Senator Lodge. Krutz and Peake (2009, 33) explain "one reason treaties were so endangered . . . is the fact that the Senate was prodded to defend its foreign policy prerogatives through the only means available to it."

The conflict over treaties during this era was marked with partisanship, much like what we see today. For example, during the failure of the Versailles Treaty, President Wilson, a Democrat, faced off against a Republican Senate, and the voting was based largely along party lines (Holt 1933). Divided partisan control of the government is one obvious reason, however during the Cold War period, Republican presidents, and Democratic Senates (and vice versa) routinely submitted, debated, and approved treaties. Ideological polarization of the two political parties is the likely culprit for the dysfunction during the earlier era. Much like today's Congress, the five decades following the Civil War were marked with ideologically polarized political parties. Figure 1.1 provides a graph of ideological polarization in the Senate based on NOMINATE scores, a popularly used measure of ideological preferences in Congress. The figure clearly shows elevated polarization during the earlier period. Such high levels of ideological polarization make the supermajority necessary for treaty ratification very difficult to achieve for any significant treaty. Treaty failures during this period were routinely stories of partisanship (Dangerfield 1933; Fleming 1930; Holt 1933; see also Prins and Marshall 2009).

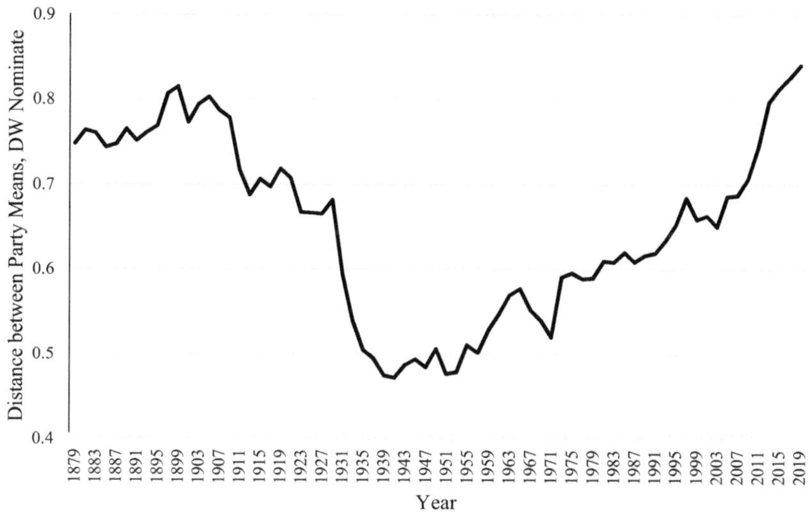

FIGURE 1.1 Senate polarization (1879–2020)

Source: Lewis, *et al.* (2022).

In the 1930s, as partisanship and ideological polarization decreased, the conflict surrounding the treaty ratification process diminished. In fact, since 1935, only four treaties have been rejected on the floor of the Senate. The floor defeats include the Convention on the High Seas in 1960; the Montreal Protocol No. 4 in 1983; the Comprehensive Nuclear Test Ban Treaty in 1999; and the UN Convention for the Rights of the Disabled in 2012. However, measuring treaty conflict based on floor failures underestimates the severity of political conflict surrounding treaties during the modern era, as numerous treaties languish in the Senate, never reaching the floor. Partisan conflict over foreign policy, more generally, decreased during the post–World War Two era, given the Cold War consensus that had the effect of contributing to the president's primacy in foreign policy (Rudalevige 2005; Schlessinger 1973). As foreign policy scholars have noted, the reemergence of hyper-partisanship over the last two decades coincides with the end of the Cold War consensus over the direction of US foreign policy (Schulz 2017; Trubowitz and Mellow 2011).

As shown in Figure 1.1, partisan polarization again reached elevated levels in the early part of the twenty-first century, with the most recent Senates setting record highs. Such high levels of partisan polarization, coupled with the breakdown of the bipartisan Cold War consensus in foreign policy, makes for an awfully difficult context to push treaties in the Senate (Myrick 2021; Schulz 2017). As a result, Senate consent to treaties is commonly subject to considerable delay or outright failure, often proving costly to the president and US foreign policy. Today, numerous treaties languish in the Senate, some for decades. Many of these treaties include significant multilateral human rights, arms control, and environmental conventions.

The twentieth century witnessed the rise of executive agreements, which constituted 94 percent of all binding international agreements completed from 1949 to 2000 (Krutz and Peake 2009). The significant increase in the use of executive agreements started during the Franklin Roosevelt administration. President Roosevelt completed executive agreements on a whole host of highly significant policies, including trading destroyers for bases with Britain in 1940 and a series of agreements with Britain and the USSR regarding the division of Europe after Germany's defeat (Ackerman and Golove 1995; Krutz and Peake 2009, 38–40). For the most part, the Congress facilitated this expansion of executive authority over international agreements, though one failed effort emerged during the 1950s to curtail their use via constitutional amendment. The Bricker Amendment fight ultimately failed, but it signaled to the president that Congress was not fully onboard with carte blanche unilateral diplomacy. Additional concerns over major commitments being completed as executive agreements and a lack of transparency in the process led to the passage of the Case Act in 1972, which requires the executive branch to report executive agreements to Congress in a timely manner. Presidents responded by including Congress in the process when pressed, often completing agreements as treaties when requested to do so by powerful senators (Krutz and Peake 2009, 48; Martin 2005).

During the twenty-first century, however, the domestic politics of international agreements changed considerably. Today, presidents submit far fewer treaties to the Senate for advice and consent than during the prior century and tend to complete their major commitments unilaterally through executive agreements or as political commitments. The main task of this book is to explain why this change has occurred, and for that, we must start with a theory.

International Relations Theory and International Agreements

The explanation for this major change in US foreign policymaking is centered on the significance of domestic politics and process. In short, while the need for efficiency may have led to the rise of executive agreements during the twentieth century (Krutz and Peake 2009), a broken domestic treaty process has cemented presidential unilateralism in US diplomacy, and US foreign policy is worse off as a result. Partisan polarization has broken the process in the Senate and provided incentives for presidents to rely overwhelmingly on their unilateral authority, weakening the international commitments they make and endangering full US participation in international law. The changing international landscape has also greatly diminished consensus in US foreign policy, heightening partisan conflict over its direction.

The idea that domestic politics often guide a state's foreign policy is not new. Liberal international relations theory is based on this general idea, as it is argued that the democratic nature of the US guides its foreign policy culminating in a grand strategy focused on liberal internationalism, in which major international conventions play a large role. Kupchan and Trubowitz (2007) argued 15 years ago that growing partisan polarization was undermining the bipartisan consensus for liberal internationalism. Numerous recently published essays sound the alarm on the dangers of polarization for the future of US foreign policy, pointing to a deterioration of US leadership which is central to the liberal order (e.g., Burns 2020; Myrick 2021; Schulz 2017; Trubowitz and Harris 2019; Walt 2019).

The significance of domestic politics in the politics of international agreements is highlighted in the two-level game theory developed by Robert Putnam (1988), who argued that the need for domestic ratification (i.e., the second level) guides diplomats during the negotiation stage of the process (i.e., the first level). The two levels are intertwined, such that "the negotiations of international agreements have the potential to affect domestic ratification and vice versa." Thus, the options for diplomats are limited (1) "by the domestic distribution of foreign policy preferences, (2) domestic institutional constraints of the executive, and (3) the executive's negotiation strategies" (Friedrichs 2022, 6–7). As Friedrichs (2022, 10) explains, "The sorting of foreign policy preferences into two homogenous partisan groups suggests that the executive branch has to anticipate domestic partisan opposition to its international endeavors due to the steady decrease of bargaining space between members of both parties." In short, partisan polarization decreases the range of options for negotiators, given the high bar for domestic ratification.

Thus, low prospects for domestic ratification may lead the president to complete major agreements using unilateral tools (e.g., executive agreements or political commitments) rather than as treaties. The commitments they can make at the negotiating table are thus weakened considerably. It follows that the partisan sorting inherent in polarization also diminishes the role of the legislature, as presidents are incentivized to avoid Congress, and Congress is unable or unwilling to check presidential unilateralism due to its own dysfunction. While this may seem to provide greater freedom for presidents, given the breakdown of institutional constraints on their behavior, it greatly limits their ability to forge long-lasting commitments during negotiations and weakens their hand at the negotiating table, since the political constraints on US presidents are well known. Moreover, on topics, like human rights, where Article II treaties are always used to finalize US participation, presidents have hit a stone wall in the Senate, meaning they almost always fail at the second level of the two-level game. William Burns (2020) succinctly states how partisan polarization presents a problem for US diplomats:

> If our elected representatives won't give a negotiated agreement a fair hearing, support it, or at least a minimum avoid undercutting it even before the ink dries, why would any friend or foe enter into any kind of good-faith negotiations with the U.S.? And why should they have any confidence that the American government will deliver on its commitments if they do?

Before we can fully engage such provocative questions, we need a firmer empirical basis to understand the domestic politics of international agreements in the United States and how those domestic politics have led to dysfunctional diplomacy. Most of the remainder of the book seeks to provide that understanding.

Plan of the Book

Using a mixed-methods approach, I provide empirical analysis of the politics surrounding treaty ratification and the use of unilateral authority in diplomacy since World War Two, with a particular focus on the twenty-first century. I employ original data on treaty ratification and the use of executive agreements from the Truman administration through the Trump administration. I also provide in-depth case studies of several key international agreements, including the Paris Climate Accord; the Iranian Nuclear Agreement; the UN Convention on the Law of the Sea; arms control and human rights treaties; and executive agreements related to security and international trade. The evidence supports the argument that the treaty process has broken down under the strain of partisan polarization. Presidents during the polarized era more often completed their agreements unilaterally, often with the intent of skirting the opposition in Congress. The norms surrounding the treaty process described in *Treaty Politics* have broken down, and the implications for US foreign policy are substantial.

In Chapter 2, I provide a descriptive analysis of recent trends in the use of the various types of international agreements, with a special focus on comparing the presidencies of George W. Bush (2001–9) and Barack Obama (2009–17). I first contrast the politics faced by each president by comparing their experiences during the push by Bush for the Moscow Treaty in 2002 and the push by Obama for the New START Treaty in 2010. The treaties are comparable because both are significant bilateral arms control treaties with Russia that eventually were approved by the Senate. However, the politics surrounding each ratification effort were markedly different and illustrate the changes resulting from increased partisan polarization. Next, I present statistics on the use of treaties and executive agreements, which indicates a shift toward greater reliance on unilateral instruments during the Bush administration that was fully realized during the Obama administration and continued during the Trump administration. The nonuse of treaties by Obama and Trump are evident. The analysis suggests that partisan polarization is largely to blame both for the disuse of treaties and the politicization of the process.

In Chapter 3, I conduct a more systematic empirical analysis addressing the effects of polarization on the domestic politics of treaties during the period of 1949 to 2020. The statistical analyses are focused on assessing the effects of polarization on the number of treaties presidents transmit to the Senate and the amount of treaty gridlock apparent during each Senate. Using a dataset of 1,000 treaties transmitted during the period, I also assess the factors that contribute to delay during the ratification process. Each analysis clearly indicates that partisan polarization plays an important role in the treaty process, diminishing the number of treaties presidents submit to the Senate and substantially increasing the delay during the ratification process.

The statistical analysis indicates that multilateral treaties are particularly problematic in terms of receiving domestic support, which means presidents are routinely rebuffed in their efforts to secure Senate approval of key international agreements on vexing transnational problems, including human rights, the environment, and arms control. As a result, the United States often finds itself on the outside of the very international organizations it designed after World War Two to deal with these sorts of international problems.

In Chapter 4, I discuss several multilateral treaties in each of these important areas, with a focus on treaties that have languished in the Senate. I start with an assessment of the UN Convention on the Law of the Sea (UNCLOS), which is a broadly significant treaty that governs international law related to issues ranging from national control of coastal waters, fishing rights, and deep seabed mining. This key treaty has languished in the Senate since 1994, largely due to ideological opposition by conservatives. The underlying themes evident in the UNCLOS battle are also apparent in my survey of numerous multilateral treaties on human rights, the environment, and arms control. While participation in multilateral treaties covering these topics has always been a difficult domestic political problem for US presidents, recent circumstances have cemented US nonparticipation in international law on these matters to its detriment.

Article II treaties represent just a small fraction of the binding international agreements completed by the United States each year. Most binding international agreements are executive agreements completed on the unilateral authority of the president. The executive agreement process cuts out the Congress, for the most part, though in many cases there is some linkage back to a delegation of power to the executive via statute. As several legal scholars have indicated, such linkages are often very tenuous and transparency is nonexistent, leaving the process open to abuse by the executive. To better understand the executive agreement process—i.e., the process by which most of the United States' legally binding commitments are made—we need a better accounting of executive agreements signed by recent presidents.

In Chapter 5, I use an original dataset encompassing all reported agreements signed during the second G.W. Bush term through the Trump administration, which includes 3,045 executive agreements. I present descriptive statistics on the topics addressed by the agreements, signatory partners, and the agency responsible for each agreement. I end the chapter with brief case studies of several significant executive agreements, including US security commitments to Iraq and Afghanistan and several trade agreements signed during the period. The case studies clearly indicate that recent presidents have relied heavily on their unilateral authority to complete far-reaching international commitments, sometimes contrary to congressional wishes.

Completing international agreements without involving Congress is attractive to presidents for a variety of reasons accentuated by partisan polarization. However, unilateral tools also have serious drawbacks, as they can be more easily overturned by successors, making for much less credible commitments than action in conjunction with the legislature. President Obama, especially, pushed the envelope of executive authority on international agreements.

In Chapter 6, I support this conclusion by assessing two of Obama's signature foreign policy accomplishments: the 2015 Iran Nuclear Agreement and the 2015 Paris Agreement on Climate Change. Both agreements were, in part, nonbinding political commitments rather than legally binding executive agreements. Essentially, Obama lacked the authority to complete the agreements as binding international law. As a result, the agreements were much weaker than they would have been if the president had sought expanded authority from Congress to complete a binding agreement or went down the treaty route. Those options were closed to Obama because the Republican-controlled Congress opposed both agreements. The weakness of Obama's unilateral approach proved to be the agreements' undoing, as President Trump, whose "America First" agenda was hostile to multilateral international agreements, made quick work of reversing Obama's signature legacies. The on-again, off-again international commitments evident in both cases highlight the degree of dysfunction for US diplomacy, as presidents seek to commit the country to major international agreements.

In the final Chapter, I present the conclusions of the study, including a summary of its primary findings. Most of the focus, however, will be on the implications of the findings for US foreign policy and prospects for the future, including recommendations for changes to the process. As far as the domestic politics of international agreements go, the United States is at a crossroads. Presidents could continue to push the boundaries of unilateral action, further undermining the democratic legitimacy of international law. Instead, they could try to undertake the more difficult work of involving Congress as seemingly required by the Constitution. The latter approach would make for more effective foreign policy and more credible commitments on the part of the United States, something agreement partners clearly value. It would also preserve the congressional role in US foreign policymaking, a valuable end that legitimizes policy decisions and upholds the separation of powers. By signaling its willingness to participate again in international agreement making, Congress, and especially the Senate, could guard its institutional role in foreign policy by avoiding the delegation of vast amounts of authority, narrowing the openings for presidential unilateralism, and more effectively policing executive authority through oversight.

US leadership in the world suffers because of presidents' inability or unwillingness to use the treaty mechanism. Ratified treaties send clearer and more credible signals of national commitment. Moreover, the United States operates from a position of strength in multilateral organizations created by treaties it has ratified. Ratification failures also come with clear costs. A treaty that is not ratified is devoid of any legal force regarding international law. The solutions to this problem developed by recent presidents make for awfully fragile commitments on the part of the United States. As I describe in this book, presidents are constrained by both domestic and international politics, as their predecessors' commitments are still US commitments and agreement partners expect the United States to keep its commitments. Failing to do so will have long-lasting reputational costs. Perhaps one lesson of the Trump presidency is that unilateral withdrawal from international agreements poses as many risks domestically and geopolitically as the Obama administration's quest to implement them by circumventing Congress.

A third possibility exists, of course. Future presidents could purposively avoid formal multilateral diplomacy altogether, refusing to enter into legally binding agreements. Past Republican presidents usually have been supportive of multilateralism and international law. Has the Trump presidency and partisan polarization changed this? The whipsaw changes from Obama to Trump and Trump to Biden in the realm of international agreements adds more fuel to concerns that the United States lacks diplomatic credibility, particularly in multilateral contexts where its leadership is important. Obama's relative weakness on international agreements, from a domestic political perspective, meant that he was unable to negotiate credible and resilient deals. Trump's penchant to eschew multilateral diplomacy lays bare this weakness—and has serious implications for the rest of the world, as it seeks to make binding international law to deal with significant transnational problems. The rest of the world will continue to write international law, whether the United States participates or not.

Notes

1 Kerry was previously the chair of the Senate Foreign Relations Committee (2009–13). The hearing was on the Iran Nuclear Accord, which is discussed at length in Chapter 6.

2 While treaties are "supreme law" under Article VI of the Constitution, and can alter federal laws, executive agreements are not, as they cannot be inconsistent with ratified treaties or federal law, nor violate the constitutional rights of Americans (see *United States v. Guy Capps, Inc.*, 204.F.2d 655, 660 [4th Cir. 1953]; *Reid v. Covert*, 354 US 1, 16 [1957]). Executive agreements, however, do trump state laws just as a treaty would.

3 I discuss the various types of executive agreements in some detail in Chapter 5. A small subset (far less than 1 percent) of executive agreements requires bicameral legislative approval, including significant trade agreements like NAFTA.

2

RECENT TRENDS IN TREATY POLITICS

The domestic politics of treaties and international agreements changed considerably during the Obama administration (2009–17). Obama submitted far fewer treaties to the Senate for approval than his predecessors, and when he sent treaties to the Senate, ratification was far from a sure thing, as his success rates on treaties submitted are the lowest of any modern president. Simply put, President Obama and the Senates that he served with had the worst treaty record in modern history. President Trump's record is similarly poor because he sent only a handful of treaties to the Senate during his presidency. As Obama's Secretary of State, John Kerry said, "You can't pass a treaty anymore."

President Trump entered office clearly hostile toward treaties. Early in his administration, a draft executive order on multilateral agreements was leaked. If implemented, the order would have created a high-level committee to review all multilateral agreements, unrelated to national security, trade, or extradition, to which the United States was party. The draft order signaled a significant change in US treaty behavior (Conrad and Ritter 2017).[1] It was clear to State Department (DOS) officials and others that the new administration was hostile to current and new multilateral agreements, particularly those involving human rights. Republican presidents before Trump were largely supportive of multilateralism and international law, even though most opposition toward these treaties typically comes from Republicans in the Senate.

Secretary Kerry's frustration with the treaty process in the Senate was clearly justified. The problem is not singularly an executive problem, but also one of shared governance, as today's hyper-partisan Senate is unable or unwilling to play its advice and consent role. When compared to the scope of US history, the recent records of the US Senate and Presidents Obama and Trump indicate an important change in the domestic politics of treaties. Obama often avoided the Senate on

DOI: 10.4324/9781003347422-2

important diplomatic matters, knowing ratification was unlikely, and when he took his treaties to the Senate, prospects were much dimmer than in the past. At first glance, the problem is not so obvious. After all, treaty rejections on the floor of the Senate are rare in the modern era. Since 1935, the Senate has rejected just four treaties in this manner. However, a much larger number of treaties languish in the Senate, as they are either ignored by the Senate Foreign Relations Committee (SFRC) or are not brought to the floor following committee action. Languishing treaties include treaties that have a great deal of support from domestic economic interests, security interests, and presidents of both political parties.[2] Historically, while most treaties are eventually approved by the Senate, considerable delay is common, and the length of the process has increased significantly in recent years (Krutz and Peake 2009; Peake 2017).

In this chapter, I present data on historical trends in the use of treaties and success rates for presidents when they submit treaties to the Senate for ratification. I compare President Obama's record on treaties with his modern predecessors, with a more detailed comparison to the record of President George W. Bush, his immediate predecessor. Before setting out to compare Obama's record in significant detail, I compare Obama's experiences during the 2010 battle for the ratification of New START to Bush's experience with the Moscow Treaty in 2002. Both treaties represent significant bilateral nuclear arms control treaties with Russia. The comparisons starkly contrast each president's experience, suggesting significant changes in the politics of treaties during the early part of this century. Partisan polarization, a condition that plagues the US Senate, is a major contributor to this change. The discussion here about Obama's record is suggestive; whereas more systematic analyses that follow in the next chapter demonstrate the significance of polarization in disrupting the treaty process. I end the chapter with a discussion of Trump's limited record on treaties, which focused more on leaving rather than completing treaties.

A New START?

> Let me also say that this new START Treaty is completely in line with a tradition of bipartisan cooperation on this issue. This is not a Democratic concept; this is not a Republican concept. This is a concept of American national security that has been promoted by Ronald Reagan, George H.W. Bush, Bill Clinton, George W. Bush, and now my administration.
>
> *President Barack Obama, November 18, 2010*

A comparison between Obama's experience on New START and Bush's experience with the Moscow Treaty illustrates the changing nature of domestic politics of treaties. At the beginning of Obama's first term in 2009, there were good reasons for optimism regarding the treaty agenda. First, President Bush had a strong record of treaty ratification, as I detail below. While President Clinton faced some difficulties in moving arms control treaties through the Senate due to conservative opposition, culminating in the failed floor vote on the Comprehensive Test Ban Treaty (CTBT) in 1999 (Homan 2016; Krutz and Peake 2009), his record was also quite strong comparatively. Second, President Obama was riding a massive electoral victory in 2008 which generated 60 Senate seats for the Democratic caucus during his first year, a majority not seen since the 1960s. Third, President Obama, Vice President Biden, and Secretary of State Hillary Clinton were all members of the Senate prior to their taking office in 2009. To get treaties through the Senate, they would need to work with familiar colleagues. This was especially the case for Biden, who had previously served as chair of the SFRC.

Despite all these factors in their favor, the Obama team struggled to achieve Senate approval of New START. During the lame duck congressional session of 2010, the Senate narrowly approved the New START treaty with Russia, the only major Article II treaty that Obama both signed and managed to ratify while in office. The treaty was an important arms control agreement that followed on a long history of arms control treaties between the United States and Russia (and previously, the Soviet Union). The three prior START treaties, ratified in 1992, 1993, and 2002 had a combined ten no votes; whereas, Obama had to negotiate significant concessions with Republicans to pass the treaty, 71–26, just several votes more than was needed. In the wake of the ratification debate, it was quite evident that other major arms control agreements that Obama championed (specifically, the CTBT) had zero chance of approval in the Senate (Peake, *et al.* 2012).

In contrast, the Moscow Treaty (or SORT), which was signed by President Bush in May 2002, was given Senate approval on March 6, 2003, by a vote of 95–0. No substantial concessions were required for Bush to get his treaty through the Senate. While the treaty was brief, the pledged reductions in weapons were substantial, requiring a reduction of nearly two-thirds of deployed warheads (Homan 2016).[3] Despite the treaty's significance, the main sticking point for Bush and the Senate was whether the president would finalize the treaty as an executive agreement or as a formal treaty. Russian President Vladimir Putin clearly preferred a "full-blown" treaty, as he wanted a binding legal commitment (Martin 2005, 448). Leaders on the SFRC, including the Democratic chairman (Joe Biden of Delaware) and the ranking Republican (Jesse Helms of North Carolina), wrote a letter to Bush requesting that the Moscow Treaty be submitted as a formal treaty, and Bush complied.

During floor debate prior to the final vote on the treaty, Biden urged his colleagues to vote against various amendments to alter the treaty to bolster its verification requirements, as the changes might have led Bush to set aside the treaty and instead complete the agreement as an executive agreement without Senate approval. The amendments were defeated, and the treaty was approved unanimously (Krutz and Peake 2009, 71–3). Kreps, *et al.* (2018) argue that Bush, who was seen as a hawk, had an easier go in persuading other hawks (i.e., Republicans) in the Senate to support his arms control treaty. Bush was seen as having credibility in dealing with the Russians, as he prioritized military spending, including on missile defense, over getting a nuclear deal done. Bush had already withdrawn from the Anti-Ballistic Missile (ABM) Treaty, solidifying this perception. Relations between the United States and Russia were also warming at the time, so a treaty with Russia was less problematic, and seen as a cornerstone of Bush's efforts to improve relations with Russia to gain allies in the war on terror. The international context, then, favored ratification (Homan 2016).

The domestic political context also favored Bush. While there was some delay in getting the treaty to the floor, once Republicans gained control of the Senate at the beginning of 2003, the treaty was quickly moved through the process. Republicans had uncontested unified control of both chambers of Congress and the White House for the first time in 50 years, so President Bush was in a powerful position to lead Congress. As the treaty moved through the Senate in 2002, Bush maintained high public approval ratings as a "wartime" president, and those ratings, while dropping off toward the end of the year and at the beginning of 2003, were still quite good. Bush was in a strong position to push Congress to support his foreign policy initiatives, including ratification of the treaty. Moreover, the treaty simply lacked controversy. It was popular among the US public, with one survey indicating that 88 percent of the US public approved the treaty. The simple fact that Bush is a Republican blunted any conservative opposition to the arms control treaty, and what little Democratic opposition that emerged emphasized that the treaty did not go far enough (Homan 2016, 103–4). Ratification was never really in doubt.

In contrast to Bush's experience with the Moscow Treaty, Obama struggled to get Senate consent for his arms control treaty with Russia, the New START. The treaties were similar in many respects, and the Obama administration believed that a follow-on treaty to Bush's, with a bolstered verification regime, would easily be approved in the Senate. There was a clear need for the treaty, given the 2009 expiration of the monitoring regime from the original START treaty and the Obama administration's efforts to reset relations with Russia. The international context favored ratification of the treaty (Homan 2016). However, Obama was seen by many Republicans as a dove given his vision of ridding the world of nuclear weapons, and therefore lacked the credibility in making a deal with the Russians that Bush had. As a result, Obama would have to pay a high premium to secure enough Republican votes for ratification (Kreps, *et al.* 2018).

Even though New START was a modest update of the arms control framework and was required to restart monitoring of nuclear stockpiles, significant opposition to Senate consent emerged in the Republican caucus, particularly among staunch conservatives led by Senator Jon Kyl (R-AZ). Republican opposition was not limited to arch conservatives, however, as Senator John McCain (R-AZ), often considered a moderate Republican willing to strike bipartisan deals, vocally opposed the treaty from his perch on the Senate Armed Services Committee. Republicans on the SFRC mostly supported the treaty, including the ranking member, Richard Lugar (R-IN), however most of the caucus was opposed. To move the resolution to approve ratification to the floor, White House negotiators had to agree to significant expenditures to modernize the United States' nuclear stockpile. In the final tally, just 13 Republicans joined all the Democrats in voting to approve the treaty (Peake, *et al.* 2012).

Republican opposition to the treaty gelled early in the process. Their concerns focused on restrictions on missile defense. In their view, the treaty did not allow the United States to convert current missile stockpiles to defensive weaponry, a limitation they believed would limit US defensive capabilities. Additionally, Republicans were concerned about the modernization of nuclear forces (Starks 2010). Another concern that Republicans linked to the treaty was the administration's new Nuclear Posture Review (NPR), which stated that the United States would not use nuclear weapons against nonnuclear states that comply with the Nuclear Non-Proliferation Treaty (NPT) and would only use conventional forces against nations that use nuclear or biological weapons against the United States, with exceptions including North Korea, Iran, Russia, and China. Republicans largely opposed these changes in the NPR and sought to use ratification of New START as a cudgel to get the administration to reconsider them (Starks and Oliveri 2010).

Obama transmitted the treaty to the Senate in May 2010 and the SFRC held hearings in June and July. The hearings were largely constructive, as it was clear that the committee chair (John Kerry, D-MA) and the ranking member (Lugar) supported ratification. Both found the treaty vital to US interests because it would restart monitoring of Russia's nuclear arsenal. Most witnesses at the SFRC hearings were in favor of the treaty, but over the course of the hearings, a few points of concern emerged. They focused on the defensive weapons issue mentioned above and verification and monitoring of Russia's stockpile. The informational hearings held by the Senate Armed Services Committee, however, were another matter, as Senator McCain used the hearings to voice opposition to the treaty.[4]

During the summer, Republican opposition formed behind the leadership of the Minority Whip, Senator Kyl. Other important senators announced their opposition, including Jim DeMint (R-SC) and James Inhofe (R-OK), both members of the SFRC. Rather than look to Senator Lugar for leadership, a consistent supporter of arms control during his long congressional career, rank-and-file Republicans looked to Senator Kyl, an arms control skeptic. Many newer members considered Kyl an expert on the topic (Cadei 2010a), given his leadership in opposing two key arms control treaties during the Clinton years, the Chemical Weapons Convention (CWC), which passed, and the CTBT, which failed in 1999. To blunt Republican opposition, Senator Kerry set aside his initial draft of the resolution for ratification, and instead put forth Senator Lugar's version, as it dealt more directly with Republican concerns. The SFRC voted 14–4 in September to report the treaty, with three Republicans voting with all the Democrats in favor, and Kerry issued the report on October 1.[5]

The 2010 midterm elections were fast approaching, and leaders decided to postpone floor consideration of the treaty until after the elections when the Senate returned from recess for its lame duck session. Democrats were beaten badly during the midterms, with Republicans picking up eight Senate seats. Senator Lugar pushed for the Democratic leaders to take up the treaty and move to floor consideration. Senator Kerry continued to negotiate with Senator Kyl, with the primary sticking point being an $85 billion nuclear weapons modernization plan. Kerry and the White House agreed to the plan, but then Kyl changed his position, withdrawing his support. Despite this switch, Kerry decided to push for floor consideration of the treaty (Rogin 2010a).

With just a week to go in the lame duck session, the Senate finally took up the treaty on December 15, 2010. Republicans produced an onslaught of amendments, including several which were designed to undermine the treaty (Rogin 2010b). In total, 11 Republican amendments were defeated, and Democrats were forced to invoke cloture to move the treaty to its final stages. The cloture motion carried, 67–28, which provided a clear signal that the treaty had the votes necessary for approval. To allay Republican concerns and get the treaty over the final hump, Obama agreed to send a letter to the Senate declaring his commitment for nuclear modernization and the missile defense program. On the last day of the lame duck session, December 22, 2010, New START was approved 71–26, with 13 Republicans and all the Democrats voting in favor of the treaty (Cadei 2010b).

At first glance, the efforts to approve New START in the Senate look very much like typical politics, with posturing and deal making to get the necessary number of votes. Democrats controlled the Senate and were able to effectively use the legislative calendar during the lame duck session to get the treaty over the finish line. Was Obama's difficulty with New START simply a result of a Democrat having to make side payments to Republicans to get support for an arms control treaty (Kreps, *et al.* 2018)? That is a plausible explanation. After all, the efforts were like Clinton's two major battles on multilateral arms control agreements during the 1990s: the successful campaign to ratify the CWC and the failed campaign to ratify the CTBT.

That Republicans were willing to spike Obama's bilateral agreement with Russia over relatively minor concerns, at a time where the only bilateral agreement had expired the year prior, signaled an important change in how Republicans would approach treaties negotiated and pushed by Democratic presidents, however. A regression analysis of Republican voting on New START clearly links Republican opposition to the treaty to ideology. While controlling for other factors, the more conservative members of the Republican caucus were far more likely to oppose the treaty than the less conservative members (Peake, *et al.* 2012). As moderate Republicans disappear from the Senate as polarization deepens, the prospects for treaty ratification continue to dim.[6] When one considers the New START experience in conjunction with Obama's overall experience on treaties, its broader implications become apparent.

Partisan Polarization and International Agreements

President Obama and the Senates he served with had the worst record in modern history when it came to successfully completing Article II treaties. Obama submitted far fewer treaties than any of his modern predecessors. Of course, that does not mean that US diplomacy came to a halt. In fact, Obama more commonly turned to unilateral tools to complete his diplomatic agreements and was emboldened to commit the United States internationally with little input by Congress. As described in Chapter 1, institutional norms developed around the treaty process during the twentieth century where presidents would send most of their significant international agreements to the Senate for approval and the Senate would give treaties submitted by the president a fair hearing, particularly when the treaty had broad support or was critical for the president to meet their diplomatic goals.

During Obama's eight-year presidency, while he only transmitted 39 treaties, the Senate managed to approve just 20 treaties, six of which were originally submitted by President George W. Bush. Neither end of Pennsylvania Avenue worked effectively regarding treaties. By comparison, the Senate, during just the two years of the 110th Congress (2007–8), ratified 38 treaties. It ratified 104 treaties during the entire Bush presidency (2001–8). Thus, President Obama's behavior on treaties presents an interesting puzzle, but so does the degree to which the Senate shirked its responsibility on advice and consent. Why did Obama practically abandon the Article II treaty process? Partisan polarization and the attractiveness of unilateral action provide much of the explanation.

Given the apparent freedom presidents have in choosing how to complete their agreements, why would they ever use treaties? After all, executive agreements afford presidents the opportunity to circumvent the treaty process, so why not always use executive agreements? The answer to this question is twofold and has more to do with domestic and international politics and less to do with the law.[7] However, given the paucity of treaties recently, a simpler answer might be that President Obama simply avoided using formal Article II treaties due to domestic political uncertainty, opting instead for the use of unilateral authority.

In terms of domestic politics, political science scholarship suggests that presidents are constrained in their use of unilateral powers if Congress is willing and able to check executive action (Howell and Pevehouse 2007; Krutz and Peake 2009). In other words, presidents are less free to act unilaterally when completing international agreements when legislative opponents can check their actions or make them pay a price for their behavior. Presidents, generally, use fewer executive agreements and more treaties when the opposing party has majority control of the Senate (Krutz and Peake 2009; Martin 2005), a trend that is counter to the popular evasion hypothesis often cited in earlier work on international agreements (Johnson 1984; Margolis 1986). This is a trend that continued with President Obama, at least in terms of treaty transmittals. Obama was most active in submitting treaties during his last Congress (the 114th, 2015–16), with 16 treaty submittals. Republicans controlled the Senate then, whereas Democrats controlled the Senate during the 111th through 113th Congresses (2009–14).

In terms of international politics, agreement partners often prefer a treaty to an executive agreement. Martin (2000) persuasively argues that treaties send more credible signals of commitment to agreement partners because they require broad domestic political support. We saw this in 2002 with the Moscow Treaty discussed above. President Putin believed that a treaty would have greater legitimacy and signal greater commitment by the United States. In 1979, President Carter transmitted the SALT II agreement to the Senate as a treaty, after floating a trial balloon that he might treat it as an executive agreement, instead. The Soviets pressured the administration to pursue a formal treaty, as they believed an executive agreement would have inferior status (Krutz and Peake 2009, 78).

Norms developed during the twentieth century regarding the topics of treaties that satisfy both domestic and international political concerns. For example, presidents submit arms control agreements to the Senate as treaties to involve the Congress and satisfy the concerns of treaty partners.[8] Similar norms exist for human rights accords, multilateral environmental agreements, and bilateral tax, extradition, and investment treaties (Spiro 2001). However, these norms have broken down, given the paucity of treaties during the Obama administration and routine skirting of congressional approval on a host of agreements that, under the norm, would require congressional input (Bradley and Goldsmith 2018). The best examples include two of Obama's most important international agreements, the Iran Nuclear Agreement, and the Paris Agreement on Climate Change. I discuss these two agreements in Chapter 6 and additional examples in Chapter 5.[9]

The norms that developed during the twentieth century came under considerable stress during the Obama presidency. The primary explanation is partisan polarization, which has two effects on the treaty process. First, it makes getting a treaty approved very difficult, given the supermajority requirement and the fact that a presidential failure provides additional incentives for the president's opponents to oppose treaties. The 67-vote threshold makes securing concessions on other issues a potent strategy, as we saw with the case of New START. Cross-party support for presidential initiatives is much less common under conditions of high partisan polarization. Relatedly, polarization exaggerates the power of anti-treaty interest groups (e.g., the Heritage Foundation) that have effectively pressured Republicans in the Senate to oppose a host of international agreements.

Second, partisan polarization reduces the capability of the Senate, and Congress more broadly, to protect its institutional prerogatives regarding international agreements. Political consensus must exist for Congress to act to constrain the president on international agreements, as presidents can act unilaterally, and Congress must typically legislate to restrain the executive. When Congress manages to legislate to check the president's unilateral behavior, their actions are subject to presidential veto, so to be successful, congressional leaders must build bipartisan supermajorities. Such consensus is improbable in today's ideologically polarized Congress. In effect, partisan polarization increases the attractiveness of unilateral action, as presidents are better situated to get away with an action members of Congress might argue is an abuse of power, due to congressional weakness. With the ability to act unconstrained due to congressional dysfunction, presidents can further push the envelope of their unilateral powers. These realities were clear during the Obama presidency and made unilateral diplomatic devices especially attractive for President Trump.

Article II Treaties during the Obama Administration

President Obama's record on treaties is easy to describe. Obama completed far fewer treaties than his modern predecessors and when Obama transmitted treaties to the Senate, he met with much less success than other modern presidents.[10] Table 2.1 presents the number of treaties and executive agreements for each two-year Congress from 1949 to 2020. Obama averaged only about ten treaty transmittals to the Senate for each two-year Congress (2009–16), compared to an average of 32 treaties per Congress from 1949 to 2008. Bush averaged 24 treaties per Congress. Prior to Obama's presidency, the lowest number of treaty transmittals in a two-year Congress was 18, in 1957–8. In all, Obama transmitted just 39 treaties, with 18 coming during his last two years in office, two of which were transmitted in January 2017, just before he left office.[11] While treaty submittals during the 114th Congress (2015–16) were greater than any other two-year period for Obama, this high is still lower than any other since the end of World War Two. Using the best publicly available data on executive agreements, at least 97.6 percent of Obama's international agreements were executive agreements.[12]

In Table 2.2, I show aggregate success rates for treaties transmitted to the Senate by presidential administration from 1949 to 2016.[13] While President George W. Bush was able to secure Senate approval for 93.7 percent of the treaties he transmitted to the Senate, the highest success rate in the table, President Obama's success rate was just 35.9 percent (see Table 2.2, column 3)—lower than all his modern predecessors. The average comparable success rate for Presidents Truman through Clinton is 76.6 percent. The percentages in column 3 reflect the percentage of treaties approved by the end of each presidency. The lowest percentage prior to Obama is President Carter, who saw only 52.3 percent of his treaties approved by the Senate while in office, but he served just a single term. In Table 2.2, column 2, I report the percentage of each president's treaties approved, even after leaving office, and Obama's success rate improves to 64.1 percent. This success rate is much lower than his modern predecessors, who average 92.5 percent. The increase in Obama's success rate is due to 11 treaties that were approved after he left office. Of course, this success rate could continue to climb as the Senate processes additional pending treaties.

TABLE 2.1 Treaties and executive agreements (1949–2020)

Congress	*Years*	*President*	*Treaties transmitted*	*Executive agreements concluded*	*% treaties*
81	1949–50	Truman	42	305	12.10
82	1951–2	Truman	39	504	7.18
83	1953–4	Eisenhower	31	369	7.75
84	1955–6	Eisenhower	20	530	3.64
85	1957–8	Eisenhower	18	419	4.12
86	1959–60	Eisenhower	26	516	4.80
87	1961–2	Kennedy	22	579	3.66
88	1963–4	Kennedy/L.B.J.	23	456	4.80
89	1965–6	L.B.J.	30	441	6.37
90	1967–8	L.B.J.	28	420	6.25
91	1969–70	Nixon	28	345	7.51
92	1971–2	Nixon	35	501	6.53
93	1973–4	Nixon	37	470	7.30
94	1975–6	Ford	29	666	4.17
95	1977–8	Carter	27	841	3.11
96	1979–80	Carter	61	699	8.03
97	1981–2	Reagan	28	665	4.04
98	1983–4	Reagan	31	618	4.78
99	1985–6	Reagan	32	736	4.17
100	1987–8	Reagan	23	821	2.73
101	1989–90	Bush	22	761	2.81
102	1991–2	Bush	41	589	6.51
103	1993–4	Clinton	39	595	6.15
104	1995–6	Clinton	36	560	6.04
105	1997–8	Clinton	60	516	10.42
106	1999–2000	Clinton	51	457	10.04
107	2001–2	G.W.B.	21	424	4.72
108	2003–4	G.W.B.	28	512	5.19
109	2005–6	G.W.B.	24	622	3.72
110	2007–8	G.W.B.	23	585	3.78
111	2009–10	Obama	8	490	1.61
112	2011–12	Obama	8	421	1.85
113	2013–14	Obama	6	348	1.69
114	2015–16	Obama	16	333	4.58
115*	2017–18	Trump	3	145	2.03
116*	2019–20	Trump	4	101	3.81
	1949–2008	*Average Cong.*	31.8	551	5.46
	2009–20	*Average Cong.*	7.5	306	2.39

Sources: https://congress.gov/treaties for treaties; Fisher (2001) for executive agreements 1949–99; Peake (2018) for 2000–16; Hathaway, *et al.* (2021, https://dataverse.harvard.edu/dataverse/executive agreements), updated through October 2021.

Note: Executive agreements are included in the dataset at the time of signature.

*Data on executive agreements for 2017–20 are preliminary, represent significant undercounts, and should be used with caution.

TABLE 2.2 Success rates on treaties transmitted to the Senate for consent (1949–2016)

Presidential administration	*No. of treaties transmitted (bilateral/multi) Column 1*	*% of transmitted treaties approved (bilateral/multi) Column 2*	*% approved during administration (bilateral/multi) Column 3*
Truman (2nd term)	82 (41/41)	85.4 (90.2 /79.5)	64.6 (72.2/56.1)
Eisenhower	100 (55/45)	93 (92.7/93.3)	83 (85.5/80)
Kennedy	30 (13/17)	90 (100/82.4)	63.3 (76.9/52.9)
Johnson	67 (23/44)	94 (87/97.7)	88.1 (87/90.7)
Nixon	92 (37/55)	96.7 (100/94.5)	80.4 (86.5/76.4)
Ford	41 (20/21)	92.7 (95/90.5)	80.5 (75/85.7)
Carter	88 (49/39)	88.6 (87.8/89.7)	52.3 (55.1/48.7)
Reagan	112 (67/ 45)	89.3 (92.5/84.4)	72.3 (74.6/68.9)
Bush I	64 (37/27)	96.9 (97.3/96.3)	79.7 (72.3/88.9)
Clinton	185 (127/58)	94.6 (98.4/86.2)	84.9 (96.8/58.6)
Bush II	97 (57/40)	95.9 (100/90)	93.7 (96.2/90.7)
Obama	39 (20/19)	64.1 (85/42.1)	35.9 (45/26.3)
Truman to Bush II average		92.5 (94.6/89.5)	76.6 (79.8/72.5)
Democrats' average (pre-Obama)		90.5 (92.7/87.1)	70.6 (77.6/61.4)
Republicans' average		94.1 (96.3/91.5)	81.7 (81.7/81.8)

Source: Data are from Peake (2018), updated.

Note: Column 2 includes the ratification success rate after the end of the administration; whereas column 3 includes the president's success rate on treaties approved while president. The end date for the Kennedy administration is November 22, 1963. The end date for the Nixon administration is August 8, 1974.

Another way to quantify treaty activity is to examine the number of resolutions for advice and consent passed each two-year Congress by the Senate. For the period between 1981 and 2008, the Senate approved an average of 33 treaties per two-year Congress. The comparable number during Obama's presidency (2009–16) is five treaties per two-year Congress, with a total of 20 treaties approved during Obama's presidency. Thus, the sum of treaties approved during the entire eight-year Obama presidency is equivalent to about 60 percent of the average two-year Congress for the period of 1981 through 2008.

In addition to submitting treaties to the Senate, presidents sometimes signal their desire for Senate approval of pending treaties by issuing a treaty priority list (see Peake, *et al.* 2012, 1307). Early during his first year in office, President Obama submitted his first and only treaty priority list to the Senate, which included 17 treaties.[14] All but one of the treaties was left over from prior administrations, with one going as far back as Carter.[15] Only six of the treaties on Obama's priority list were approved, for a success rate of 35 percent. As a point of comparison, Bush's success rates on his treaty priority lists issued in 2005 and 2007 were 81 and 85 percent, respectively (Peake, *et al.* 2012). When we add together the treaties listed on Obama's priority list and the treaties Obama transmitted, we get a total of 55 treaties, of which only 20 (36.4 percent) were ratified during his presidency.[16] This poor record is despite Obama's party having control of the Senate for the first six years of his presidency. President Trump never issued a treaty priority list. Of course, as discussed below, treaties simply were not a Trump priority. President Biden did not submit a treaty priority list during his first year, suggesting that the practice is probably dead.

Why was Obama's record on treaties so poor? The answer relates primarily to the political context in which Obama governed. Put simply, the polarized and partisan US Senate presents very difficult prospects for success, especially for policies that require supermajority support like treaties. However, Bush also faced a polarized Senate, though to a somewhat lesser degree. The fact that Bush is a Republican and that most opponents to treaties in the Senate are also Republicans may also explain why Obama met with less success. Republican senators are more apt to oppose a Democratic president's foreign policies than the foreign policies of one of their own, and we saw this play out in our comparison of Bush's Moscow Treaty and Obama's New START. In the modern era, Republican presidents have been slightly more successful in the treaty process. As shown in Table 2.2, Republican presidents receive approval on about 82 percent of their treaties prior to leaving office. The comparable percentage for Democrats is 71 percent. Clearly, partisanship plays a role in the treaty process.

A second possibility focuses on Obama's lack of leadership on treaties. John Bellinger (2012), former Legal Advisor in the DOS during the Bush administration, argues that Obama's "weakness on treaties" is largely a result of the administration's lack of effort pushing for their ratification and its sluggishness in transmitting treaties to the Senate. Indeed, the White House could have done more to shepherd treaties through the Senate, but it is unlikely that such efforts would have been fruitful given the polarized partisan context and the general trends in treaty failures noted here. The weak record cannot be explained by a lack of presidential effort. For example, Obama promised early on to push hard for ratification of the CTBT. His efforts on behalf of the treaty stalled in the wake of the battle for New START, and some suggest that his lack of effort on behalf of the test ban treaty in the face of concerted Republican opposition is what stalled it (Homan 2016; Jones and Marsh 2014). Given that the CTBT failed on a floor vote in 1999 after a hard push for ratification by President Clinton during a period that was less polarized, it is hard to imagine that Obama was in a better position to push for the treaty against concerted Republican opposition.

The partisan political context is the most important domestic political variable that affects the treaty ratification process, particularly when a treaty is controversial (Kelley and Pevehouse 2015; Krutz and Peake 2009). Recent analysis by Peake (2017) finds that high partisan polarization contributes to delay in bilateral treaties receiving Senate consent; so, even the more mundane bilateral treaties are often held up because of partisan polarization. The partisan context was particularly problematic during Obama's tenure as president. During his tenure, each successive Senate set a record in terms of partisan polarization, as measured by NOMINATE scores, and this impacted treaty approval (Peake *et al.* 2012). Because treaties require two-thirds support, the president must be able to build a broad bipartisan coalition—something difficult to do when the parties are highly polarized. Moreover, treaties are clearly seen as presidential initiatives such that a successful ratification is a win for the president and his party. Given the "team-play" that plagues the polarized Senate (Mann and Ornstein 2012), opposition party members, particularly Republicans, are reluctant to provide the president a clear victory that a significant treaty approval would provide.

The challenge is especially difficult for a Democratic president pushing a liberal and internationalist agenda, as Republican senators are free to oppose the president openly on the floor of the Senate and in committee. A Republican president, however, may have an easier go getting the Senate to approve multilateral treaties, should they be so inclined. Democratic senators are more likely to support multilateral treaties no matter the president's party, given their more liberal ideology, while Republicans are less likely to openly oppose a Republican president, even on treaties that might not fit their ideological preferences. Analysis of arms control agreements confirms that Democratic presidents must overcome significant partisan obstacles in the Senate to ratify their treaties, while Republicans do not. Such obstacles have increased as the Republican Party has grown more ideologically conservative in recent decades (Böller 2022; Kreps, *et al.* 2018).

We can see this difference in the aggregate success rates on multilateral treaties reported in Table 2.2, column 3, where Democratic presidents have an average success rate of 61.4 percent and Republican presidents have an average success rate of 81.8 percent. This dynamic has played out during ratification politics of human rights treaties (Baldez 2014). In looking at the four UN human rights conventions that the United States has ratified, we see that three were approved by the Senate, after lengthy delays, only when a Republican president pushed for ratification. This was the case with the Genocide Convention, which was approved by the Senate in 1986, after languishing in the Senate for nearly 40 years. President Reagan, a Republican, announced his support for the convention in 1984 and was able to push Republicans, who controlled the Senate, to approve it in 1986 (LeBlanc 1991). President George H.W. Bush, also a Republican, asked for and received Senate approval of two UN human rights treaties: the UN Convention Against Torture (in 1990) and the International Covenant on Civil and Political Rights (in 1992). Thus, Republican presidents are more often able to draw on support from the opposition party, whereas doing so is more difficult for Democratic presidents. This is especially the case for Obama, whose success rate on multilateral treaties was just 26.3 percent. George W. Bush's success rate on multilateral treaties, however, was quite robust (90.7 percent).

An additional component of the political context relates to the policy agenda. Given the overwhelming focus of Obama on the economy and other domestic policy priorities in 2009 and 2010, his focus was elsewhere. By the time he could turn his focus to treaties in late 2010, his party was beset with massive midterm losses in Congress, further dimming prospects on approving additional treaties. When he focused on foreign policy during his first two years, Obama's attention was largely on Iraq or Afghanistan, where he relied entirely on executive agreements rather than treaties. Obama's focus on the economy necessarily limited the amount of attention and political capital he could spend on treaties. Prior research on treaty politics suggests that presidential political capital spent on behalf of treaties can be decisive in the ratification effort. Such efforts include going public, i.e., giving speeches on behalf of the treaty, and using resources to negotiate with key senators (Homan 2016; Lantis 2009). Obama expended much political capital to get New START approved, and with other prominent issues dominating the political agenda, he lacked the political capital to spend on marshaling additional treaties through the Senate.

Even so, other modern presidents have had to deal with crowded policy agendas and have much more substantial treaty records. President Carter, who has the second lowest treaty success rates presented in Table 2.2,[17] dealt with several foreign policy crises, including the Iranian hostage crisis which dominated news and presidential attention for months during 1980, his last year in office. Carter was able to get approval for 31 treaties during the 14-month hostage crisis. He also dealt with high unemployment and a crowded domestic agenda, yet he was able to get the Senate to narrowly approve the controversial Panama Canal treaties in 1978. Carter expended significant political capital to push that treaty through the Senate (Krutz and Peake 2009, 119). President Clinton, Obama's most recent Democratic predecessor, transmitted 185 treaties during his two terms, and his success rates shown in Table 2.2 are very high. Clinton expended substantial political capital to push key multilateral treaties, including the International Convention on the Elimination of All Forms of Racial Discrimination (CERD) in 1994, the CWC in 1997, the Convention on Nuclear Safety in 1999, and a UN convention on desertification in 2000. He also oversaw the expansion of NATO membership to much of Eastern Europe and successfully ratified the START II treaty with Russia. Of course, the Senate also worked much more effectively during the Carter and Clinton presidencies, approving 54 treaties during Carter's four years and 172 treaties during Clinton's eight years.

A final component of the political context is the broader foreign policy environment in which presidents must push their treaty agenda. During the Cold War years, a broad consensus existed in US politics that largely supported liberal internationalism in foreign policy, including arms control and nonproliferation. Treaties are an important component of the liberal international order. Moreover, the unifying threat of the Soviet Union and communism largely muted congressional opposition to internationalist foreign policies, as well as provided presidents with substantial leeway in implementing their diplomatic agendas. This Cold War consensus on foreign policy largely disappeared in the wake of the dissolution of the Soviet Union in 1991. Increased partisan polarization, which coincided with the end of the Cold War consensus, is certainly related to this explanation (Trubowitz and Mellow 2011). It is difficult to disentangle the effects of polarization from the impact of this major change in the international political context given their concomitance.

In sum, a combination of factors contributed to President Obama's poor record on treaties. First, Senate Republicans were more prone to oppose treaties pushed by a Democratic president. Second, and perhaps most important, due to partisan polarization, the Senate was in particularly bad shape during Obama's presidency for doing anything, let alone approving treaties that require supermajority support. Moreover, the clear consensus supporting liberal internationalist foreign policy no longer existed. Third, Obama's attention was focused elsewhere on more pressing issues, particularly the struggling economy. Finally, as is suggested by the data presented above on the paucity of treaties during the Obama presidency, along with his reliance on executive agreements, President Obama had an alternative to the cumbersome and now highly politicized treaty process. While the alternative certainly existed for Obama's predecessors, the incentives for avoiding the Senate treaty process were not so great for them as they were for Obama.

Treaties during the Trump Administration

In 2017, President Donald Trump entered office hostile toward international agreements, especially multilateral treaties. He routinely referred to various agreements signed by his predecessors as the "worst deals ever" (Brown and Irwin 2018; Gordan 2018). His "America First" approach to foreign policy presented a direct challenge to US global leadership, particularly on issues where international agreements are especially relevant. President Trump's aversion to traditional forms of diplomacy, including treaties and binding multilateral agreements, had profound implications for US foreign policy. In one of his first official foreign policy acts, Trump withdrew from the Trans-Pacific Partnership (TPP) on January 23,

2017. The TPP was a massive free trade agreement between the United States and 11 other Pacific states, which importantly excluded China (Mui 2017).[18] Early in 2017, as referenced above, a draft executive order that disparaged multilateral agreements was leaked. The order would have required the reassessment of dozens of existing agreements to which the United States was party and clearly signaled Trump's hostility toward multilateralism. Thus, it is unsurprising that Trump's record on treaties is quite limited. During his single term, Trump submitted just five treaties to the Senate and only one of those treaties was approved during his presidency.[19]

In fact, a review of Trump's brief record on treaties indicates that he withdrew or unsigned as many Article II treaties as he submitted to the Senate, and he threatened to withdraw from and questioned the value of numerous other agreements, including NATO, the most significant security agreement to which the United States is party (Bellinger 2019). Richard Haas (2020) argues that the Trump doctrine is essentially the "Withdrawal Doctrine," citing Trump's withdrawals or threats of withdrawal from a host of international agreements as the only guiding principle of the administration's foreign policy.

Trump withdrew from the following ratified treaties: the Optional Protocol to the Vienna Convention on Diplomatic Relations; the Treaty of Amity with Iran; the Intermediate-Range Nuclear Forces (INF) treaty with Russia; and the Open Skies treaty. The last two of these treaties are important components of the arms control legacies of former Republican presidents, Ronald Reagan and George H.W. Bush. Trump also unsigned the Arms Trade Treaty in April 2019, a significant arms control treaty signed by Obama in 2016. Trump delayed action on renewing the New START treaty with Russia.[20] Trump's opposition toward arms control agreements is unsurprising and mirrored the skepticism apparent in the very conservative Republican Senate majority (Böller 2022). Trump formally began US withdrawal from the World Health Organization (WHO) on July 6, 2020. However, US participation in the WHO was through a joint resolution of Congress, passed in 1948, so the Constitution of the WHO was not an Article II treaty under domestic law, but rather a congressional-executive agreement (Gostin, *et al.* 2020).[21] Trump also withdrew from the UN Educational, Scientific, and Cultural Organization (UNESCO), another congressional-executive agreement (Hathaway 2020).

President Trump's hostility to binding international agreements extended to other forms of international agreements, including the Paris Agreement on Climate Change and the Iran Nuclear Agreement, which I discuss extensively in Chapter 6. He reveled in dismantling US participation in each of these signature Obama agreements. Trump also repeatedly threatened to leave the WTO, NAFTA, and the bilateral trade agreement with South Korea (Brown and Irwin 2018; Hathaway 2020).

Much like Obama, Trump relied on executive agreements to complete the lion's share of his international agreements. Public reporting of executive agreements as of this writing indicates that the Trump administration completed at least 246 executive agreements, which is likely a substantial undercount. Thus, at least 98 percent of Trump's binding international agreements were executive agreements, a figure that is even higher than Obama's percentage.[22] As more and more executive agreements are publicly reported, this percentage will increase.

If President Trump had desired to submit and push for treaties, he would probably have met with greater success than Obama. After all, his party controlled the Senate during his presidency. Moreover, as a Republican, Trump would likely have received support from fellow partisans in the Senate, and Democrats normally support treaties during the ratification process. In fact, the Senate approved 12 treaties during Trump's presidency, including 11 that were left over from the Obama administration. The 11 treaties were uncontroversial, however, and several of them, especially the tax protocols, had the strong support of business groups. Even so, they were held up by Republicans in the Senate during the Obama administration, with the logjam only breaking once a Republican occupied the White House.[23] Concerted efforts to push treaties and formalize multilateral cooperation were anathema to Trump's "America First" approach to foreign policy.

Conclusion

In this chapter, I reviewed recent trends in the use of treaties and executive agreements by presidents, with a focus on comparing the presidents of the twenty-first century, G.W. Bush, Obama, and Trump. The analysis of the data indicates a slight shift toward greater reliance on unilateral instruments during the Bush administration, followed by a full-throttle charge toward unilateralism during the Obama administration, which was continued by Trump, who focused more on withdrawing from treaties than on making them. While Bush's use of treaties is comparable to that of his predecessors with only a slight decrease, Obama nearly abandoned the use of treaties, completing far fewer of them than any modern predecessor who served at least a full term.[24] Trump continued the downward trend, submitting just a handful of treaties to the Senate during his single term. Moreover, Obama's record of success with treaties does not compare favorably to his modern predecessors. His success rates are worse than any of his modern predecessors, as most of his treaties were ignored by the Senate while he was in office. The Senate, for its part, approved far fewer treaties during the Obama and Trump presidencies.

The situation has not improved during President Biden's first year and a half in office. As of May 2022, Biden had submitted just two treaties. Why have recent presidents largely abandoned the use of treaties? Secretary of State John Kerry certainly had a legitimate complaint when he stated, "You can't pass a treaty anymore," as the recent Senate has proven as dysfunctional on treaties as it has on other forms of policymaking. The source of that dysfunction lies in the hyper-partisanship that characterizes the institution these days. The analysis and discussion suggest that partisan polarization is largely to blame both for the disuse of treaties and the politicization of the process when Obama chose to submit a treaty to the Senate, as we saw with Obama's effort to push for his signature bilateral arms control agreement with Russia, the New START.

But a dysfunctional Senate brought about by partisan polarization is only part of the story. Presidents largely retain the freedom to complete their international agreements unilaterally, without Congress. Doing so is even more attractive when Congress is dysfunctional because it is unlikely that the legislature could force the president's hand legislatively, given the fortification provided the president by the veto and the high bar required to override. In the chapters that follow, I turn toward quantitative statistical analysis of the data on treaties, as well as more detailed case analysis of significant international agreements during the Obama and Trump presidencies.

Notes

1 Readers can read the draft executive order at: www.apps.washingtonpost.com/g/documents/world/read-the-trump-administrations-draft-of-the-executive-order-on-treaties/2307/. While the order was never implemented, it caused quite a stir in the international law community because it signaled a shift in thinking regarding multilateral commitments and US leadership. It also suggested that high-level officials in the White House had serious misunderstandings regarding the purpose of international law, particularly regarding human rights (Bellinger 2019; Sullivan 2017).

2 The best example of a significant stalled treaty is the UN Convention on the Law of the Sea, a treaty I discuss extensively in Chapter 4. President Obama pushed for action on the treaty in 2012, but to little effect.

3 The treaty was far-reaching, yet lacked "the complex verification measures, reporting mechanisms, and timetables of past accords" (Homan 2016, 91).

4 In total, the SFRC held nine hearings and Armed Services held five hearings on New START. In 2002, the SFRC held four hearings and Armed Services held two hearings on the Moscow Treaty.

5 The report is available at: www.congress.gov/congressional-report/111th-congress/executive-report/6.

6 Homan's (2016) account of Obama's success on New START suggests it was a great victory in the sense that Obama was the first Democratic president to successfully ratify a bilateral arms control treaty with Russia or the Soviet Union. While Democratic presidents clearly face greater political obstacles on arms control treaties from conservatives in the Senate (Böller 2022; Kreps, *et al.* 2018), Presidents Kennedy, Johnson, and Clinton were all able to secure significant multilateral arms control treaties. Carter was unsuccessful with SALT 2, but that was largely due to Soviet actions on the international stage (their invasion of Afghanistan in 1979) and not opposition from conservatives in the Senate. In fact, Carter was nearing successful ratification according to contemporary accounts, until Soviet actions changed the calculus in the Senate (Kreps, *at al.* 2018).

7 In fact, legal scholars often punt on this question, stating there are no clear textual reasons within the law, in particular the Constitution, to guide presidential behavior here. My contention is that absent clarity in the law, presidents are freer to act and any constraints on their behavior are much more likely to be political than legal. As I have previously argued, treaties and executive agreements may be seen as legally interchangeable, but they are not so politically (Krutz and Peake 2009, 80–2).

8 There is precedent for presidents to submit arms control agreements to the Congress for bicameral approval, as Nixon did with the original SALT accord in 1972 (Krutz and Peake 2009, 78). The Senate jealously guards its turf on these kinds of agreements, especially.

9 Numerous other examples exist, where Obama clearly skirted these topical norms, and little controversy resulted. In 2013, the Obama administration acceded to the Minamata Convention on Mercury, an important multilateral treaty on environmental protection. They did so unilaterally, and there was no objection from the Senate, despite unclear authority on the part of the executive and the fact that multilateral environmental agreements, under the previously described norm, historically are done as Article II treaties (Bradley and Goldsmith 2018). Despite persuasive evidence that these subject area norms for Article II exist (Spiro 2001), some legal scholars dismiss them because they can find no basis in the Constitution for their special treatment (Ramsey 2017). The norm appears to have developed because of congressional efforts to push for treaties on certain topics, pass statutes requiring congressional approval in some areas (e.g., trade and fisheries), whether the agreement might affect the laws of the states (i.e., federalism issues, which may occur in instances of taxes and extradition), and legal concerns about whether or not the treaty is self-executing.

10 For a list of all treaties transmitted by Presidents Obama and Trump, see table 1 in the appendix: https://dataverse.harvard.edu/dataverse/jeffreypeake.

11 One of the treaties transmitted during the 111th Congress was submitted by President Bush in January 2009, just prior to Obama's inauguration. Obama transmitted two of the treaties during the 115th Congress in January 2017, just prior to Trump's inauguration.

12 This is a difficult number to estimate. The table reports far fewer executive agreements than were completed by the Obama administration during its second term and for the Trump administration. Publicly available data are used for these counts and the DOS simply does not accurately report executive agreements in a timely fashion. I discuss this transparency problem in greater detail in Chapter 5 and the problem is analyzed extensively by Hathaway, *et al.* (2020).

13 Trump is excluded here because he only transmitted five treaties to the Senate.

14 For Obama's 2009 priority list, see table 2, in the appendix: https://dataverse.harvard.edu/dataverse/jeffreypeake.

15 I am referring to the Convention for the Elimination of All Forms of Discrimination Against Women (CEDAW), which was transmitted to the Senate by Carter in 1980 where it has been pending ever since. I discuss CEDAW at length in Chapter 4.

16 When you include the Obama transmitted treaties approved since he left office, the sum of approved Obama-favored treaties is 31, and the approval rate increases to 56.4 percent.

17 Carter's low success rate in column 3 is partly attributable to the fact that he only served a single term. Obama served two full terms.

18 The TPP was not transmitted to the Senate as an Article II treaty. Obama signed the agreement on February 3, 2016. He planned to push Congress to pass the controversial agreement as a congressional-executive agreement during the post-election period at the end of 2016. The TPP was a politically fraught issue during the 2016 election. Though Hillary Clinton, the Democratic nominee, had supported the TPP as Secretary of State, she modified her position during the campaign. Most Democrats in Congress also opposed the deal. The most important opponent, however, was Trump, who had continually voiced disdain for the TPP throughout 2015 and 2016 (Behsudi 2016). In the wake of Trump's 2016 victory, Obama abandoned his efforts to lobby Congress for TPP and Senate leaders pronounced the agreement dead in Congress (Mauldin 2016). Trump ended US participation in the agreement with his official withdrawal.

19 Trump's only treaty approval was the protocol to include North Macedonia as a member of NATO. The other four treaties include a fisheries agreement with Pacific states, an extradition treaty with Croatia, the Beijing Convention, and the Beijing Protocol. The last two treaties replace the Montreal Convention and are important updates to international law on civil aviation and terrorism. Trump waited until June 18, 2020, to submit the last three of these treaties, so it is not surprising they were not approved by the Senate before he left office. At the time of this writing (May 10, 2022), four of Trump's five treaties remain pending in the Senate, although two were recently reported by the SFRC (the fisheries agreement and the treaty with Croatia) and will probably be approved before the end of the 117th Congress.

20 President Biden formally extended New START for five years by executive agreement on February 3, 2021.

21 On his first day in office, President Biden reversed Trump's withdrawal from the WHO, which under the 1948 joint resolution would not go into effect until July 6, 2021, a year after Trump's announcement (Keaten 2021). The legality of Trump's unilateral withdrawal is questionable, given the requirements set forth in the 1948 law—requirements he failed to meet (Gostin, *et al.* 2020). Using similar reasoning, legal experts questioned the ability of Trump to follow through on his threats to unilaterally withdraw from the North American Free Trade Agreement (NAFTA), something he threatened to do numerous times in 2017 before successfully renegotiating the deal in 2019 (Aleem 2017). Given that US participation in NAFTA (and the WHO) was through statute, the president cannot unilaterally reverse US law without a clear delegation by Congress or by following procedures laid out in the agreement. It remains unclear, however, if a president were to act unilaterally, if Congress or the courts could stop such an action. It would likely take legislation, which could be vetoed by the president, so the effort would require a bipartisan supermajority. Even in the case of unilateral withdrawal from duly ratified treaties, presidents retain a great deal of discretion under domestic law if they follow the process outlined in the treaty (Krutz and Peake 2009, 35–6).

22 I did not include the three treaties submitted by Obama in January 2009 in making this calculation. President Trump only submitted five treaties and my count of executive agreements completed during his presidency is 246, for a total of 251 agreements.

23 The 11 Obama treaties ratified during the Trump years include two extradition treaties (with Serbia and Kosovo); two maritime boundary agreements with Pacific island

nations; a multilateral convention on the blind; a UN convention on receivables financing; the accession of Montenegro into NATO; and four tax protocols (with Japan, Spain, Switzerland, and Luxembourg).

24 I made the full-term qualification here because President Kennedy submitted 30 treaties to the Senate, but he served slightly less than three years before he was assassinated; and President Ford submitted 41 treaties to the Senate during his two and a half years as president. Obama submitted just 39 treaties in eight years. Of course, President Trump set a new low bar for treaties.

3

THE EFFECTS OF PARTISAN POLARIZATION ON TREATY POLITICS

I have argued that partisan polarization is the primary explanation for changes in treaty politics that have occurred since the end of the twentieth century. Norms that governed the treaty process last century have deteriorated. The discussion of the Obama and Trump years suggests that both the legislative and executive branches share in the blame for this deterioration and the resulting dysfunction. In this chapter, I conduct a more systematic empirical analysis that assesses the impact of polarization on the domestic politics of treaties. The chapter includes a series of statistical analyses focused on testing the effects of polarization. First, I model the number of treaties presidents transmit to each Senate. Second, I model the median time taken in the Senate Foreign Relations Committee (SFRC) to process treaties during each Senate.[1] Finally, I disaggregate the analysis to the treaty level to assess treaty gridlock during the Senate approval process for all treaties submitted by presidents from 1949 to 2020. The statistical analyses confirm that partisan polarization plays an especially important role in the treaty process, structuring presidential decisions on submitting treaties and the ability of the Senate to process treaties once they are submitted.

Presidents are largely free to choose how to complete their international agreements in domestic law. Evidence suggests presidents often base their decisions regarding the form their agreements will take on tradition, as well as domestic and international political considerations and the need for efficiency in processing international agreements (Krutz and Peake 2009). During the second half of the twentieth century, the lion's share (94 percent) of international agreements were completed as executive agreements, typically without any input from Congress; however, presidents continued to use Article II treaties to complete upwards of 40 percent of the most significant agreements (Krutz and Peake 2009). As shown in Chapter 2, this dynamic changed during the twenty-first century, as recent

DOI: 10.4324/9781003347422-3

presidents have relied almost exclusively on unilateral instruments to complete their diplomatic agreements. Presidents still submitted some of their agreements to the Senate for approval, and many languished in the Senate, often ignored by the SFRC.

As discussed in Chapter 1, the treaty approval process begins and ends with the president. First, a member of the executive branch signs the international agreement, and then the administration determines whether to submit the agreement to the Senate as an Article II treaty or to consider the agreement an executive agreement in terms of the domestic ratification process. The standard bureaucratic process is governed by the Circular-175 process laid out in the *Foreign Affairs Manual* (Krutz and Peake 2009, 82–3); however, the process is much less transparent and standardized as required by both the *Manual* and the statutory transparency regime (Hathaway, *et al.* 2020). Bradley and Goldsmith (2018) estimate that more than 99 percent of executive agreements over the past several decades exclude Congress (also see Hathaway 2009), including most so-called congressional-executive agreements. In most cases, executive agreements enter into force upon signature by the president's agent.[2]

Second, if it is determined that the agreement will be finalized as an Article II treaty, the president transmits it to the Senate for advice and consent via a transmittal document which summarizes the treaty and provides arguments for approval, along with a memorandum from the DOS and the text of the treaty. By Senate rule, the treaty is then referred to the SFRC, the committee with exclusive jurisdiction over treaties. Typically, the SFRC will hold hearings on a treaty and report a resolution of ratification to the floor of the Senate, which will often include reservations, understandings, or declarations (RUDs), however this process can take a great deal of time. Then the treaty moves to the floor. Amendments to the resolution of ratification, or to the treaty itself, can occur on the floor, though most treaties, once reported, pass without much difficulty, and successful amendments are rare. While failure on the floor is rare and many pass with a division vote (i.e., no roll call),[3] many treaties languish for long periods of time either at the transmittal stage (i.e., between signature and presidential transmittal), the committee stage, or both. Dozens of treaties have been ignored by the SFRC or are not taken up by the floor but remain pending.[4] Others are withdrawn by the president or returned by the Senate.[5] Given that more than 95 percent of treaty failures occur due to Senate inaction, we cannot rely on floor vote failures to provide much insight on the Senate treaty process. The final step in the process is when the president deposits the ratification documents, formally ratifying the treaty under international law.

Of the 1,000 treaties transmitted by presidents from 1949 to 2020,[6] 913 were eventually approved by the Senate, for an overall treaty success rate of 91.3 percent. Of the 87 treaty failures, 63 (72.4 percent) never made it out of the SFRC. The remainder were either never scheduled for full floor action after being reported by the committee (20) or failed when they came up for a vote (four). Over

90 percent of treaties are eventually approved by the Senate. Such a high passage rate masks a substantial amount of treaty gridlock, which becomes apparent when we examine the amount of time treaties languish in the process outlined above. First, the median time between executive signature and presidential transmittal of a treaty is 187 days, or about six months. Once a treaty is transmitted, it may wait months before the SFRC acts. The median time in committee is 204 days. Once a treaty is reported by the SFRC, however, if the full Senate takes up the treaty it often does so quickly, as the median number of days from SFRC report to full Senate vote is eight.[7] These statistics indicate that the committee stage is most vital for treaties and an assessment of treaty politics in the Senate is correct to closely examine the committee stage.

What explains variation in presidential behavior on treaty transmittals and gridlock in the Senate treaty process? In Chapter 2, I highlighted the significance of partisan polarization. The evidence from the Obama presidency suggests that partisan polarization affects presidential decisions on treaties and structures the politics at play in the Senate as presidents seek approval for their treaties. What other factors influence the process? Does the partisan polarization explanation hold when subjected to systematic statistical analysis with appropriate controls? To address these questions, I run a series of regression analyses, testing the following hypothesis: as partisan polarization worsens in the Senate, presidents will use fewer treaties and treaty gridlock (delay in the Senate) will increase. I also address other factors including presidential resources (i.e., public approval ratings and the number of presidential partisans in the Senate), the ideology of the SFRC chair, and, in the disaggregate analysis, some treaty-specific variables.

Explaining Presidential Treaty Usage

Why have recent presidents submitted fewer treaties for approval by the Senate? Given that treaties require the support of two-thirds of the Senate, any explanation should focus on the prospects for receiving Senate consent. The discussion of President Obama's disuse of treaties in Chapter 2 highlights the importance of partisan polarization, which has made the prospects of the Senate doing anything difficult, let alone processing treaties which require such a high bar to approve. The prospect of Senate support is the basis for the evasion hypothesis, which states that as prospects for ratification diminish, presidents will use fewer treaties. Early studies that tested and found support for the evasion hypothesis focused on partisan variables, including divided government, that is, when one party controls the presidency and the other party controls the Senate, or the number of presidential partisans in the Senate. As the number of the president's partisans in the Senate decrease (or during divided control of the presidency and the Senate), presidents should use fewer treaties. Under such conditions, presidents evade the treaty process by completing their agreements unilaterally, due to the lower prospects for Senate approval (Margolis 1986).

However, the hypothesized relationship between partisan control and treaty usage does not hold up to empirical scrutiny. During the period (1949–2020), the mean number of treaties transmitted during a Senate controlled by the president's party is 25.7. When the other party controls the Senate, the mean number of treaties is 30.4.[8] Prior research on the use of treaties indicates that the basic partisan component of the evasion hypothesis is not supported in the data, whether researchers examine treaty submittals, the use of executive agreements, or a ratio measure accounting for both the number of treaties and executive agreements as a share of all international agreements (Krutz and Peake 2006; Martin 2000, 2005; Shull 2006).

But why? Theories related to the use of unilateral presidential powers suggests that presidents are less inclined to rely on their unilateral powers during divided government because the majority party in Congress is more likely to challenge the president on their usage (Howell 2005, 433). Thus, when the president's party controls the Senate, majority party leaders are likely to grant the president leeway in how they finalize their international agreements. Another theory suggests that treaties have opportunity costs for presidents, such that they will push other legislative priorities, primarily electorally important domestic priorities, rather than treaties when opportunities are propitious for legislative success, such as when their party controls the Congress (Kelley and Pevehouse 2015).

While the basic partisan evasion hypothesis is unsupported by the data, that does not mean presidents are unlikely to consider the prospects for Senate consent when deciding on whether to submit treaties. Recall, for example, Secretary of State John Kerry's statement regarding the impossibility of getting treaties approved by the Senate, when providing testimony on why the Iran Nuclear Agreement was not a treaty: "I spent quite a few years ago trying to get a lot of treaties through the United States Senate, and frankly, it's become physically impossible. You can't pass a treaty anymore." The Constitution's supermajority requirement increases opportunities for treaty opponents to delay or even kill a president's treaty. More generally, Senate counter-majoritarian rules embolden the minority party such that spiking or significantly delaying a treaty may not be a matter of party control, but rather the willingness of treaty opponents to use all the parliamentary tools at their disposal to block a treaty. A more cohesive minority party also allows members of the minority to demand changes to a president's treaty or to condition approval on concessions on other issues, as we saw with the case of New START in 2010 (Boller 2021).

In sum, passing treaties requires building a broad bipartisan coalition, prospects for which are less likely under conditions of partisan ideological polarization (Krutz and Peake 2009, 161). When conditions are poor for building bipartisan coalitions, the prospects for speedy consent in the Senate are substantially diminished. As a result, partisan polarization is likely to play an important role as an explanation for the president's use of treaties, such that as polarization increases, presidents use fewer treaties.

Other factors are likely to play a role in treaty usage. The SFRC is particularly important to the treaty process in the Senate, and the committee chair determines the committee's agenda and how it will proceed on treaties submitted by the president. The data on treaties indicate that, for the median treaty, 86.4 percent of the time in the Senate is spent in the SFRC. If delay occurs, it will normally occur in the committee. Thus, the most important senator in the treaty process is the chair of the SFRC, who controls the committee's agenda. Conservatives are most inclined to oppose far-reaching international agreements, given their historical hostility to internationalism (Auerswald and Maltzman 2003; DeLaet and Scott 2006). Krutz and Peake (2009) demonstrate that treaty delay increases, and presidents use more treaties as a share of all international agreements, when the SFRC chair is more conservative. Thus, any analysis attempting to isolate the effects of partisan polarization on the treaty process must account for the ideology of the SFRC chair. The expectation is that presidents will use fewer treaties when the chair is more conservative, however the opposite relationship could emerge as presidents may want to avoid upsetting a conservative committee chair by using unilateral alternatives to complete their binding international agreements.

Another factor that may influence the use of treaties by presidents could include their political resources. A president's political capital, which is often expressed as their public approval ratings, may embolden them to use treaties rather than skirting the Senate. Additionally, the data in Table 2.2 clearly indicate that Democratic presidents tend to use treaties more regularly than Republican presidents, and this was especially the case with Presidents Truman, Carter, and Clinton. Thus, the analysis should control for the president's party. Finally, the international context may demand more treaties from the president during a given Senate. When new states are added to the United Nations, the need for Article II treaties increases irrespective of the domestic political situation.

I estimate a statistical model to explain the number of treaties presidents transmit to each Senate for the 81st Congress (1949–50) to the 116th Congress (2019–20).[9] The dependent variable is the number of treaties as shown in Table 2.1 and the unit of analysis is each two-year Senate (N=36). Because this is a simple count variable, I use a count model rather than ordinary least squares (OLS) regression.[10] I regress the number of treaties per Congress on partisan polarization in the Senate,[11] the size of the president's party in the Senate,[12] and the SFRC chair's ideology.[13] I include three additional control variables: the president's average approval rating over the two-year Congress in the Gallup Poll,[14] an indicator variable for the president's party (Democrat = 1) during each Congress, and the count of new UN members during each two-year period.[15]

The results are presented in Table 3.1 and clearly support the main hypothesis: as polarization increases, presidents transmit fewer treaties to the Senate. The results indicate a substantively important marginal effect of partisan polarization. Increasing polarization by one standard deviation leads to a decrease in the expected number of treaties by 38 percent.[16] The most polarized Senate of the

TABLE 3.1 Count model for the number of treaties transmitted per Congress (1949–2020)

Independent variable	*Coefficient*	*Robust standard error*	*z score*	*Marginal effect (%)*
Partisan polarization	−4.877	1.287	−3.79★★	−38
SFRC chair ideology	0.588	0.228	2.57★★	+24
Num. of presidential partisans	−0.017	0.009	−1.73★★	−12
Presidential approval	−0.011	0.007	−1.28	
Democratic president	0.37	0.174	2.13★★	+45
Growth in UN membership	0.11	0.017	0.68	
Constant	7.52★★			
	N = 36			
	Log likelihood: −133.04			
	Model chi-squared: 20.16			
	Pseudo R-squared: 0.09			
	★$p < 0.10$; ★★$p<0.05$ (one-tailed)			

Note: The marginal effect represents the effect on the expected number of treaties with an increase of the independent variable by one standard deviation. For the Democratic president indicator variable, the marginal effect is the percentage increase for going from 0 to 1 (Republican to Democrat).

period, the 116th, which has a polarization score 2.26 standard deviations above the mean, is predicted to have about 85 percent fewer treaties than average, or about five treaties. The actual number of treaties for the 116th Senate is four.

The results indicate that the SFRC chair's ideology is also an important factor, as presidents transmit more treaties to the Senate when the chair is conservative, a finding that is somewhat counterintuitive, since we would expect the prospects for treaty passage to decrease under a conservative chair. A one standard deviation increase in the chair's ideology (more conservative) increases the number of treaties by 24 percent. The SFRC chair may play an important role in constraining the president's inclination to avoid the Article II treaty process, leading presidents to submit more treaties when the chair is conservative, when controlling for other factors.

As presidential resources increase (i.e., their party size in the Senate or their public approval ratings), presidents submit fewer treaties. The results for the number of presidential partisans variable are significant and in the opposite direction of the evasion hypothesis.[17] When a president's political resources increase, the Senate may grant the president increased leeway in determining how they finalize their international agreements. Thus, presidents may be less constrained in completing international agreements unilaterally. Alternatively, presidents may instead focus on other legislative policy efforts, with a focus on fulfilling campaign promises when their political capital is higher, eschewing the opportunity costs of treaties (Kelley and Pevehouse 2015). The model also indicates that Democratic presidents submit more treaties than Republican presidents, as expected. The UN growth variable is insignificant.

Treaty Gridlock

Partisan polarization is an important consideration as presidents consider whether to submit treaties to the Senate. As clearly stated in the quote from Secretary Kerry, it is likely that presidents and their advisors expect a polarized Senate to be less able to complete action on treaties, even when their own party holds most of the seats as was the case for six of the eight years during the Obama presidency. Kerry's statement suggests, however, that historically (i.e., before polarization was a problem) most treaties made it through the Senate and were approved. The treaty approval process can be marked with substantial delay. When controlling for other factors, does partisan polarization contribute to treaty gridlock, or the delay experienced by treaties as they work their way through the Senate?

Before considering what may impact treaty gridlock, a pressing question is why study treaty gridlock in the first place? If most treaties are eventually ratified, what does it matter if a treaty is held up by a few months or even years? As a general statement, gridlock in treaty ratification means that presidents are less able to achieve their diplomatic goals. The existing status quo that led the executive to sign the treaty is maintained until the treaty is ratified. Even the more mundane bilateral treaties deal with important problems that remain unresolved while the treaty remains unratified, including, for example, unfavorable tax and investment conditions for US businesses. Moreover, delayed ratification allows opponents of a treaty to increase their efforts to change or defeat it. The data clearly indicate that the longer the treaty languishes in the Senate, the chances for ratification diminish each year. Thus, uncertainty around the issues dealt with by the treaty increases. The longer a treaty languishes, the more costly it may be for the president to get key senators to support the treaty. During the 1990s, for example, SFRC Chair, Jesse Helms (NC-R) held up several of President Clinton's treaties, including the CWC and START II, moving them through committee only after he secured the president's commitment to sign on to his DOS reorganization plan, which Democrats in the Senate opposed (Hersman 2000, 88–90).

Treaty delay may also negatively impact the president's political reputation, both at home and abroad. Treaties that stagnate may make the president look ineffective as a foreign policy leader, which may diminish the perception that the United States is worthy of partnership. This may especially be the case for multilateral agreements where US negotiators led the talks, but then seem incapable of getting an agreement they coauthored approved in the Senate. As I show in the next chapter, this accurately describes what happened with the UN disabilities convention (CRPD) and the UN law of the sea treaty (UNCLOS). On issues such as human rights or arms control, the United States may be seen as an international scofflaw because if its unwillingness to ratify and participate in key international agreements like the CEDAW or the CTBT (Baldez 2014; Patrick 2019). US diplomats are handcuffed during negotiations because of the significant uncertainty in the domestic ratification process. That it took the United States nearly 40 years to ratify the Genocide Convention was a source of embarrassment for US diplomats during most of the Cold War (LeBlanc 1991). More generally, a protracted delay in ratifying an important treaty could have "a corrosive effect on American prestige" (Krepon and Caldwell 1991, 4). Taking a leading role in shaping international law is difficult under such circumstances.

Explaining Trends in Treaty Gridlock

Gridlock in the treaty process, if it emerges, will likely be found in the SFRC, as treaties spend most of their Senate lifespan in the committee. I empirically assess treaty gridlock in two ways. First, I calculate the median length of time treaties submitted to a particular Senate spend in committee, prior to the committee's issuing a positive report to send the treaty to the Senate floor.[18] I model this median length of committee delay in the aggregate, using the same variables as in the analysis above for the number of treaties transmitted per Senate. The unit of analysis for the model is each two-year Senate. The expectation is that polarization will increase the median number of days treaties spend in the SFRC. Second, I disaggregate the data to the individual-treaty level and conduct an analysis of treaty delay. The unit of analysis is the treaty (N=1,000), and the dependent variable is the number of days each treaty spends before the SFRC.[19] The disaggregated analysis allows for the inclusion of treaty-specific variables which have been shown to be important in explaining treaty gridlock (Krutz and Peake 2009; Peake 2017).

The results of the aggregate analysis are presented in Table 3.2, where the dependent variable (median days treaties spend before the SFRC) is regressed on partisan polarization, the ideology of the SFRC chair, the number of presidential partisans, average presidential approval, the president's party (Democrat=1), and growth in UN members. To normalize the dependent variable, I used its natural

TABLE 3.2 OLS regression model of the natural log of median days to SFRC report per Congress (1949–2018)

Independent variable	*Coefficient*	*Standard error*	*t statistic*
Partisan polarization	2.610	1.051	2.48**
SFRC chair ideology	−0.060	0.278	−0.22
Num. of presidential partisans	−0.006	0.013	−0.44
Presidential approval	−0.006	0.008	−0.67
Democratic president	0.230	0.201	1.14
Growth in UN membership	−0.029	0.017	−1.64*
Constant	4.371**		
	N = 35		
	Model F-statistic: 3.63**		
	Pseudo R-Squared: 0.32		
	*p < 0.10; **p<0.05 (one-tailed)		

log value.[20] The results indicate party polarization has a statistically significant and positive effect on aggregate treaty gridlock. Clearly, the median treaty takes far longer to process in committee as partisan polarization increases. The other variables, however, do not appear to impact treaty gridlock in the aggregate, nor do presidential resources have much effect.[21] However, during periods of significant UN growth, when the international demand for treaties is greater, the SFRC processes treaties more quickly. This is likely due to the nature of treaties with new states, as they often lack much controversy because they are bilateral treaties where diplomats are focused on setting up new consulates and amending or writing new tax and extradition treaties.

Treaty Gridlock at the Individual Treaty Level

The treaties dataset includes treaty specific information at the individual treaty level (N=1,000), which allows us to isolate the impact of partisan polarization on treaty gridlock, while controlling for treaty-level factors and other politically relevant variables that might vary by treaty or time. Salient treaty-level factors include whether the treaty is bilateral or multilateral, whether the treaty is a new treaty or an amended or updated treaty, and the broad topic associated with the treaty. Moreover, I include politically relevant variables at the time of presidential transmittal to determine their impact on the Senate's processing each treaty.[22]

The disaggregated analysis accounts for several individual characteristics of treaties, as these characteristics might contribute to treaty gridlock. Multilateral treaties are likely to take longer to process in the SFRC. It is often multilateral treaties that evoke conservative opposition and an examination of the 37 pending treaties before the Senate listed on the DOS website indicates that 35 are multilateral treaties.[23] New treaties are likely to take longer to process than treaties that represent amendments, updates, or changes to existing treaties.[24] I also account for the general topic area of the treaty, adopting the topic codes used in prior work (Krutz and Peake 2009, 151). The topics are mutually exclusive and broken down as follows: security, sovereignty, economic, legal, and norms.[25] Treaties on international norms are likely to take longer, on average, as they deal with issues that are often controversial in US domestic politics and are the focus of conservative opposition (Patrick 2019). Conversely, economic treaties are likely to move through the process more quickly because their ratification is likely to have the support of US business groups and other powerful constituencies. Finally, I analyze the full set of treaties and then analyze separately the subset of treaties that are considered particularly significant and coded as important.[26] The expectation here is that the effects of polarization, as well as other variables, are likely to be more pronounced for the subset of important treaties.

The discussion to this point has focused largely on the impact of partisan polarization and the preferences of key players in the ratification process (e.g., the

SFRC chair), in addition to the political resources available to the president. In the analysis that follows, to account for the president's political resources, I include variables for the president's approval rating at the time of transmittal, as well as the partisan makeup of the Senate.[27] I also include the partisan polarization variable and the SFRC chair's ideology, using the same variables described previously. Finally, I include an indicator variable for the president's party. Democratic presidents, historically, are more inclined to submit treaties. Because opponents to treaties are typically conservatives, Republicans in the Senate are more likely to oppose treaties submitted by Democratic presidents, which is likely to extend the time required to process such treaties (Böller 2022; Homan 2016; Kreps *et al.* 2018). Thus, each treaty receives a code of 1 if it was transmitted by a Democrat and a 0 if it was submitted by a Republican.

The broader policy context is also likely to matter. The policy agenda-setting literature suggests that issues compete for attention both from the president and within the Congress (Peake 2016). Comparative analysis of the treaty process provides important insights here. For example, Boockmann (2006) finds that high unemployment decreases the likelihood of ratification success of ILO conventions in wealthy countries. In the US setting, the state of the economy, especially when it is struggling, is the issue most likely to dominate the president's agenda and compete with a president's foreign policy priorities. Presidents are likely to alter their own policy agenda in response to heightened public concern for the economy that results from high unemployment (Eshbaugh-Soha and Peake 2011). As a result, the president's attention to foreign policy may diminish and the White House may deploy fewer resources in the Senate on behalf of treaties. To control for issue competition, I include a variable to account for the unemployment rate at the time of the treaty's transmittal, as reported by the Bureau of Labor Statistics. I also include a variable to account for the size of the treaty agenda, which is simply the number of important treaties submitted during the same Senate (Krutz and Peake 2009, 151).

I use duration analysis, also referred to as hazard analysis, to assess the independent effects of the set of independent variables on the committee stage of treaty ratification process.[28] The dependent variable is the duration (in days) from presidential transmittal to SFRC report. The dates of transmittal and SFRC report are the instrumental data for the analysis.[29] In a hazard model, the coefficients demonstrate the impact of the variables on the underlying hazard rate. Thus, I report hazard ratios rather than the coefficients, although the significance tests relate to the coefficients. Hazard ratios reflect the probability of the process terminating. In the case of treaties, terminating the process has a somewhat counter-intuitive meaning, as it reflects the SFRC reporting the treaty to the floor.[30] Hazard ratios greater than 1.0 with a significant positive coefficient indicate an effect that speeds up the process (i.e., the committee report) and, therefore, decreases duration. Hazard ratios below 1.0 with a significant negative coefficient indicate an effect that slows the process, thus increasing duration.

TABLE 3.3 Hazard model for treaty duration in the SFRC stage of ratification process (1949–2020)

Independent variables	*All treaties (model 1)*			*Important treaties (model 2)*		
	Hazard ratio	*z score*	*Impact on duration (%)*	*Hazard ratio*	*z score*	*Impact on duration (%)*
Partisan effects						
Partisan polarization	0.309	−1.91**	+10	0.009	−3.93**	+38
SFRC chair's ideology	0.861	−1.28*	+6	0.930	−0.28	
Democratic president	0.867	−1.66**	+16	0.527	−3.44**	+77
Agenda competition						
Unemployment	0.915	−3.08**	+14	0.883	−2.11**	+19
Size of treaty Agenda	1.002	0.16		0.997	−0.17	
Presidential resources						
Presidential approval	1.007	2.71**	−11	1.001	0.18	
Num. of president's party	0.998	−0.43		1.013	1.13	
Treaty characteristics						
Multilateral	0.692	−4.98**	+42	0.741	−1.67**	+30
New treaty	0.697	−5.26**	+40	0.985	−0.09	
Security	1.067	0.47		1.442	1.84**	−36
Sovereignty	0.889	−0.89		1.475	1.58*	−37
Economic	1.052	0.59		1.967	3.21**	−59
Norms	0.675	−3.03**	+54	0.740	−1.43*	+37
Gamma	−0.001	−14.50**		−0.001	−7.69**	
	No. of subjects: 1,000			No. of subjects: 282		
	No. of failures (reports): 937			No. of failures (reports): 258		
	Total time at risk: 740,492			Total time at risk: 308,348		
	Log-likelihood: −1706.4			Log-likelihood: −485.1		
	Chi-squared (13): 118.15**			Chi-squared (13): 91.24**		
	Predicted median duration: 251			Predicted median duration: 318		

Note: *p < .1; **p < .05 (one-tailed). The dependent variable is the time (in days) from the point of treaty transmittal to when the SFRC first reports on the treaty. Hazard ratios below 1.0 indicate an increase in duration, whereas a hazard ratio above 1.0 indicates a decrease in duration. Impact on duration indicates the percentage effect on the baseline estimate of the median duration to committee report when the independent variable of interest is moved from its mean value (or 0 if a dummy variable) to one standard deviation above its mean (or 1 if a dummy), with all other variables held at their mean values. Legal treaties are the reference category for treaty topic. Analysis was conducted in STATA 14. Impacts were computed using "mfx" command therein.

I report the results of two duration models in Table 3.3. The first model reports the results for the entire dataset (N=1,000) and the second model reports the results for just the important treaties (N=282). The results for both models support the primary hypothesis underlying this chapter. As partisan polarization increases, treaties take longer to process in the Senate. In both analyses, the partisan polarization variable has a statistically significant hazard ratio below 1.0, meaning that treaties take longer to process when polarization is higher. Increasing the value of polarization from its mean to one standard deviation above its mean, while holding all the other variables at their mean value, increases the duration by 10 percent, or about 24 days. Increasing the value of polarization from its minimum value to its maximum value is estimated to increase duration by a whopping 47 percent, or 118 days (about four months). As expected, the impact of polarization is especially pronounced for the important treaties. A one standard deviation increase in polarization increases duration by 38 percent, or 121 days (four months). The maximum impact, moving from the minimum value of polarization to the maximum, more than doubles the duration for the subset of important treaties. The other key hypothesis related to the importance of the SFRC chair receives only modest support, however, as the substantive effects are substantively marginal in the full set of treaties and are insignificant when we examine just the subset of important treaties.

Another significant partisan effect is that of the president's political party. Treaties transmitted by Democratic presidents take substantially longer to process. The hazard ratios are well below 1.0 in both analyses and statistically significant, indicating that the effect is to slow the process considerably. In terms of the impact, treaties transmitted by Democrats take 16 percent longer to process through committee for the full set of treaties. The effect is especially pronounced for important treaties submitted by Democrats, which take 77 percent longer to process in the SFRC than important treaties submitted by Republicans.

The president's political resources also appear to impact the duration of the treaty process, but the effect is limited to the president's popularity. The number of presidential partisans variable, while correctly signed, does not appear to significantly impact duration.[31] The president's approval rating, however, has a statistically and substantively significant impact on the duration of the treaty process, decreasing the duration for treaty consideration. The effect dissipates, however, when the model is restricted to the subset of important treaties. The agenda-setting hypothesis is partly supported in both models. While the size of the treaty agenda had no impact on duration, high unemployment significantly increases the time it takes to process treaties, as expected. The hazard ratio for the unemployment variable is below 1.0 and statistically significant, indicating that higher unemployment adds to treaty duration. The strong relationship holds for the subset of important treaties. During times of high unemployment, the focus of the president and Congress is likely spent on handling the economic situation rather than treaties pending in the Senate.

The characteristics of individual treaties also matter. For the full dataset, multilateral and new treaties take about 40 percent longer to process in the SFRC, though only in the case of multilateral treaties do we see this impact carry over to the subset of important treaties. It is also apparent that the general topic of the treaty is important. Treaties on international norms (e.g., the environment or human rights) tend to take much longer to process. For the subset of important treaties, security, sovereignty, and economic treaties are all processed more quickly than are legal treaties, the reference category, while norms treaties take longer. I estimated each model again, including just a single indicator variable for a specific topic in each estimation in turn, to compare the impact of a single topic against the rest of the treaty dataset. The estimations indicate that norms treaties are processed much more slowly than are other treaties and economics treaties are processed much more quickly.

Some treaties face obstacles on the floor that may not emerge in committee. In some cases of treaty failure (24), the SFRC issued a positive report, but the full Senate failed to consider the treaty (20) or considered it and voted it down (4). To verify the results from the SFRC model to the full time for Senate approval, I estimated the same duration models using the time from presidential transmittal to full Senate approval. The results are very similar, although the statistical significance and substantive effects of the partisan polarization variable increase in both sets of treaties. The effects of other relevant variables also increase in the full Senate approval model, except for the SFRC chair's ideology, which is insignificant.[32] The results from the SFRC stage of the model are verified when we examine the full Senate process.

Conclusion

Partisan polarization has a pernicious impact on the treaty process in the US Senate, providing a potent explanation for dysfunctional diplomacy. Examining a 70-year period with data on 1,000 treaties confirms that partisan polarization in the Senate impacts the process in two ways. First, presidents are less inclined to transmit treaties to the Senate as polarization increases, which means they are likely to rely more on unilateral diplomatic tools under such conditions. Scholarly accounts of the US Senate indicate the chamber works less effectively due to increasing partisan polarization and the team play that results, and it is perfectly rational for presidents to alter their behavior as a result (Lee 2009; Mann and Ornstein 2012; Wallner 2020). Second, partisan polarization greatly contributes to treaty gridlock once presidents send their treaties to the Senate. While Secretary Kerry's "physically impossible" intonation was an exaggeration, the analysis clearly supports the notion that polarization inhibits the ability of the Senate to process treaties and the effect is especially apparent on the most important treaties. Today's Senate, as polarized as it is, is much less able to uphold its Article II responsibilities of advice and consent on treaties.

At its base, such a finding is unsurprising. Partisan polarization, a condition that seems to have broken Congress and US politics more generally, distorts the treaty process by undermining basic norms that developed around the process last century as the United States grappled with its international leadership role. Such a breakdown in the treaty process could have profound implications for US diplomacy as partisan polarization continues to worsen and complaints about a dysfunctional Senate become commonplace. Understanding these implications requires a more in-depth examination of the politics surrounding some of the recent treaty failures. How is it that the United States, with its strong domestic laws promoting equality for the disabled, be one of the few states in the world that has not ratified the major UN convention protecting the rights of persons with disabilities? Ditto for the rights of women. Why has the United States, with the world's largest economy and most fearsome navy, and territory on two oceans and interests spanning the globe, failed to ratify the most significant piece of international law dealing with the law of the sea? And why is the United States on the outside looking in on major international issues having to do with environmental protection and climate change? The dysfunctional Senate treaty process resulting from partisan polarization is a big part of the answer.

As will become apparent, another major implication of partisan polarization is the increased use of unilateral tools by presidents to complete the United States' international commitments. In looking at a broken Senate process, presidents who are determined to complete international agreements must do so unilaterally. Such unilateral commitments are considerably less valuable when they are deemed illegitimate by one of the two major political parties. They also lack domestic political legitimacy when presidents enter them without the imprimatur of Senate approval or any support from the other political party. Finally, international commitments are much less durable when they are completed with the stroke of a pen rather than through joint action with the Congress. The implications of fragile international commitments are profound.

Notes

1 Earlier versions of the two aggregate analyses appeared in Peake, *et al.* (2012). The aggregate analyses presented here are updated and include a slightly different statistical model, with stronger results.
2 Executive agreements and other unilateral tools of diplomacy are discussed at length in Chapters 5 and 6.
3 The full Senate has voted down only four treaties since 1935 (see Chapter 1).
4 The DOS maintains a list of pending treaties at: www.state.gov/treaties-pending-in-the-senate/. As of this writing (April 2022), the list was updated through October 2019, and included 37 treaties, with the longest languishing treaty having been transmitted in 1949 (an International Labor Organization (ILO) treaty). The list includes two of the most recent treaties that failed floor votes: the CTBT and the disabilities convention. The list does not include three of Trump's pending treaties, submitted in 2020, or the two treaties transmitted by Biden through April 2022. Thus, the most current number of pending treaties is 42.
5 During the period (1949–2020), 19 treaties were returned to the president by simple resolution. Presidents withdrew from 25 additional treaties over the period, with six of these treaties superseded by a new treaty while the treaty awaited action in the Senate. I could not determine the disposition of one treaty in the dataset: Conventions Concerning the International Exchange of Publications and Documents (Executive Document G, 88-1, transmitted in 1963). I treated it as pending in the analysis.

6 A treaty is counted based on transmittal documents and then subsequent action by the SFRC. In some instances, presidents submitted multiple treaties in a single transmittal document. This typically happened when the president transmitted a convention, along with an associated protocol (or update) to the convention since it was signed. While technically this would involve more than one treaty, I treat such cases as a single treaty. However, when the president submitted multiple agreements together in one document, the transmittal document might separate them (this practice was common earlier during the period) or the SFRC may decide to process each treaty separately. When the SFRC determined to process the treaties separately (i.e., as separate treaty documents), I count them separately, otherwise I treat them as a single treaty. Treaties reported together but processed by the Senate separately are denoted on the Congress.gov website by their treaty document number and a letter. For example, President G.W. Bush transmitted an amendment and a protocol to the Convention on Certain Conventional Weapons (CCW) and the Geneva Protocol III in one transmittal document (Treaty Document 109–10). The Senate separated these treaties and processed them as three treaties. Thus, I treated them as three separate treaties. Finally, there are two treaties that are included twice in the dataset because they were transmitted twice decades apart by different presidents. The first is the Genocide Convention, which was transmitted by President Truman in 1949 (Executive Document O, 81–1) and then again by President Nixon in 1970 (Treaty Document 91–12). The convention was eventually approved in 1986. The second is the Convention Concerning the Abolition of Forced Labor, originally transmitted by President Kennedy in 1963 (Executive Document K, 88–1) and then again by President George Bush in 1991 (Treaty Document 102–3). The convention was approved three weeks following its second transmittal, after languishing for nearly three decades in the Senate.

7 I use medians here, rather than means, because outliers with very large values tend to distort the mean. For example, the mean number of days for signature to transmittal is 601 and the mean number of days for transmittal to SFRC report is 425. I provide graphs in prior work showing the distribution of days to transmittal and ratification for treaties processed within three years (Krutz and Peake 2009, 139; Peake 2017, 842). The graphs clearly demonstrate that most treaties are processed at each stage close to the median values, but the rightward tails of the distributions are quite long, meaning that outliers (treaties that take years to process at each stage), distort the mean significantly.

8 A difference of means test indicates that the differences in these mean values are not statistically significant.

9 The data that support the findings of this chapter are openly available in Harvard Dataverse at https://dataverse.harvard.edu/dataverse/jeffreypeake.

10 There is evidence of significant overdispersion, so I use a negative binomial regression model, which is preferred to the Poisson regression model in such a situation (see Long and Freese 2006, 377). I tested for autocorrelation and stationarity and found the variable is stationary, with no autocorrelation present. I ran the same models using Poisson regression and OLS regression and obtained similar results in the variables of interest.

11 I use the NOMINATE scores for the congressional political parties available at: https://voteview.com/data. The variable is the absolute difference between the Democratic mean and the Republican mean first dimension ideology score (Lewis *et al.* 2022). The mean of the variable over the period is 0.622, with a standard deviation of 0.096, a minimum of 0.476 (82nd Senate) and a maximum of 0.839 (116th Senate).

12 I use this website to calculate the president's party variable: www.senate.gov/history/partydiv.htm. For the 81st through 85th Senates, I calculate the percentage of seats due to the Senate only having 96 members at the time.

13 To measure the chair's ideology, I used the first dimension NOMINATE score for each chair, available on the Voteview website cited in note 11. NOMINATE scores range from −1 (most liberal) to +1 (most conservative).

14 Presidential approval data come from www.presidency.ucsb.edu/statistics/data/presidential-job-approval.

15 The growth in UN membership is available at: www.un.org/en/about-us/growth-in-un-membership. I also lagged this variable by one two-year period to allow for time to negotiate and submit new treaties, but the results did not change.

16 Interpreting the effects of independent variables is not as straightforward in count models as it is in OLS regression. I used the listcoef command in Stata (Long and Freese 2006, 378).

17 The results are confirmed when an indicator variable for divided partisan control of the presidency and Senate is included instead of the number of presidential partisans variable. Divided government is positive and statistically significant, meaning presidents submit more treaties when the other party controls the Senate. The results for the other variables also increase in strength, with presidential approval becoming statistically significant in the negative direction (opposite of the evasion hypothesis expectation). I use the presidential partisans variable in order to be consistent with prior research.

18 I calculated the length of time between a treaty's transmittal to the Senate by the president and the date the chair of the SFRC issued the report. The aggregate measure of treaty gridlock for a given Senate is the median number of days it took for treaties transmitted during that Senate to be reported out of committee. The median is more appropriate than the mean number of days, given the existence of outliers, particularly among treaties transmitted but never approved.

19 I also ran duration models on the time from presidential transmittal to full Senate approval. The results are very similar, although the statistical significance and substantive effects of the partisan polarization variable are higher. The substantive interpretations remain the same, no matter which time variable we examine.

20 Tests indicate that OLS is appropriate (the dependent variable, which is a time series, is not autocorrelated and is stationary). However, the dependent variable is not normally distributed—it is highly skewed. I logged the dependent variable, which normalized it, making OLS appropriate. President Trump's last Senate (the 116th) was dropped from the analysis because only one treaty transmitted during that two-year period has been successfully reported out of the SFRC by the time of the analysis (December 2021). The N for the analysis is 35.

21 Replacing the presidential partisans variable with an indicator variable for divided control of the presidency and Senate yields the same results.

22 The data that support the findings of this chapter are openly available in the Harvard Dataverse at https://dataverse.harvard.edu/dataverse/jeffreypeake.

23 The median number of days to SFRC report for multilateral treaties is 281.5; whereas the same value for bilateral treaties is 201. Due to outliers, the mean value for days to SFRC report are much higher. For multilateral treaties, the mean value is 1,096 days (i.e., three full years) and for bilateral treaties it is 440 days. A difference of means test indicates a statistically significant difference. Treaties completed with one other state are coded as bilateral. Treaties completed between the United States and more

than one other state are coded multilateral, as are treaties made through international organizations (e.g., the UN or Organization of American States (OAS)) or between the United States and multilateral organizations.

24 A difference of means test indicates, on average, that new treaties take significantly longer to process in committee. New treaties are treaties where no existing treaty exists on the topic with the partner state or set of states. Thus, a tax or extradition treaty that replaces one that is existing, no matter how old, is not considered new for the purposes of the analysis. If it is a tax treaty in an entirely new area of taxes (e.g., regarding estate taxes rather than income taxes), it is considered a new treaty. Each transmittal document and accompanying DOS memo was read carefully to determine if the treaty represented a new treaty or replaced or amended an existing treaty. The one exception is that I coded protocols that added new states to NATO as new treaties because this substantially altered the US relationship with the newly added states (i.e., it made them formal allies).

25 A difference of means test for each of the categories indicates that economic treaties are processed significantly more quickly, on average, and norms treaties are processed significantly more slowly. Security treaties (n=80) include alliances, basing agreements, peace agreements, and arms control treaties. Sovereignty treaties (n=97) include border and territorial agreements, the creation of international organizations unspecific to a topic (e.g., the OAS), and treaties dealing with diplomatic procedures. Economic treaties, by far the largest category (n=473), include transportation agreements (e.g., shipping and aviation), fisheries conventions, tax conventions, commodity agreements, and communications agreements. Legal treaties (n=237) include mutual legal assistance treaties, copyright and trademark conventions, extradition treaties, and terrorism conventions. Finally, norms treaties (n=113) include human rights conventions, labor rights agreements, environmental and conservation (but not fisheries) conventions, and rules of war (but not weapons prohibitions).

26 I used a process like Krutz and Peake (2009, 151) to code if a treaty was important. For the twentieth-century treaties, I adopted the code used by Krutz and Peake (2009), along with a reading of the transmittal document and DOS memo, which led me to change the code on a handful of treaties. A reading of the two memos, as well as contemporary media accounts helped me determine which treaties were of particular significance since 2000, yielding a total of 282 important treaties.

27 The presidential approval value is the approval rating reported by the Gallup Poll in the most recent poll prior to the president transmitting the treaty. The presidential partisans variable is the same as in the other analyses: the president's share of seats in the US Senate.

28 I employ hazard analysis, as duration data typically violate the assumptions of traditional OLS regression because they often include a non-normally distributed dependent variable that is time dependent (see Bennet and Stam 1996). Examination of the histogram of days to report (the dependent variable) clearly indicates that the data are skewed to the right, that is, most treaties are processed within a year, but some take many years or even decades to process. There are a variety of hazard models available, which differ based on the distribution of the rate at which the duration processes end. Examination of the hazard function confirm that most treaties are processed quickly, and, as time goes on, the likelihood of the process ending (with a committee report) decreases exponentially. This suggests that a parametric hazard model is more appropriate (specifically one that specifies a hazard function that is monotonic) rather than

the standard Cox regression model. I used the Gompertz distribution model (Cleves, *et al.* 2010, 267). Running the models using the Cox model yields the same substantive results. The Akaike information criterion (AIC) approach to model selection also points to using the Gompertz distribution model (Cleves, *et al.* 2010, 282).

29 For treaties that are withdrawn, superseded by another treaty, returned to the president, or defeated on the floor by a floor vote, the date of this event occurring is the date used in the analysis to determine duration, however these treaties are not treated as having passed committee. In duration analysis parlance, they are not coded a 1 on the "failure" indicator variable, which in the case of this analysis is the committee process ending via report.

30 Thus, in the analysis, reporting the treaty terminates the process in committee, but means the actual ratification process may continue to the floor and the treaty is not "terminated."

31 An indicator variable for divided control of the presidency and the Senate is statistically significant in the full dataset but is insignificant in the subset of important treaties. The effect is that it speeds the consideration of treaties, which is in the opposite expected direction. I use the number of presidential partisans variable in order to be consistent with the other analyses in the chapter. Including divided government only increases the statistical significance of partisan polarization.

32 I only report the SFRC duration results to save space and because the substantive results are the same as the Senate approval model.

4

THE UNITED STATES ON THE OUTSIDE

Multilateral Conventions

The destructive effects of treaty gridlock are apparent when one considers recent advancements in international law on issues typically dealt with through multilateral treaties. In recent decades, the United States has signed but failed to ratify numerous important human rights, environmental, and arms control conventions that are supported by the vast majority of countries. Other significant treaties in these areas of international law remain unsigned by the United States, primarily due to opposition among domestic political actors and an unwillingness or inability of presidents to push for their ratification. As a result, the United States often finds itself on the outside of the very international organizations it designed after World War Two to deal with numerous vexing international problems. In this chapter, I survey significant treaties that remain unratified by the United States. As with the quantitative analyses presented in Chapter 3, I focus my examination here on treaties signed by the president and submitted to the Senate.[1]

US ambivalence toward international law is as old as the republic. The Senate's rejection of the Treaty of Versailles following World War One is, perhaps, the best early example, and clearly partisan politics played an important role in its defeat. Following World War Two, congressional resistance toward participation in international law remained significant, as "many legislators resisted legal obligations that might constrain the nation, challenge the Constitution, or infringe on the states' rights in the US federal system" (Patrick 2019, 102). Such fears nearly led the Congress to propose an amendment to the Constitution severely limiting the impact of ratified treaties on domestic law and curtailing presidential authority on executive agreements. Known as the Bricker Amendment, the effort failed by just one vote in the Senate in 1954 (Krutz and Peake 2009, 44). The effort was a clear indication that conservatives in the Senate would continue to resist multilateral conventions they believed threatened US sovereignty (Johnson

DOI: 10.4324/9781003347422-4

2006, 58), or, in their words, were akin to "a tyrannical world government" (Tananbaum 1988, 157). Given the supermajority requirement in the Senate for treaty approval, which emboldens intense minorities, this ambivalence works against the ratification of far-reaching treaties, particularly multilateral human rights, environmental, and arms control treaties. For example, it took nearly 40 years for the Senate to finally approve the Genocide Convention in 1986, even though US negotiators took the lead in writing the treaty (Krutz and Peake 2009, 122; Leblanc 1991).

Stewart Patrick (2019, 102) argues that the United States' dominance during the latter half of the twentieth century led to a US desire to restrict the actions of other states through international law, while at the same time limiting such constraints on its own international behavior. Patrick refers to this as US "exemptionalism" (rather than exceptionalism) in international law, which is underpinned by three primary factors: "power, culture, and institutions." America's status as a superpower, and as the sole superpower following the end of the Cold War, meant that it has substantially more options on the international stage, as well as obligations, such that it should not be constrained in the same manner as "lesser actors." Moreover, in terms of culture, Americans "insist that their country's founding political and legal principles are inherently universal—and ought to be shared globally." Thus, international law is not necessary to constrain the actions of a benevolent global power (103). Finally, constitutional design creates checks and balances and inherent institutional competition regarding the ratification of treaties not found in most other Western democracies. The supermajority requirement for Senate approval, as shown in Chapters 2 and 3, contributes substantially to treaty gridlock and the inability for the United States to fully participate in international law, even when such participation is broadly popular.

Recent opposition to US participation in multilateral conventions focuses on the issue of sovereignty. The view is plainly laid out in the Trump administration's early draft executive order that was leaked in 2017, which, if published, would have ordered the State Department (DOS) to reconsider US participation in existing multilateral treaties. "The basic premise of the draft order . . . [was] that the United States had become party to multilateral treaties that 'were not in our national interests' and involved 'ceding sovereignty'" (Patrick 2019, 117). Sovereignty claims underscore conservative opposition to a whole host of multilateral treaties throughout the modern era, particularly in human rights, including such notable cases as the Genocide Convention and the Convention for the Elimination of All Forms of Discrimination Against Women (CEDAW), which has languished for over 40 years (Baldez 2014). The United States is the only country that remains outside of the UN Convention on the Rights of the Child (CRC), for similar reasons. Republican hostility to multilateralism, based in sovereignty concerns, was placed into the 2016 Republican Platform, which states that the party opposed the adoption "of treaties that would weaken or encroach upon American sovereignty" (Patrick 2019, 117).

Conservatives making these claims view sovereignty very narrowly. Participation in multilateral conventions is an expression of sovereignty by the state signatory. There are tradeoffs, of course, as explained by Patrick (2019), whereby signatory states cede some autonomy of action, but in exchange receive benefits in the form of influence over international law in a particular area or the ability for its citizens to more fully benefit from global commerce, travel, etc.[2] The United States is party to over 600 multilateral conventions on a host of key issues, ranging from environmental protection, to peaceful uses of outer space, to pandemic responses. In each case, the United States cedes some freedom of action in exchange for influence and predictability (Patrick 2019, 118).

Yet, despite these benefits, the United States remains outside of numerous key multilateral conventions, diminishing its influence on international governance in the areas of the global commons, in particular the law of the sea, as well as human rights and the environment.[3] To a lesser extent, the US failure to ratify key arms control agreements limits its capacity to lead international progress on curtailing nuclear arms proliferation and the use of munitions that indiscriminately kill civilians, including cluster bombs and land mines. In many cases, the policy disputes surrounding the issues involve legitimate disagreements on the wisdom of the treaty, given the limits the treaty would place on US policy or its economic costs. However, as we will see, this is often not the case, and arguments resting on claims of threats to sovereignty are particularly weak.

Thus, even under ordinary circumstances, with a functional Senate unhampered by partisan polarization, US domestic politics present a significant challenge for presidents seeking to cement US participation in international law through treaties, especially on controversial topics that require multilateral action to solve. Add to this the extreme partisan polarization apparent during the twenty-first century and the challenge has become especially acute. In this chapter, I survey numerous multilateral conventions that the United States has failed to ratify, focusing on the issues of human rights, the environment, and arms control. While participation in multilateral treaties covering these topics has always been a difficult domestic political problem for US presidents, recent circumstances have cemented US nonparticipation in international law to its detriment.

The UN Convention on the Law of the Sea

To illustrate the difficulties recent presidents have faced in moving multilateral treaties toward ratification, before I turn to each of the aforementioned issues, I offer a discussion of the broadly significant UN Convention on the Law of the Sea (UNCLOS). The discussion of UNCLOS highlights the problems that a polarized Senate presents to the president seeking ratification of important multilateral treaties. Despite substantial support for UNCLOS across the political, military, and business spectrum, conservative Republicans in the Senate have been able to scuttle attempts to ratify the treaty, as sovereignty and other specious arguments have greater pull with the party recently. Patrick (2019, 21) finds that these sovereignty concerns, in the case of UNCLOS, "are excessive," and that the United States does not risk subordinating domestic law and its Constitution to international law by ratifying the treaty. Rather, ratifying "a treaty is an exercise . . . [not] . . . an abdication of sovereign authority."

The UNCLOS is the best example of a currently stalled treaty that has far-reaching significance for US diplomacy, security, and commercial activity. The convention addresses several key issues, ranging from environmental protection to exploitation of resources in the seabed, to freedom of navigation on the high seas. There are 168 parties to the convention, including all major maritime powers, except the United States. In practice, the United States adheres to the provisions of the convention, treating it as customary international law. Yet, by failing to ratify the treaty, the United States has no direct role in setting international law governing 70 percent of Earth's surface (Almond 2017).

UNCLOS was originally drafted by the UN in 1982.[4] President Reagan did not sign the treaty, largely due to concerns related to deep seabed mining rights. To secure US signature, the parties renegotiated the convention to address these specific concerns and President Clinton signed the agreement on July 29, 1994. He transmitted the convention to the Senate for advice and consent the following October. The Democratic SFRC chair at the time, Claiborne Pell (D-RI), supported the convention but was unable to move on the treaty due to the intervening midterm congressional elections, in which the Democrats lost their Senate majority (Hudzik 2010). The opportunity for speedy ratification was lost, as the new SFRC chair, Jesse Helms (R-NC), was a staunch opponent of the treaty. Helms was the most conservative SFRC chair in modern history (Krutz and Peake 2009, 160), and a devoted sovereigntist, and his opposition to multilateral treaties upheld numerous multilateral conventions pushed for by President Clinton. Helms held the gavel for nearly eight years, so UNCLOS was ignored by the committee for nearly a decade. There was no action on the treaty, despite its support from a broad coalition of interests, including an extensive range of business groups (e.g., the Chamber of Commerce), the oil industry, fishing interests, every branch of the US military, every living president, shipping interests, and environmental groups.

In 2004, at the behest of President George W. Bush, and with a new Foreign Relations chair in the Senate who was more amenable toward multilateral treaties (Richard Lugar, R-IN), the convention was finally reported out of committee. Despite unanimous support in committee, with a 19–0 vote, Senate leaders were unable to secure floor time for the treaty due to opposition from conservative Republicans and it did not receive a vote before the end of that Senate. Following urgent calls for ratification by President Bush and a host of business, military, and environmental interests, in late 2007, the SFRC, this time led by Joe Biden (D-DE), again reported the convention with an overwhelmingly favorable vote (Krutz and Peake 2009, 194–5). Ratification of UNCLOS was particularly urgent at the time, because if the United States did not ratify the convention, it would be shut out of the committee created by the convention to govern many of the key issues. Questions regarding the Arctic were especially significant, given US territorial interests off the coast of Alaska which were expanding due to melting sea ice resulting from climate change and challenges presented by Russian claims in the region. On the Senate floor, however, enough Republicans were stridently opposed to the convention, despite its broad domestic support, backing in the SFRC, and the efforts of President Bush, such that the treaty did not receive floor consideration before the end of Bush's presidency (Hudzik 2010).

After President Obama called for its ratification and included it in his 2009 treaty priority list, the convention was again revived by SFRC chair John Kerry (D-MA), who held committee hearings on the treaty in June 2012. The three-and-a-half-year delay in holding hearings, however, effectively doomed this latest ratification effort. Obama was in a good political position in 2009 to push for ratification, given his party controlled a healthy majority in the Senate; however, his focus was on economic recovery, the Iraq and Afghanistan wars, and his reset with Russia, which included ratification of New START. In 2012, Obama finally got around to pushing for UNCLOS in his public statements, citing its increased importance because of climate change and the opening of sea lanes in the Arctic and the convention's relevance to Chinese expansionist moves in the South China Sea (Colin 2016). By that time, of course, Republicans held a stronger hand in the Senate, and they were able to effectively kill consideration of UNCLOS in July 2012 when 34 senators stated on the record their strong opposition to the treaty, including 31 who wrote a letter expressing their opposition to then Senate majority leader, Harry Reid (D-NV) (Wong and Lengell 2012; Wright 2012). Even if the treaty had finally made it to the floor, it would have failed, given the 67-vote requirement.

During the 2014 midterms, Republicans won control of the Senate, ending any chance for Obama to move the convention forward. Unsurprisingly, the Trump administration did not support the convention. Trump's hostility toward multilateral treaties doomed the convention during his presidency. While President Biden supported UNCLOS while in the Senate and as vice president, it is unlikely Republicans will alter their opposition to the treaty no matter how much pressure he puts on the Senate to ratify the treaty. The arguments by conservatives against the treaty have only grown more vociferous over time and it is unrealistic to expect Biden to succeed in persuading conservative Republicans where President Bush failed. When considered against the backdrop of Obama's inability to move treaties through the Senate and the ever-growing partisan polarization in the Senate, it seems that the prospects for the ratification of UNCLOS will remain dim for some time.

Patrick (2019, 123), summarizes the reasons for Republican opposition thus: the UNCLOS "would undermine 'American sovereignty' by transferring 'ownership' of the high seas to the UN, allowing global bureaucrats to veto US naval operations, and require US deep-sea mining companies to pay exorbitant royalties to an unaccountable International Seabed Authority." Of course, these concerns "have no basis in fact" (Patrick 2019, 129), as evidenced by the support for the convention by the US Navy and the very businesses opponents were purporting to protect. Ratification of UNCLOS would provide a permanent seat to the United States on the International Seabed Authority and other important bodies, allowing it to block rulings it opposed and defend its interests (Hudzik 2010; Nevitt 2021).[5] Failure to accede to the treaty, therefore, diminishes US power in shaping international rules regarding these critical issues, rules that it already follows as customary international law.

What are the costs of the nonratification of multilateral treaties, generally, and the UNCLOS specifically? For many of the treaties discussed in this chapter, US negotiators took the lead in writing the conventions, and, thus, Americans played an important role in developing international law on the environment, human rights, arms control, and the global commons. The inability of the United States to fully ratify conventions it takes the lead in negotiating undermines that leadership role. As explained by Kaye (2013), "by excluding itself" the United States forfeits its influence over "global problem solving." Why should negotiators take US concerns seriously when writing international law if the United States is unlikely to ever become party to the treaty? For example, in the case of UNCLOS, the United States plays a bystander role in determining global regulations related to significant issues like extended exclusive economic zones, and in the case of the Arctic, maritime boundaries along the continental shelf that are in dispute between the United States, Russia, and Canada. Other states determine international law governing vast areas of the oceans and seas surrounding US sovereign territory (Nevitt 2021).[6] This is a serious and growing problem, given the increased relevance of issues addressed by UNCLOS due to climate change and competition between the United States and China in the Pacific and the United States and Russia in the Arctic.

Moreover, failure to ratify multilateral treaties that have been ratified by the vast majority of states "carries reputational costs, undermining faith in the country's dedication to the international rule of law and the credibility of its commitments" (Patrick 2019, 129). This reputation hit makes it difficult for the United States to use international law to challenge China's claims in the South China Sea or Russia's claims in the Arctic, especially when these adversaries, both parties to UNCLOS, can point to the United States' failure to ratify the convention (see Cardin 2016; Cronin and Ha 2018; Darmawan 2021). Failure to ratify UNCLOS is an "unforced error" on the part of the United States, which provides great power competitors (i.e., China and Russia) opportunities to claim that Americans flout international law, when the United States is upholding it (Nevitt 2021). Climate change is accelerating these concerns, and the United States has no seat at the table in the international bodies that formulate international law to address them.

Recent presidents' experience with UNCLOS follows a familiar pattern when presidents push significant multilateral treaties on human rights, arms control, and the environment. According to data provided on the DOS's website, multilateral treaties make up the bulk of treaties currently pending before the SFRC.[7] Updated most recently in October 2019, the list includes 37 pending treaties, of which 32 are multilateral treaties. Since the update, there are five additional pending treaties, of which three are multilateral, giving us a total of 42 pending treaties, of which 35 (83 percent) are multilateral. Among the multilateral treaties, eight are environmental conventions, six are arms control conventions, and five are human rights conventions. Thus, most pending multilateral treaties fit within the three issues I examine more closely below.[8]

Human Rights Treaties

Multilateral conventions addressing human rights issues have always presented challenges for ratification in the United States. Recall that the Genocide Convention was first submitted to the Senate by President Truman in 1949 but was not given Senate approval until 1986. If the United States struggles to ratify a convention banning the heinous crime of genocide, surely other human rights treaties would present a struggle. It is puzzling that the United States, with a relatively strong domestic human rights record in recent decades and acting as a long-time champion of human rights abroad, would struggle with acceding to international law on these issues. Moravcsik (2005) argues that this paradox is largely due to four factors, including US superpower status; its democratic stability obviating the domestic need for human rights protections; the presence of an intense minority long opposed to human rights conventions; and the fragmentation of power in US political institutions, which empowers minorities to block changes to the status quo. The United States is the only country where all four of these factors come into play.

The United States "stands apart from other mature democracies in resisting major human rights treaties." This is part of US exemptionalism discussed above, whereby the United States insists that other states adopt human rights protections for their citizens, while avoiding "external constraints or supervision" of its own behavior (Patrick 2019, 125). Senate rules embolden intense minorities, allowing them to block action on treaties that are broadly popular, and such is the case with most of the multilateral human rights treaties submitted to the Senate over the past five decades (Kaufman 1990; Krutz and Peake 2009, 122; Moravcsik 2005). The intense partisan polarization plaguing the Senate in recent decades only exacerbates the problem, as Republicans look for every opportunity to defeat policies pushed by Democratic presidents. Meanwhile, the world moves on making human rights law without direct US participation.

This observation is not intended to be a partisan claim. The facts indicate that opposition to human rights treaties always comes from the political right in the United States, and it is usually Democratic presidents that push for Senate ratification of human rights treaties. When Republican presidents have pushed for approval in the Senate, they have more often met with success than Democratic presidents. This is because the locus of support for these treaties is among Democrats in the Senate and Republicans, typically, are less likely to oppose a Republican president pushing a treaty than they would a Democratic president. Thus, a Republican president is more likely to be able to build the bipartisan majority required for Senate approval of a treaty. As shown in Table 2.2 in Chapter 2, Republican presidents have higher success rates on treaties than Democratic presidents, and the difference is especially pronounced for multilateral treaties (61.4 percent for Democrats versus 81.4 percent for Republicans). Moravcsik (2005) observed that major multilateral human rights treaties only receive approval in the Senate when Democrats hold a significant majority (55+). No Republican-controlled Senates have approved a human rights treaty and of the 12 conventions Moravcsik examined, only one (the Convention Against Torture (CAT)) was originally transmitted to the Senate by a Republican president. A substantial Democratic majority appears to be a necessary but insufficient condition for human rights treaty approval.

The United States has ratified just four of the ten most significant UN human rights conventions, an abysmal record in comparison to other world powers. In three of the four successes, including the Genocide Convention (approved in 1986), the CAT (1990), and the International Covenant on Civil and Political Rights (ICCPR, 1992), it took a Republican president to push the Senate to finally ratify the treaty. President Clinton is the only Democratic president to successfully ratify a major UN human rights treaty: the International Convention on the Elimination of All Forms of Racial Discrimination (CERD) in 1994. His efforts to push that treaty meant that he was unable to focus on pushing for the ratification of a similar convention banning discrimination against women (Baldez 2014).

Three of the ten treaties remain pending in the Senate, i.e., they were signed by the United States and transmitted by the president to the Senate for approval. The pending major human rights treaties include the International Covenant on Economic, Social and Cultural Rights (ICESCR), the CEDAW, and the Convention on the Rights of Persons with Disabilities (CRPD). Each of these treaties has 171 or more parties, so the United States remains one of just a few states worldwide not to have ratified them. The remaining three major UN human rights treaties include CRC, the Convention on the Protection of Migrant Workers (CMW), and the Convention for the Protection from Enforced Disappearance (CED). While Clinton signed the CRC in 1995, he did not submit it to the Senate due to significant Republican opposition (Blanchfield 2015b).[9] The United States stands alone as the only member of the UN that is not party to the CRC (Mehchu 2021).[10] The United States has not signed the CMW or the CED. The middle category of these ten UN conventions, those treaties that remain pending in the US Senate, are the most interesting subset for the purposes of this study, and I address each below.

The Carter administration represents a watershed moment in US foreign policy and human rights. President Carter submitted to the Senate four UN human rights convention: ICCPR, ICESCR, CERD, and CEDAW, and publicly urged the Senate to approve the Genocide Convention. The UN convention dealing with economic, social, and cultural rights (ICESCR) was submitted by President Carter on February 23, 1978. Carter transmitted three other human rights accords on the same day including the convention dealing with civil and political rights (ICCPR), which was eventually approved in 1992; the convention to eliminate racial discrimination (CERD), which was approved in 1994; and the American Convention on Human Rights, which remains pending in the Senate.[11] The ICESCR focuses on positive human rights, i.e., the right of individuals to receive benefits from government, including such things as minimal standards in healthcare, education, employment, and income. Negative human rights, however, oblige governments to protect basic liberties, including the freedoms of speech, press, religion, and political participation. Companion to the ICESCR, the ICCPR is focused on negative rights, which are also enshrined in the Constitution and consistent with the classical liberal approach, while positive rights are not (Patrick 2019, 126). It is not surprising that the ICCPR, with its focus on negative rights, was eventually approved by the Senate, whereas the ICESCR was not. While both conventions are meant to implement the basic rights recognized by the UN in the Universal Declaration of Human Rights (UDHR) of 1948 (MacNaughton and McGill 2012),[12] the separation of political rights (negative) from socioeconomic (positive) rights was by design (Lewis 2009).

Typically, conventions, and laws more generally, that deal with positive rights are significantly more controversial in the United States than those that protect negative rights, although this is not a perfect dichotomy, as conventions banning discrimination can involve both negative and positive rights and have also been controversial in the United States. While not perfect, the positive–negative rights dichotomy helps explain why the United States has ratified the ICCPR, which focuses on negative rights, but not the ICESCR, which focuses on positive rights. Given this focus, the ICESCR remains "the most controversial human rights treaty for the United States," according to Lewis (2009, cited by MacNaughton and McGill 2012, 368). She persuasively argues that despite its initial support for socioeconomic rights through the UDHR, US policy, given the history of US racial discrimination and pronounced economic inequality, has been overtly hostile to the formal codification of the rights protected by the ICESCR.[13]

Opponents to the ICESCR contend that socioeconomic rights are not human rights but are rather lofty policy goals that should be governed by the domestic political process and not subject to international law. Such a belief is a basic tenet of US conservatism and forms the basis for Republican opposition to ratification (Alston 1990). The fact that the United States has not ratified the treaty coincides with this hostility to legal guarantees of positive rights, and given the difficulty presented by the treaty ratification process, US accession soon is unlikely. Thus, the languishing of the ICESCR is not, primarily, a result of Senate dysfunction or specious claims to US sovereignty, as is the case for other human rights conventions.

CEDAW was concluded in 1979 and signed by the Carter administration on July 17, 1980. Carter subsequently transmitted the convention to the Senate for its advice and consent on November 12, 1980. CEDAW is the only UN convention focused on the rights of women, specifically, and at the time of this writing there are 190 parties to the convention, making it one of the most widely ratified UN treaties. The nonparty states include the United States, Iran, Palau, Somalia, Sudan, and Tonga.[14] The convention calls on states "to take measures to eliminate discrimination against women in all areas of life, including political participation, employment, education, healthcare, and family structure" (Blanchfield 2015a). CEDAW, when compared to other human rights treaties, is particularly ambitious in its mandate on states to eliminate discrimination, however its enforcement mechanisms are weak (Englehart and Miller 2014).[15]

CEDAW is an interesting nonratification case for several reasons. First, the treaty has been taken up several times by the SFRC and a resolution of ratification was reported twice, in 1994 and 2002, yet the treaty has never made it to the full Senate for a vote. Second, as is the case in other areas of human rights, the United States has a strong domestic record of protections for discrimination against women. In fact, US laws are consistent with the requirements of CEDAW, so ratification would not require changes in domestic law. The primary benefits for the United States would be increased influence on human rights law, as nonratification presents costs to US leadership and legitimacy on the issue. Moreover, supporters cite advancements in women's rights abroad because of CEDAW and US ratification would further legitimize women's rights as human rights (Baldez 2014, 6–8). Empirical analysis demonstrates that CEDAW has improved women's rights in party states, particularly in political equality, making it one of the more successful UN human rights conventions (Englehart and Miller 2014; Simmons 2009). Third, the arguments against CEDAW follow similar patterns as with other human rights treaties. Sovereigntists and conservatives are concerned about its impact on US domestic law, with a particular focus on abortion, although their concerns regarding the CEDAW monitoring committee and the convention's impact on domestic law are overblown (Baldez 2014). Each of these concerns has been addressed in proposed reservations and understandings attached to the resolutions of ratification. Opponents also point to the fact that many parties to the convention have poor women's rights records and that the United States already has a strong legal regime protecting women (Blanchfield 2015a).

Why has the United States failed to ratify CEDAW? Lisa Baldez (2014) suggests there are three explanations typically used to explain ratification of treaties. First, institutionally, ratification barriers are particularly pronounced in the United

States, as I have already described. But that does not explain why the United States has ratified some human rights conventions, but not CEDAW. It does, however, magnify the impact of a unified minority standing in opposition to the treaty, which is clearly the case with CEDAW. Second, scholarship suggests that countries that already adopt the norms of a convention are more likely to ratify it. This argument helps explain why the United States has not ratified the ICESCR, with its focus on positive rights, but has ratified the ICCPR, the CAT, and the Genocide Convention. The norms explanation does not explain the CEDAW case, however, as its goals are broadly consistent with US values. "From a norms-based perspective, the United States is the only 'real' outlier among the . . . countries that have not ratified CEDAW—the only advanced industrial democracy that has failed to do so" (Baldez 2014, 27). Of course, the same could be said for other human rights treaties. The third explanation is based in cost–benefit analysis. States ratify treaties when the costs of meeting the treaty's requirements are low. Given that US domestic laws are consistent with CEDAW, the legal costs of implementing the treaty are low. That said, political costs could be quite high, given the intense domestic political disputes that we see surrounding US ratification and the protracted political fight necessary to overcome opposition in the Senate.

US diplomats took a leadership role in writing CEDAW during the late 1970s and there was bipartisan consensus supporting such a role. However, that consensus quickly broke down, and arguments for and against CEDAW became part and parcel to domestic political conflict in the United States. As the two parties became more ideologically polarized during the 1990s and 2000s, Republican opposition to CEDAW hardened. While Republican moderates initially supported the convention during the 1990s, by 2002, no Republicans supported its ratification (Baldez 2014, 31). That CEDAW moved nowhere immediately following President Carter's transmittal to the Senate is unsurprising, given it was just a few short days after he lost reelection to Ronald Reagan. As a lame duck, Carter's political capital was at its nadir, and other foreign policy priorities were ascendant at the time. Women's rights advocates were focused almost entirely on the doomed ratification of the Equal Rights Amendment (ERA) (Baldez 2014, 154–5). The Reagan administration did not support CEDAW, and it received no attention in the Senate during his presidency. Republican moderates, however, pushed President George Bush to support CEDAW, and the situation was ripe for ratification given its widespread support in Congress.[16] However, the administration decided, instead, to focus on marshaling support for two other major UN human rights treaties, the CAT and the ICCPR, ratified in 1990 and 1992 respectively, and it "remained silent on CEDAW" (Baldez 2014, 166–7).

The focus on other, less controversial UN human rights conventions continued during the Clinton presidency. While President Clinton supported ratification of CEDAW, and Democrats held a substantial majority in the Senate at the outset of his presidency, the administration elected to prioritize ratification of CERD instead. This was a missed opportunity for proponents of CEDAW. Sixty-eight senators sent a letter to President Clinton urging ratification, and the SFRC held its first formal ratification hearings on the convention in September 1994, reporting the treaty to the floor with a 13–5 vote. The hearings indicated that the locus of opposition centered on abortion. Opponents were concerned that "U.S. ratification of CEDAW would strengthen the status of abortion rights in international law." Their concerns, at least in terms of the treaty's impact on domestic law, were addressed in the numerous reservations and understandings included in the resolution of ratification, including a specific understanding related to abortion (Baldez 2014, 167–70; Blanchfield 2015a).[17]

In the wake of the Democrats' massive losses in the 1994 midterm elections, Senator Jesse Helms (NC-R) became chair of the SFRC, which doomed Senate consideration of CEDAW for the next eight years. Baldez (2014, 175) quotes Helms as saying, "if I have anything to do with [CEDAW]—and I think I do—it will never see the light of day on my watch." Despite a push for hearings on CEDAW, led by bipartisan group of women senators in 2000, the SFRC sat on the treaty until Helms lost the gavel.

In 2002, the SFRC again held ratification hearings. The SFRC chair, Senator Joe Biden (DE-D), a long-time proponent of the convention, moved to consider committee approval of the treaty despite an unwillingness of the George W. Bush administration to participate in the hearings. Even though the treaty was placed on Bush's first treaty priority list "as generally desirable and should be approved," Secretary Colin Powell, indicated that while the goals of the convention are laudable, its impact on domestic law and the reach of the monitoring committee needed further study. Proponents of the convention linked support for CEDAW with the US efforts in Afghanistan to free women from the Taliban's oppressive rule. Opponents, however, emphasized that the issue needed further study, and maintained their abortion-related concerns; without President Bush's support, all the Republicans on the committee voted against the resolution for ratification. The resolution passed the committee in a party-line vote, 12–7 (Baldez 2014). The Democrats' slim majority control of the Senate was short-lived, as Republicans regained the majority following the 2002 midterms and the treaty went nowhere during the remainder of the Bush presidency.

President Obama supported ratification of CEDAW, including it in his 2009 treaty priority list; however, he did not forcefully push for Senate approval during his presidency. Democrats regained the majority in the Senate following the 2006 midterms and held that majority through most of Obama's presidency. Despite Democratic control of the SFRC for much of the intervening period, and a supportive administration, there has been no further action on CEDAW since the 2002 report. In November 2010, the Senate Judiciary Committee's Subcommittee on Human Rights and the Law held a hearing on ratification of CEDAW, but only the SFRC can advance a treaty through the Senate. When considered in conjunction with other multilateral treaties that have stalled in the Senate in recent decades, it is unsurprising that CEDAW remains pending. Even though it has broad Democratic support, the issues addressed by the convention remain controversial domestically (Baldez 2014, 182).

As shown in Chapter 2, President Obama met with only limited success getting treaties approved by the Senate, even though his party controlled the Senate for six of eight years. The Obama administration pushed for the ratification of the UN convention on disability rights (CRPD) in 2012, only to be rebuffed. That experience surely diminished the prospects for ratification of CEDAW during the Obama administration. President Trump opposed ratification of CEDAW. President Biden has listed ratification of CEDAW as a foreign policy priority, but the SFRC has not moved on the matter as of this writing (May 2022).[18] Thus, even with the support of Democrats and Democratic Party control of the Senate, Democratic presidents have not pressed for ratification of CEDAW, as obtaining the supermajority required for Senate approval remains out of reach due to the intensity of Republican opposition.

The UN CRPD was the first human rights treaty of the twenty-first century, negotiated and completed by the UN during the George W. Bush administration. The CRPD was the only one of the ten UN conventions to reach the Senate floor and fail in a floor vote.[19] President Obama signed the convention in June 2009 and transmitted it to the Senate in May 2012. The delay in transmittal contributed to the treaty's failure, as it was not until late 2012 that the CRPD made it to the floor of the Senate. Obama clearly failed to take advantage of the large Democratic majority in the Senate during 2009 and 2010, and the delay doomed the treaty. As described in Chapter 2, President Obama's first-term agenda was largely focused on the struggling economy, his major healthcare reform policy, and, in foreign policy, New START and the Afghanistan and Iraq wars. By the time Obama got around to finally transmitting the treaty, it was a presidential election year and domestic politics were even more likely to dominate how the Senate handled a human rights treaty, even one as innocuous as CRPD.

The convention is a far-reaching treaty based on US domestic disabilities law (the Americans with Disabilities Act (ADA)), and, as such, did not require any changes to US law.[20] The SFRC held hearings on the CRPD in July 2012 and reported the convention to the floor, with reservations, in a 13–6 vote (American Bar Association 2022). Despite its seemingly innocuous nature, the treaty failed on the floor, marking the first time that a treaty had been rejected outright on the Senate floor since the Comprehensive Test Ban Treaty (CTBT) failed in 1999. The locus of opposition to the convention was conservative Republicans, as 38 voted against the treaty. There were 61 votes in favor, including all the Democrats and a handful of Republicans. Proponents were just six votes shy of the constitutionally required supermajority to approve the treaty. The failure was a real media spectacle, as one of convention's greatest champions, former Senate Majority Leader Bob Dole (R-KS), had come to the floor of the Senate to celebrate its approval, only to be embarrassed when the vote failed (Cox and Pecquet 2012). According to Taylor (2019, 184), the treaty's "defeat was a shock" to Democratic leaders.

SFRC Chair Kerry (D-MA) "had anticipated quick passage because the treaty was much less controversial than the UN Convention on the Law of the Sea, which he had unsuccessfully attempted to get through the Senate earlier in the Congress."

Opponents argued spuriously that the treaty potentially violated US sovereignty, even though the treaty was based on US law, had no enforcement mechanism that could apply to the United States, and it was US diplomats that took the lead at the UN in negotiating the final agreement. Moreover, the United States already had a strong legal regime of protections for the disabled, on which the treaty was based (Kanter 2019). Opponents also claimed that the treaty threatened the rights of families to homeschool their children (Baker 2015; Taylor 2019), would lead to leftists in the UN dictating US social policy, and force the United States to expand access to abortion. The opposition to the CRPD by homeschooling advocacy groups was particularly effective in flipping several Republicans, who had initially signaled their support for the treaty (Taylor 2019).

These arguments against the convention, when looked at objectively, have no basis in fact. Patrick (2019, 98–9) calls these claims "absurd" and "groundless" and "hysteria," largely because the CRPD "explicitly protected the independent decisions of parents and required no changes in U.S. law," including the laws of the various states.[21] The ratification instrument that failed the Senate vote indicated this express point, as well. While the United States would be bound to provide data for the UN committee that monitored compliance, such reporting had no legal status in the United States. Moreover, the resolution of ratification included numerous reservations and understandings that accounted for each of the primary arguments opponents leveled against the treaty (Blanchfield and Brown 2015; Kanter 2019). Opponents also complained that the vote's timing was problematic, as it was held during the lame duck session of 2012. Republicans argued that the new Senate should be given the opportunity to vote on the treaty during the next Congress. The argument, however, was also unfounded, as the Senate, since 1970, had ratified 19 treaties during lame duck sessions, including the New START treaty in 2010 (Baker 2015).

Taylor (2019) reports that during the 113th Congress (2013–14), the Foreign Relations Committee continued to push hard to bring the CRPD back to the floor. However, despite numerous reservations added to the resolution of advice and consent which put to rest the homeschooling issue, the polarized atmosphere of the Senate meant that opponents were not budging, and additional specious arguments against the treaty mounted. While the SFRC managed to report the resolution for advice and consent, along with 13 reservations, understandings, and declarations with a 12–6 vote in 2014 (Kanter 2019, 333), the treaty was set aside by Senate leadership for lack of the necessary floor votes (American Bar Association 2022; Taylor 2019). Without the necessary votes, the treaty was dropped, and the committee focused on processing other, less controversial treaties, with only modest success. Republicans took control of the Senate following the 2014 midterm elections. The new Republican chair of the SFRC, Bob Corker

(R-TN), had already announced his opposition to the convention in late 2013 and voted against both the 2012 and 2014 reports, thus dooming any prospect for ratification of the CRPD during the remainder of Obama's presidency (Cox 2013). Trump never pushed for the treaty's ratification or made any public remarks regarding the convention and efforts to revive the treaty have stalled during the early Biden administration.[22]

The political circumstances surrounding the ratification debate for the CRPD spelled its doom. Enough Republicans, pushed to the right by extremist interest groups, led by homeschool advocacy groups and the Heritage Foundation, became inalterably opposed to the CRPD such that ratification efforts stalled toward the end of the Obama administration. In her account of the debate, Kanter (2019) points to overt hostility of Republicans to international law as the primary hurdle to ratification. Even though each of the Republican concerns have been addressed through reservations or shown as irrelevant, ratification of the treaty would be seen as a win for Democrats. Thus, the CRPD, the treaty that promotes human rights for the disabled based on US domestic law long championed by Republicans, is unlikely to pass any time soon largely due to Republican hostility to international law.

Currently, 184 states are party to the CRPD. While protections for disabled Americans at home remain strong, as is the case with other human rights accords, nonratification means that US diplomats lack a seat on the UN committee overseeing advancements in those protections worldwide. This diminishes US influence in the global advancement of rights for the disabled (Brett 2021). Moreover, while the United States can lobby other governments to adopt domestic laws like the ADA, such efforts ring hollow when the United States has not ratified the major international convention dealing with the issue. As is the case with CEDAW and women's rights, the United States has effectively ceded leadership on the issue of disability rights with its inability to ratify the CRPD. More broadly, the paradox in US human rights policy persists, largely owing to domestic opposition by an intense minority empowered by supermajority rules and extreme partisan polarization that has paralyzed the Senate on major issues.

Environmental Treaties

Environmental conventions are another category of multilateral treaties where the United States is often unable to ratify and fully participate in global efforts to solve transnational problems. Perhaps the quintessential global problem is climate change, and while the United States is party to the UN Framework Convention on Climate Change (UNFCCC), the US Senate rejected consideration of the Kyoto Protocol,[23] the major follow-on convention to the UNFCCC. US participation in agreements done at Copenhagen (2009) and Paris (2015) has been domestically controversial such that the resulting agreements were largely nonbinding in nature and were not completed as Article II treaties. I provide extensive discussion of the Paris Accord on Climate Change in Chapter 6. The UNFCCC was completed alongside two other UN environmental conventions, including the Convention to Combat Desertification, which was submitted to the Senate by President Clinton in 1996 and ratified in 2000, and the Convention on Biological Diversity (CBD), which was submitted for approval by Clinton in 1993, but remains pending in the Senate. Several other important environmental treaties languish in the Senate, including conventions focused on the production and trade in hazardous chemicals (e.g., pesticides), conservation of specific species, protection of the Antarctic, and marine pollution.

The CBD is a tremendously important treaty focused on the conservation of biodiversity, including plant and animal species, ecosystems, and genetic diversity. The United States is the only UN member state that is not party to the convention. US diplomats took the lead in initially calling for the treaty, and then writing the eventual document. President George Bush, however, refused to sign the CBD when it opened for signature in 1992, citing intellectual property (IP) and other industry concerns. There was also little appetite among the Republican Party to push for the treaty during an election year (Jones 2021). President Clinton signed the treaty in June 1993 and transmitted it to the Senate for approval the following November. The SFRC reported the treaty in July 1994 with a bipartisan vote (16–3), forwarding the resolution for ratification to the full Senate; however, the treaty was successfully blocked for consideration by Republican leaders (Jones 2021). Republicans took control of the Senate in the wake of the 1994 midterm elections. With Senator Helms leading the SFRC, the treaty was effectively dead. No presidents since Clinton have pushed publicly for ratification of the CBD, though President Obama included the convention on his 2009 treaty priority list.

Republican opposition to CBD continues to stymie Senate consideration. Their concerns largely center around sovereignty and IP rights. Legal scholars discount these concerns, however, citing that the proposed understandings account for the IP concerns and the treaty, itself, does not cede sovereign authority over environmental policies. In fact, US negotiators weakened the language in the agreement regarding resource exploitation, which addressed the sovereignty concerns directly (Jones 2021). Moreover, US conservation policies are already congruent with the CBD, so ratification would require no changes in domestic law (Patrick 2019). Given current threats to biodiversity resulting from climate change, US participation in global governance on the issue is important given its expertise and environmental footprint. By not ratifying the convention, however, the United States is unable to fully participate in setting global rules as the world confronts these threats (Saunders and Meek 2021).

More focused environmental treaties also languish in the Senate, including two key conventions on hazardous chemicals. The Rotterdam Convention on trade in hazardous chemicals was signed by President Clinton in 1998, and submitted to the Senate in 2000, and the Stockholm Convention on persistent organic pollutants (POPs) was signed by President George W. Bush in 2001, and submitted to the

Senate the following year. Both conventions were supported by Democratic and Republican presidents, appearing on both President Bush's and President Obama's treaty priority lists. In June 2003, the SFRC held hearings on the two conventions, but the committee failed to report either treaty to the floor. The Obama administration lobbied for ratification in 2010, but those efforts stalled due to a partisan dispute over domestic regulation of chemicals by the Environmental Protection Agency (EPA) (Schor 2010). The Trump administration opposed ratification and President Biden, as of this writing, has not pushed for ratification.

Most countries are party to the conventions, as the Rotterdam Convention has 165 parties and the Stockholm Convention has 185 parties.[24] The Rotterdam convention "aims to ensure that importing nations know about and agree to imports of chemicals that are banned or severely restricted in the exporting country," including POPs. The Stockholm convention bans or severely restricts the production, trade, and disposal of numerous POPs deemed as hazardous to human and environmental health (Yen 2013). While the ratification of both conventions has bipartisan support and backing from the chemical industry, neither has made much headway in the Senate largely due to inconsistencies between US domestic law governing POPs and the rules created by the conventions,[25] as well as disputes over EPA processes in regulating hazardous chemicals. As a nonparty state to the conventions, the United States significantly reduces its influence over the listing of additional POPs on the ban lists (Schor 2010). By not joining the agreements, the United States cedes any influence over how other countries employ POPs and other hazardous chemicals, while creating a disparate regulatory regime that may be at odds with the remainder of the world (Angelo, *et al.* 2012).[26]

Other key multilateral environmental treaties languish in the Senate, including the Agreement on the Conservation of Albatrosses and Petrels (ACAP, Treaty Doc. 110–22); the Antarctic Liability Annex (Treaty Doc. 111–2); and the 1996 London Protocol to the London Ocean Dumping Convention (Treaty Doc. 110–5). The ACAP was submitted by the Bush administration in 2008 and Obama included the agreement on his treaty priority list, but the SFRC has taken no action on the treaty. According to the general counsel's office of National Oceanic and Atmospheric Association (NOAA), "the U.S. participated actively in the negotiation of ACAP due to its interest in seabird conservation in general and its status as a 'Range State' of several of the listed species and continues to participate as an observer in ACAP meetings," but its influence is limited as a nonparty state.[27]

The Antarctic liability annex was signed by the Bush administration in 2005 and transmitted by Obama in April 2009. Obama included it on his 2009 treaty priority list, yet the agreement has received no attention by the SFRC, even though the United States stands to benefit from the agreement due to its expansive scientific interests in the Antarctic (Angelo, *et al.* 2012). The London Protocol was signed by the Clinton administration in 1998 and submitted to the Senate by Bush in 2007. The Bush administration pushed for ratification and the SFRC unanimously reported the treaty to the full senate in September of 2008, yet that Congress ended before the treaty could be brought to the floor for a vote. The protocol, which effectively replaced the outdated London Convention, represents a significant advancement in enforcing bans on illegal dumping of wastes in the world's oceans, a practice that presents substantial threats to the global environment. Significant benefits would accrue to the United States, should it ratify the agreement, including uniform regulatory standards, which would benefit US industries, and the protection of its vast coastlines and ocean resources (Angelo, *et al.* 2012). According to the EPA website, the United States participates in the annual meetings to set regulations in accordance with the London Protocol, yet because it is a nonparty, its participation is limited to observation and consultation.[28]

Other than the general difficulty presented by polarized politics in the Senate contributing to treaty gridlock assessed in Chapter 3, it is unclear why the United States has failed to ratify these environmental treaties. In each case there is strong bipartisan support across both Democratic and Republican administrations, and in most cases industry groups are supportive of ratification. While conservative groups, like the Heritage Foundation, oppose ratification of environmental treaties citing sovereignty concerns, their opposition to this specific set of treaties is more muted than their opposition to the human rights treaties and UNCLOS (Groves 2021). However, the costs of nonratification are evident. As a nonparty state to these treaties, the United States is unable to directly influence global governance on a host of environmental problems. As a result, the United States has ceded its role as a global leader in protecting the world's environment.

Arms Control Treaties

As a superpower, US participation in multilateral treaties on conventional and nonconventional arms is of particular importance. During the Cold War, the United States took the lead in negotiating groundbreaking multilateral agreements, particularly in the area of nonconventional weapons, including biological, chemical, and nuclear weapons. For example, the United States led in negotiating and enforcing the Nuclear Nonproliferation Treaty and the Nuclear Test Ban Treaty. Since the end of the Cold War, however, the United States has been less keen on ratifying major multilateral arms control agreements, even when it leads the negotiations. The problem has been especially pronounced during the twenty-first century. According to Delaet and Scott (2006), following the end of the Cold War, arms control has become a much more partisan issue, with conservatives free to oppose treaties proposed by Democratic presidents. For example, a pitched partisan battle took place over the CWC during the Clinton administration, even though the convention was signed by President George Bush, a Republican, and submitted for Senate approval by President Clinton. While Clinton was able to obtain Senate approval for the CWC in 1997, he spent a great deal of political capital in doing so (Krutz and Peake 2009, 136–8).

The fight over the CWC was a precursor to a much more protracted and ultimately unsuccessful fight over the Comprehensive Test Ban Treaty (CTBT), which failed on a floor vote in the Senate on October 13, 1999, 48 for and 51 against. The CTBT represents a significant step forward in the nuclear nonproliferation regime, yet the United States remains a nonparty state. The failure of CTBT was one of the most significant foreign policy failures of the Clinton administration. The president was certainly stung by the defeat, stating, "Never before has a serious treaty involving nuclear weapons been handled in such a reckless and ultimately partisan way" (Krutz and Peake 2009, 132–3). Media reports at the time make it clear that the treaty failed primarily due to partisanship, suggesting that Republicans largely opposed the treaty because its failure represented a major defeat for Clinton (Deibel 2002; DeLaet and Scott 2006, 177). Republicans cited policy differences, and President George W. Bush opposed ratification of the convention, and even considered withdrawing from the treaty, while maintaining a moratorium on nuclear testing (Shanker and Sanger 2001).

President Obama included the CTBT on his 2009 treaty priority list and vowed to lobby hard for the treaty's approval in the Senate, though such efforts were abandoned in the wake of Obama's bruising battle over New START and continuing Republican opposition to the treaty (Jones and Marsh 2014). President Trump opposed ratification, while maintaining the testing moratorium (Arms Control Association 2020), although in 2020 his administration apparently considered renewed nuclear tests (Canfil 2020; Hudson and Sonne 2020a). President Biden has long supported the CTBT, having voted in favor of the convention in 1999. According to the DOS, Biden supports Senate approval of the treaty and has vowed to make it a foreign policy priority (Jenkins 2021). Partisan headwinds, of course, remain strong, and conservative groups and Republicans maintain their opposition to the CTBT (Groves 2021).

Currently, 185 countries have signed and 170 have ratified the CTBT. The convention requires that all the 44 countries that hold specific nuclear technologies, called Annex 2 countries, must ratify the agreement for it to enter into force. Eight of the 44 listed countries have yet to sign and ratify the CTBT, including the United States. The other Annex 2 countries that have failed to ratify include China, Egypt, India, Iran, Israel, Pakistan, and North Korea (Arms Control Association 2020). "The United States, once the champion of nuclear nonproliferation and lead proponent in pushing the treaty at the United Nations, is grouped with states suspect of nuclear proliferation" (Krutz and Peake 2009). The situation is at odds with the clear US policy against nuclear proliferation, a stance it has publicly declared it is willing to use all means necessary to uphold.

The United States has signed, but not ratified, three regional nuclear-free zone pacts. President Clinton signed the South Pacific and the African accords in 1996, but did not submit either treaty to the Senate for ratification. President Obama submitted both treaties to the Senate in May 2011 and signed the Central Asia accord in 2014 and submitted it to the Senate a year later. The treaties are significant nonproliferation pacts because they effectively ban nuclear weapons (i.e., their manufacture, possession, testing, or deployment) in each of the respective regions. The agreements fit with President Obama's policy on the non-first use of nuclear weapons, as laid out in the 2010 Nuclear Posture Review. Conservative Republicans opposed this policy, however, and their opposition to arms control has doomed Senate approval for any of the three treaties (Center for Arms Control and Non-Proliferation 2011).

Global arms control efforts have shifted to regulate the manufacture, trade, and use of certain types of conventional arms. Since the end of the Cold War, two major UN treaties were completed to ban weapons that often indiscriminately kill civilians, including land mines and cluster munitions. The United States has not signed the Mine Ban Treaty (MBT) of 1997, despite broad bipartisan support in the Senate for signature and ratification during the Obama administration (Whitlock and Kessler 2010). The US military opposes the treaty because they believe it would compromise their ability to defend South Korea from a North Korean invasion. In 2014, President Obama's administration issued an executive order banning the use of land mines outside of the Korean peninsula, although that policy was reversed by President Trump in 2020 (Dwyer 2020). Despite President Biden's promise to reinstate Obama's partial ban, prospects for US signature, let alone ratification, are dim. Currently, there are 164 parties to the MBT, including every other NATO member. However, nonparty states include major US rivals China, Russia, and Iran.[29]

The Convention on Cluster Munitions (CCM) of 2008 is like the MBT in that it seeks to ban an entire classification of conventional weapons. The Bush administration was initially supportive of the CCM, in principle, and issued an executive order to the Pentagon to phase out the use of cluster munitions and destroy most of the US stockpile. The United States, however, allowed their transfer to allies, and the weapons have been used by the Saudis in the Yemen civil war. President Obama did not sign the treaty, again due to opposition by the Pentagon, and, in 2017, the Trump administration reversed the Bush-era policy of phasing out US use of the weapons (Rogin 2017). Currently, there are 110 parties to the CCM, but major US rivals, including China, Russia, and Iran, also remain outside of the convention.[30]

The final category of recent arms control conventions addresses the trade in conventional arms. The United States has signed but failed to ratify two conventions in this category, including an OAS convention against illegal manufacturing and trafficking in arms (CIFTA) and the UN Arms Trade Treaty (ATT). CIFTA, the first multilateral treaty of its kind in the world, focuses on coordinating policing efforts to combat the illegal weapons trade in the Americas. President Clinton signed the convention in 1997 and submitted it to the Senate in 1998, where it has languished for more than 20 years. 31 of 34 OAS members have ratified CIFTA.[31]

The ATT, which was completed by the UN in 2013, focuses on regulating international arms transfers and combating illegal arms trafficking. It is the first ever treaty regulating the global trade in conventional weapons, marking a significant achievement in global arms control efforts (Olabuenaga 2019). The Obama administration signed the ATT in September 2013 and Obama submitted it to the Senate in November 2016. Obama's three-year delay in submitting the treaty is indicative of the degree of domestic opposition to the ATT, despite US diplomats shaping much of the negotiation at the UN (Stohl 2019). In short, the convention stands little hope for US ratification due to the opposition by the NRA and the Heritage Foundation, who claim the treaty threatens Second Amendment rights and violates US sovereignty (Finn 2013; Groves 2021; Stohl 2019).[32] Opposition in the Senate to the ATT appears to be bipartisan, as 50 senators, including five Democrats, sent the Obama administration a letter opposing its ratification (Jett 2014). In 2019, President Trump "unsigned" the ATT, officially withdrawing the United States from the treaty and requested its return by the Senate (Galbraith 2019). There are 110 countries party to the ATT, and while the United States is still listed as a signatory on the UN website, there is a note from the Trump administration indicating the United States does not intend to become party to the treaty.[33] Trump's actions weaken international efforts to regulate international arms transfers and undermine US leadership on the issue (Stohl 2019). President Biden or any future president could reverse this decision, of course.

Not only has the United States been unable to ratify several key arms control agreements during the twenty-first century it has also begun to unravel the arms control regime built during the Cold War. The United States has left more arms control agreements since 2000 than it has ratified, beginning with President George W. Bush's termination of the Anti-Ballistic Missile (ABM) Treaty in 2002. President Trump decided to end US participation in two key treaties: the Intermediate Nuclear Forces (INF) treaty and the Open Skies Treaty.[34] The INF was a bilateral treaty with the Soviet Union, signed by President Reagan in 1987, which banned US and Soviet (Russian) deployment of intermediate-range nuclear weapons. As a result, nearly 3,000 nuclear warheads were destroyed. Citing Russian cheating and the fact that the treaty did not include China, another major nuclear rival, Trump announced its termination in 2019. The move was supported by NATO allies but derided by arms control advocates (Seligman and Gramer 2019). The Open Skies treaty was signed in 1992. It is an important multilateral treaty that allows mutual reconnaissance flights to reduce the likelihood of accidental war. The Trump administration, again citing Russian cheating, announced US withdrawal from the treaty in 2020, a move derided almost universally, except for conservative Republicans (Hudson and Sonne 2020b). Even if President Biden tries to revive the INF or rejoin the Open Skies Treaty, the chances for Senate ratification appear low, given the general Republican opposition to arms control over the past two decades (Pifer 2021).

Conclusion

What should we make of the inability of the United States to fully participate in international law? The United States, the world's sole superpower, sits on the sidelines while the rest of the world implements key multilateral treaties designed to address some of the most vexing transnational issues, ranging from environmental degradation to disability rights to nuclear proliferation. Time and again, US diplomats take the lead during treaty negotiations, securing major concessions to improve chances for US ratification often having the effect of weakening the treaty, only to have their efforts voided when the president is unable to secure the Senate's approval. Often, opposition in the Senate centers around an intense minority pushing specious claims that the treaties endanger US sovereignty or will somehow usurp domestic law at the behest of some faceless UN body. This opposition, always coming from the ideological right (i.e., Republicans), is empowered by the supermajority requirement for treaty ratification. Such is the case, even with environmental treaties signed and submitted by both Republican and Democratic presidents and supported by affected industries. US behavior on multilateral treaties is the epitome of dysfunctional diplomacy.

The problem has gotten so bad that recent Democratic presidents hardly push for Senate ratification of multilateral treaties any longer. President Obama, for instance, managed to obtain the Senate's approval for just one multilateral treaty dealing with human rights, the environment, or arms control, despite including seven such treaties on his 2009 treaty priority list and submitting an additional six multilateral treaties on these topics during his presidency.[35] The assessment of Obama's efforts on behalf of these treaties suggests Obama did not make a concerted push for their ratification, outside of his efforts on behalf of the CRPD. Given Obama's early experiences with the CRPD and the UNCLOS, as well as his costly, but successful push to ratify New START followed by the Republican rebuff of his efforts to revive the CTBT, it is unsurprising that he did not take a leading role in pushing for the ratification of other multilateral treaties. When it came time to finalize his other key diplomatic priorities, including addressing climate change and nuclear proliferation in the Middle East, Obama had other diplomatic tools available which allowed him to skirt Republican opposition in Congress. I discuss these unilateral diplomatic tools in the next two chapters.

President Trump did not support or introduce a single multilateral treaty dealing with arms control, the environment, or human rights, and he opposed most of the pending treaties on these topics. In his single term in office, Trump left as many treaties as he submitted to the Senate, no matter the topic, such that observers have labeled his approach to treaties as the "Withdrawal Doctrine" (Bellinger 2019; Haas 2020). While President Biden extended the New START treaty with Russia, he has made precious little headway in pushing for the ratification of any of the multilateral treaties discussed in this chapter. Through June 2022,

Biden has submitted just two treaties, suggesting there are limits to his claim that "America is back," at least as it relates to international lawmaking.

Notes

1 Significant multilateral treaties that remain unsigned by the United States or signed, but never sent to the Senate, are another category that fall outside of this analysis. For example, the United States signed but is not party to the Rome Statute (it was never submitted to the Senate). The Rome Statute is the convention that established the International Criminal Court (ICC). Other important examples include the Mine Ban Treaty (MBT), and the Convention on the Rights of the Child (CRC), among others. The US relationship with the ICC is an interesting one, worthy of in-depth analysis, but beyond the scope of this book (Kaye 2013).

2 The range of benefits from participation in multilateral conventions is extensive. The benefits range from the ability of Americans to drive on foreign roads, to receiving help in returning abducted children taken abroad, to limiting pollution in the oceans, and exploitation of fishing resources, just to cite a few (see Patrick 2019, 118).

3 As demonstrated in Chapter 3, multilateral treaties also take significantly longer to get through the Senate, and this is especially the case for treaties categorized as norms treaties, which include human rights and environmental treaties. According to Patrick (2019, 120), of the 32 multilateral treaties deposited by the United States with the UN Secretary General between 1945 and 1989, only eight were ratified within a decade of their conclusion and the average treaty that was ratified took about ten years.

4 For a timeline of the history of UNCLOS, see: www.state.gov/law-of-the-sea-convention/.

5 It is hard to overstate the significance of UNCLOS for commercial and military reasons. The military concerns for the United States are obvious, given the significance of its navy and policy of protecting freedom of navigation rights. Commercial interests go well beyond deep seabed mining, as well. For instance, as Almond (2017) describes, because the United States is not party to the convention, US telecommunication companies must seek international sponsors to protect their interests from interference by coastal states when laying fiber optic cable on the ocean's floor.

6 The problem is especially pronounced regarding the Arctic continental shelf and melting sea ice resulting from climate change. All the Arctic states (Canada, Denmark, and Russia), but not the United States, are party to UNCLOS and have representation on the special committee set up to manage claims by each of the states. It is no small matter, as vast unexplored energy reserves exist in the disputed territories. In citing former Exxon-Mobile CEO and Trump's first Secretary of State Rex Tillerson, Almond (2017) summarizes, "in the absence of treaty ratification . . . the United States suffers from the dual disadvantage of having both a cloud over the international status of US claims and a weakened ability to challenge other states' conflicting claims."

7 The list of pending treaties is available at: www.state.gov/treaties-pending-in-the-senate/ and the updated list of treaties at: www.congress.gov/treaties.

8 There are four International Labor Organization conventions that are still pending in the Senate, with the last of these submitted in 1998 by President Clinton. There are five multilateral economic conventions, one on the safety of UN personnel; the UNCLOS; the Vienna Law of Treaties Convention; and a convention on damage of cultural property in wartime, which was completed in 1954 but not submitted to the Senate until 1999. The list also includes one multilateral fisheries convention and two recent conventions dealing with terrorism in civil aviation.

9 The CMW and CED are not as widely supported as the other treaties discussed here, having only 56 and 62 state parties, respectively, according to the UN Treaty Collection available here: https://treaties.un.org/pages/Home.aspx?clang=_en.

10 By the time Clinton got around to signing the CRC in 1995, Senator Helms (NC-R) chaired the SFRC and his opposition to UN conventions was well known. The CRC initially had bipartisan support, as evidenced by Senate Resolution 231 introduced in 1990 calling on the president to sign the CRC. It had 60 cosponsors, but President George Bush refused to sign the convention. Clinton submitted two optional protocols to the CRC to the Senate in 2000, which focused on combating the use of children in the armed services and the sexual exploitation of children. Both optional protocols were approved by the Senate in June 2002.

11 The American Convention on Human Rights, also known as the Pact of San José, failed to move beyond the hearings stage in the Senate. Hearings were held alongside the three other human rights treaties transmitted with it in November 1979. Opposing arguments to the treaty were centered on its binding nature having to do with US domestic law, i.e., it was seen as an infringement on US sovereignty, which could impact states' rights, involve an international body in oversight of human rights in the United States, and possibly curtail abortion rights and use of the death penalty (Diab 1992). While 23 countries have ratified the treaty, the United States and Canada stand out as key members of the Organization of American States (OAS) that have not done so. President Carter elected not to spend the political capital necessary to push for Senate approval, as much of his treaty-related efforts focused on getting approval for the Panama Canal treaties (Shaver 2010).

12 President Franklin Roosevelt's 1941 "Four Freedoms" speech includes both negative and positive rights. The speech emphasizes the freedoms of speech, worship, from want, and from fear. These basic freedoms provide the basis for the UDHR, as well as Article 55 of the UN Charter (Lewis 2009).

13 The stain of racism in the United States explains much of the US ambivalence toward joining human rights conventions during the twentieth century, including the Genocide Convention, the ICESCR, and, of course, the CERD (Moravcsik 2005). Political violence targeting Blacks in the United States arguably fits the definition of genocide, as laid out in the Genocide Convention (LeBlanc 1991; Lewis 2009). During the years in which the Genocide Convention was considered by the Senate (it was transmitted in 1949), political violence targeting Blacks, often by government entities, was common enough to spark questions from global human rights activists and provide fodder for those questioning US exceptionalism. The issue was also tied to Cold War rhetoric, as it provided a counterpoint used by the Soviets to embarrass Americans on the world stage. Racial animus and the desire to uphold segregation in the United States undergirds the early opposition to human rights law (Lewis 2009, 117–19).

14 See the UN treaty page at: https://tbinternet.ohchr.org/_layouts/15/TreatyBodyExternal/Treaty.aspx?Treaty=CEDAW&Lang=en, and Blanchfield 2015a.

15 CEDAW requires parties to report to the CEDAW Committee on their progress in advancing women's rights and equality every four years. The committee consists of 24 independent experts and makes nonbinding recommendations to the states. There is no mechanism for enforcing these recommendations. A 2009 optional protocol, ratified by 106 states but not signed by the United States, permits individuals or groups to file complaints with the committee, who may then investigate and issue a report (Blanchfield 2015a, 3).

16 For example, in 1991, the House of Representatives voted overwhelmingly to urge the Bush administration to complete its legal study of CEDAW. The vote was 374 to 48 and included 114 Republicans voting yes. Thus, a majority of House Republican caucus supported ratification (Baldez 2014, 165).

17 It is interesting that Senate approval of CERD in 1994, which focused on racial discrimination, was completely uncontroversial, whereas CEDAW was cited as problematic for its impact on domestic law and private behavior. CEDAW's language was based on CERD and has many of the same provisions with respect to a monitoring committee, reporting mechanism, and so on. The United States issues its required reports faithfully and fully complies with CERD, yet this compliance "has not prompted anyone to raise any alarms about the erosion of US sovereignty or dramatic threats to the way of life" as we see in arguments against CEDAW (Baldez 2014, 171).

18 See https://joebiden.com/womens-agenda/.

19 Keep in mind failed floor votes on treaties are quite rare in the modern Senate. The CRPD is one of only four treaties since 1935 to reach the floor and fail on a final vote of approval. As described in Chapters 3, most treaties that fail in the Senate, fail for lack of attention in the SFRC or an inability of proponents to move the treaty to a final vote.

20 While the treaty was largely based on US law, it still has important policy consequences for Americans. For example, the treaty helps ensure disabled Americans who live and travel abroad are afforded basic rights (Powell 2012). Kanter (2019), a noted expert on the ADA, notes how the CPRD is expansive in its protection guarantees, particularly as it pushes states to adopt legal protections for the disabled.

21 The hysterics were widespread, ranging from home schooling advocacy groups, who had outsized influence over conservative Republicans, to floor statements by Republican Senators (Taylor 2019). After the treaty was killed on the floor, Senator Orrin Hatch (R-UT) warned his colleagues to stay vigilant, calling the treaty a "threat to American sovereignty and self-government," which "would endorse an official ongoing role for the United Nations in evaluating virtually every aspect of American life" (quoted in Patrick 2019, 99). Of course, the treaty would do no such thing. For a detailed accounting of the arguments for and against the CRPD, see Blanchfield and Brown (2015); Kanter (2019).

22 While there have been calls for Biden to push for Senate approval of the CRPD, there has not been much of any response by the administration, as of this writing in early 2022. Biden made public remarks celebrating the anniversary of the ADA on July 26, 2021 but did not mention the CRPD. Secretary of State Anthony Blinken's statement on International Day of Persons with Disabilities, on December 2, 2021, mentioned numerous US initiatives to promote disability rights abroad, but notably does not mention the CRPD (www.state.gov/on-the-international-day-of-persons-with-disab ilities).

23 President Clinton signed the Kyoto Protocol in 1998 but did not submit it to the Senate for approval due to significant opposition from Republicans in the Senate. The economic costs of the convention were far too great, according to its opponents, and they would be entirely borne by developed nations. Democrats also opposed presidential submission of the treaty, given that the protocol had no chance for approval (Dewar and Sullivan 1997). President George W. Bush unsigned the Kyoto Protocol in 2001.

24 For further information on the Rotterdam Convention, see www.pic.int/Home/tabid/855/language/en-US/Default.aspx. For information on the Stockholm Convention, see www.pops.int/.

25 For example, the Stockholm Convention's regulations on POPs would require amendments to US domestic laws governing pesticides and toxic substances, in particular the Toxic Substances Control Act and the Federal Fungicide, Insecticide, and Rodenticide Act. These laws use different approaches to assess risk, and as a result, several of the POPs banned recently by the Convention are still lawfully produced and deployed in the United States, and US manufacturers export these chemicals to states that may not have appropriate methods for safe use and disposal. The Stockholm Convention uses a health-based risk assessment, whereas domestic law uses cost–benefit (i.e., economic) analysis. Ratification of the convention would require changes to US law, making it a controversial issue (Morales 2014). Numerous attempts to amend domestic law so that it conforms with the two conventions have failed over the years (Yen 2013).

26 The Basel Convention, which governs the transboundary movement and trade in hazardous wastes, is another important convention relating to pesticides that the United States has failed to ratify. It was signed by President Bush in 1989 and given Senate consent in 1992. It is a rare case because the Senate approved the treaty, but the president decided not to ratify it, citing need to adjust domestic law prior to fully ratifying the treaty. The United States is the only OECD country that remains outside of the convention (Patrick 2019, 121).

27 See www.gc.noaa.gov/gcil_seabirds_agree.html.

28 See www.epa.gov/ocean-dumping/ocean-dumping-international-treaties.

29 See www.icbl.org/en-gb/the-treaty/treaty-status.aspx.

30 See www.clusterconvention.org/.

31 See www.oas.org/en/media_center/press_release.asp?sCodigo=S-010/18.

32 Threats to the Second Amendment are overblown, as no treaty can supersede protections in the US Constitution. In fact, the ATT in no way governs the domestic trade, manufacture, or possession of arms. The convention states that parties have "the sovereign right of any State to regulate and control conventional arms exclusively within its territory, pursuant to its own legal or constitutional system" (Olabuenaga 2019; Stohl 2019).

33 See https://treaties.un.org/Pages/ViewDetails.aspx?src=TREATY&mtdsg_no=XXVI-8&chapter=26&clang=_en.

34 The total number of US ratifications of arms control treaties during the twenty-first century is two: the Moscow Treaty and the New START Treaty, both discussed in Chapter 2. Trump's two withdrawals discussed here, added to Bush's termination of the ABM Treaty yields three arms control treaty withdrawals. This does not count Trump's removal of US signature from the ATT or his abrogation of the Iran Nuclear Accord of 2015. The Iran Nuclear Accord was not an Article II treaty, which I discuss extensively in Chapter 6.

35 The lone success was the International Treaty on Plant Genetic Resources for Food and Agriculture (Treaty Doc. 110–19), which was submitted by President Bush in 2008 and approved by the Senate in 2016.

5

EXECUTIVE AGREEMENTS

Implementing US Diplomacy

The most obvious difference between recent presidents and their predecessors in terms of behavior on international agreements is their nonuse of Article II treaties. US diplomacy has continued apace, as twenty-first century administrations completed executive agreements at a pace like their predecessors. The recent abandonment of treaties documented in this book may be indicative of the inability of US political institutions to construct and implement effective foreign policy through the system of shared power. Despite the abandonment of Article II treaties by recent presidents, we have little understanding of the nature of recent executive agreements and how they compare to treaties. We know that executive agreements are often used to complete major international commitments, and that has been the case for as long as presidents have been signing them, going as far back as the eighteenth century (Krutz and Peake 2009). We lack, however, a clear empirical understanding of the extent to which executive agreements have replaced treaties in finalizing major US commitments. The trends analyzed in Chapter 2 and by prior scholarship do not sufficiently address this important question. Does the departure from the treaty signal a change in how presidents complete major international agreements? Does the shift away from treaties mean that executive agreements are now used with greater frequency in dealing with significant matters, in which previously the norm had been to use treaties?

Answering these important questions requires an analysis of the thousands of executive agreements completed in recent years. In this chapter, I first discuss how executive agreements differ from Article II treaties. I then examine a comprehensive dataset of publicly reported executive agreements completed from 2005 to 2020, which includes 3,045 executive agreements. Various data challenges exist in accurately cataloging executive agreements, which I discuss. The examination suggests that recent presidents completed numerous highly important agreements

DOI: 10.4324/9781003347422-5

unilaterally. I end the chapter by taking a closer look at some of the key executive agreements completed during this period, including security agreements with Afghanistan and Iraq, as well as several trade agreements.

Executive Agreements

Executive agreements are binding international agreements that US presidents, or their agents, complete with other states or groups of states without submitting the final agreement to the Senate for supermajority approval. Executive agreements and treaties differ in terms of domestic law, but both forms of agreement are binding under international law such that international law makes no distinction between the two forms of agreement. The main difference under domestic law is how they are completed: treaties require supermajority support in the Senate, while executive agreements do not. While treaties are subject to the vagaries of the Senate, executive agreements usually enter into force upon the signature of the executive branch official. Historically, this explanation has been dissatisfying to some. For example, Schlesinger (1973, 104) recounts a story when during an SFRC hearing a senator asked a State Department (DOS) official for clarification on the differences between the forms of agreement, and the official responded that "a treaty was something they had to send to the Senate to get approval by two-thirds vote. An executive agreement was something they did not have to send to the Senate." The senator was dissatisfied with this explanation and remarked that it reminded him "of the time when as a boy on the farm he asked the hired man how to tell the difference between male and female pigeons. The answer was: 'You put corn in front of a pigeon. If he picks it up, it's a he; if she picks it up, it's a she.'"

Legal scholars consider treaties and executive agreements, for the most part, as legally interchangeable (Setear 2002). What is the practical difference, then, between a treaty and an executive agreement? Prior research suggests that the differences are largely political rather than legal (Krutz and Peake 2009). For example, treaties provide more credible signals to agreement partners and have greater legitimacy because they have the endorsement of the legislature. They are considered more enduring and more likely to bind future presidents to the agreement (Martin 2000; Milner 1997). Executive agreements, on the other hand, allow presidents to complete important commitments in an efficient manner, something the treaty power, as constructed by the Constitution, does not afford. This efficiency can result in more rational foreign policy and provides US presidents the flexibility required to navigate international relations as a world superpower.

The DOS's Office of the Assistant Legal Advisor for Treaty Affairs categorizes Article II treaties submitted to the Senate as treaties, and all other legally binding international agreements as "agreements other than treaties," or executive agreements. Executive agreements can be broken down into three categories: (1) congressional-executive agreements, which are pursuant to a previous act of Congress and may (very rarely) require congressional approval via joint resolution;

(2) agreements pursuant to an existing treaty; and (3) sole executive agreements, completed based on the president's constitutional powers. Congressional executive agreements are further broken down into three subtypes: (1) agreements where Congress provides *ex ante* authorization to the president to complete agreements in a particular policy area; (2) agreements where Congress legislates on a foreign policy matter, instructing the president to verify certain facts before the agreement can take effect; and, (3) agreements where the president seeks *ex post* approval by submitting the agreement to Congress (rather than just the Senate) for bicameral approval.[1] The third category requires only majority approval from both chambers, rather than the two-thirds Senate majority required by the treaty clause. Major trade agreements (e.g., NAFTA) are often completed using the third subtype.

Executive agreements, which make up an estimated 94 percent of binding international agreements completed since 1949, are commonly used to finalize consequential binding legal commitments. For example, the recent US commitments to the security of both Afghanistan and Iraq were governed entirely by executive agreements completed by the Bush and Obama administrations. According to estimates by Bradley and Goldsmith (2018), the breakdown for all binding international agreements since 1945 is as follows: about 6 to 7 percent are treaties; about 80 to 85 percent are congressional-executive agreements; about 1 to 3 percent are executive agreements pursuant to a treaty; and the remainder (about 5 to 10 percent) are sole executive agreements. Thus, while most international agreements are executive agreements, most of these executive agreements involve Congress in some fashion, whether through *ex post* or *ex ante* approval. Presumably, this makes them less problematic and more legitimate, as they involve some means of legislative authorization.

Oona Hathaway (2009), however, argues that *ex ante* authorization only gives the perception of congressional involvement, when in fact there is little if any actual interbranch cooperation that exists once power is delegated to the executive. In her view, Congress has incrementally delegated away its authority over international law, such that the president has become the "sole actor" in making international law. Thus, Hathaway makes a persuasive case that even *ex ante* congressional-executive agreements often violate the norm of legislative involvement in agreement making.[2] She much prefers the *ex post* variety, which happen to make up less than one half of 1 percent of the executive agreements she analyzed for the period of 1980 to 2000 (Hathaway, 2009, 150).[3] Bradley and Goldsmith (2018) argue that the links to law provided to legally justify *ex ante* congressional-executive agreements are often vague, and in many cases, not provided at all by the DOS when it reports the agreement publicly or to Congress. Moreover, when links are made, they are often tenuous, as the statutes often do not mention making binding international agreements. Like Hathaway, they estimate that less than 1 percent of agreements are of the *ex post* variety. Given the findings of this legal scholarship, it is safe to conclude that the overwhelming majority of recent congressional-executive agreements are of the *ex ante* variety and in many cases stem from tenuous or vague authority delegated to the executive decades before the agreement was finalized.

While seemingly minor, the problem described here is serious when one considers the extent to which presidents are pushing the envelope of delegated authority in the modern era, and the importance of transparency in providing congressional oversight of the executive. The lack of an effective transparency regime makes congressional oversight of diplomacy very difficult, as many agreements go unreported or their basis in law is unclear (Hathaway, *et al.* 2020). Systematically accounting for the president's use of executive agreements is difficult due to the lack of transparency in reporting by the executive branch, despite statutes requiring transparency (e.g., the Case Act of 1972). Often, agreements are reported months or even years late or not at all. And, when the agreements are reported, it is often unclear where the executive gains its legal authority to make international law (Harrington 2016). As Bradley and Goldsmith (2018) describe, this lack of transparency makes holding the executive accountable under the law quite difficult. When one considers the various types of executive agreements discussed above, getting firm counts of each type is also difficult, especially given the blurred distinctions often made between the types (Ramsey 2017).

Executive Agreements Dataset

Despite these difficulties, I set out to catalog executive agreements completed during the period of 2005 through 2020, to include the second term of the G.W. Bush administration, the Obama administration, and the Trump administration.[4] The counts discussed in the analysis below most definitely represent undercounts, particularly for the Trump years, so any conclusions drawn must be considered in that vein. Publicly available data are used for these counts and the DOS simply does not publicly report executive agreements in a timely or complete fashion.[5] The primary data source is the DOS website, including archived versions, supplemented by data provided by Hathaway, *et al.* (2021), which include information gleaned from DOS nonpublic cover memos for agreements reported to Congress from 2005 to 2017.[6]

The grand total of executive agreements included in the dataset is 3,045. The data include 1,207 executive agreements signed during the last four years of the Bush administration, 1,592 executive agreements signed during the Obama administration, and 246 executive agreements signed during the Trump administration.[7] These totals undercount the actual totals, given the irregular rate at which executive agreements are reported, i.e., they are often reported late so the Trump years in the dataset are probably missing several hundred agreements. Even with these significant problems, the data discussed below provides as complete an accounting of recent presidents' use of executive agreements currently available and the data include over 3,000 agreements covering a 16-year period.

The publicly available information on each agreement includes a summary, signing date(s), partners, etc., which allows the collection of individual-level data necessary to effectively describe recent presidents' use of this unilateral tool. When the text of the agreement was available, the agreement was read more carefully if the codes were not apparent in the summary data. Data were collected on the following information: signature date;[8] in-force date; agreement partner; region;[9] whether the agreement was bilateral or multilateral;[10] the broad type of agreement;[11] a more specific subtopic of the agreement;[12] the agreement's policy area;[13] and the agency that completed the agreement.[14] A team of undergraduate students entered each agreement and its relevant information into a spreadsheet for the initial data collection. A second team of students cross-checked the data again when the Hathaway study's data became available. I cross-checked all the agreements in the spreadsheet with the data sources to ensure accuracy in data entry and coding, and repeated agreements were discarded. To compare the dataset here with an earlier era, I make some comparison to data collected by Caruson and Farrar-Myers (2007), which cover agreements reported to Congress from 1977 to 1996.

Agreement Topic

In Table 5.1, I break down the number of agreements signed every two years by broad topic of agreement. Security agreements are the largest category equaling 44.7 percent of the total executive agreements. They include status of forces agreements (SOFAs) and other military personnel agreements; basing and military construction agreements; military cooperation and training agreements; agreements dealing with weapons and other military hardware, including research and development; military assistance agreements; and agreements dealing with nonproliferation of weapons of mass destruction, other arms control agreements, and nuclear safety agreements. A larger percentage of Bush's executive agreements were in the security category than is the case for Obama and Trump (47.9 percent vs. 42.7 percent), a difference that is partly attributable to Bush's multi-front "global war on terror."

Economic agreements represent the second largest category, constituting 30.1 percent of the total. A slight majority (52 percent) of the economic agreements involve foreign assistance, which are authorized by foreign aid statutes. Other economic agreements include transportation agreements (18.6 percent); tax agreements (13.9 percent); trade and investment agreements (12.6 percent); and communications agreements (2.8 percent). Caruson and Farrar-Myers (2007) found a similar share of economic agreements in their dataset for the period 1977 to 1996. The third largest category, at 15.9 percent, includes cultural, educational, and scientific exchange agreements. Most of the agreements in this category are related to cooperation in science and technology. The remaining agreements in this category relate to cultural and educational exchanges, environmental

TABLE 5.1 Executive agreements by topic (2005–2020)

Years	*Security*	*Sovereignty*	*Economic*	*Legal*	*Cultural, educ., & science*	*Total executive agreements*
2005–6	304	16	195	25	82	622
Bush	(48.9%)	(2.6%)	(31.4%)	(4.0%)	(13.2%)	
2007–8	274	19	173	34	85	585
Bush	(46.8%)	(3.2%)	(29.6%)	(5.8%)	(14.5%)	
2009–10	211	25	154	17	83	490
Obama	(43.1%)	(5.1%)	(31.4%)	(3.5%)	(16.9%)	
2011–12	161	16	136	40	68	421
Obama	(38.2%)	(3.8%)	(32.3%)	(9.5%)	(16.2%)	
2013–14	148	13	116	15	56	348
Obama	(42.5%)	(3.7%)	(33.3%)	(4.3%)	(16.1%)	
2015–16	159	16	90	16	52	333
Obama	(47.7%)	(4.8%)	(27.0%)	(4.8%)	(15.6%)	
2017–18	72	10	29	3	31	145
Trump	(49.7%)	(6.9%)	(20.0%)	(2.1%)	(21.4%)	
2019–20	32	16	23	4	26	101
Trump	(31.7%)	(15.8%)	(22.8%)	(4.0%)	(25.7%)	
Total Bush	578	35	368	59	167	1,207
	(47.9%)	(2.9%)	(30.5%)	(4.9%)	(13.8%)	
Total Obama	679	70	496	88	259	1,592
	(42.7%)	(4.4%)	(31.2%)	(5.5%)	(16.3%)	
Total	104	26	52	7	57	246
Trump	(42.3%)	(10.6%)	(21.1%)	(2.8%)	(23.2%)	
Total	1,361	131	916	154	483	3,045
	(44.7%)	(4.3%)	(30.1%)	(5.1%)	(15.9%)	

Note: The 2008 (Bush) totals include seven agreements signed by the Bush administration in January 2009, prior to Obama's inauguration. The 2016 (Obama) totals include 25 agreements signed by the Obama administration in January 2017, prior to Trump's inauguration. Percentages reported in parentheses are row percentages.

cooperation, and protection of archeological and cultural property. Sovereignty agreements constitute the smallest percentage of the executive agreements (4.3 percent), and include primarily diplomatic agreements, including consular and visa agreements, boundary agreements, and friendship agreements. Finally, there is the legal category, which constitutes just 5.1 percent of the total number of executive agreements, and includes agreements primarily relating to crime prevention, including narcotics, terrorism, and claims.

Overall, the patterns indicate that security agreements, in particular military cooperation agreements and arms control agreements, are more common during this period than for presidents during the latter part of the twentieth century. Data from 1977 to 1996, reported by Caruson and Farrar-Myers (2007, 635), indicate that security agreements constituted roughly 15 percent of all executive agreements, though there was an upsurge during the Clinton years, where the share of security agreements was 29.4 percent. By far, the largest category of security agreements in the dataset involves military cooperation, at 34.6 percent of the total share of security agreements. While the dataset does not include agreements during the first George W. Bush term, it is very likely that security agreements significantly increased as a category during the twenty-first century due to the initiation of two wars and the "global war on terror" following the events of September 11, 2001. Arms control and nuclear safety issues were clear foreign policy priorities during this period, and this is indicated in the dataset. Between 2005 and 2020, the United States completed 310 arms control and nuclear safety agreements as executive agreements, accounting for 22.8 percent of all security agreements in the dataset. SOFAs are also quite common in the dataset, as the data include 213 of these agreements, or 15.7 percent of all the security agreements. The high number of SOFAs is unsurprising given the extent to which US forces are dispersed across the globe. Weapons research and development (11.3 percent) and military assistance (8.8 percent) are also relatively common in the dataset.

Law enforcement and criminal assistance agreements, which fall in the legal category, are also more common during recent years than they were during the 1977 to 1996 period. While still a relatively small share of executive agreements, overall, at 5.1 percent, most of these involved agreements related to crime prevention cooperation.[15] During the earlier period covered by Caruson and Farrar-Myers (2007), the legal agreements were overwhelmingly related to the drug war. The dataset here includes only 25 agreements related to narcotics and 18 agreements specific to combating terrorism.

Agreement Partners

The United States signed executive agreements with 192 different states during the period, which accounts for virtually all members of the UN. Only 173 (5.7 percent) of the executive agreements in the dataset are multilateral, and most of these are with international organizations such as the European Union (EU), an EU agency, or NATO. In comparison, 72 treaties were signed during this period and then submitted to the Senate, of which 31 (43 percent) were multilateral. In terms of raw numbers of executive agreements signed, the top-ten partners included Panama (148); Afghanistan (86); Japan (85); South Korea (69); Russia (68); the United Kingdom (68); Mexico (63); Australia (62); Colombia (60); China (50); and Italy (50). The United States also signed a comparably large number of agreements with France (47); Indonesia (45); Jordan (44); Israel (44); Canada (43); Germany (43); Peru (38); Ukraine (38); and India (38). The list of top agreement partners includes several key allies (Japan, South Korea, Australia, and leading NATO members), two key rivals (Russia and China), and several countries in which the United States is a key provider of foreign assistance.[16]

A substantial share of the agreements with the United States' top agreement partners includes security agreements. In the case of Panama, 133 of the 148 agreements in the dataset include separate SOFAs, which upon reading are very specific and less significant than most SOFAs. There are only 80 other SOFAs signed with other states in the entire dataset combined, and they tend to be much broader in nature, including the 2008 SOFA with Iraq that caused some controversy, as I discuss below. Thus, the large number of SOFAs with Panama inflates the overall total agreements with Panama and the number of SOFAs in total. The remaining 15 agreements with Panama include agreements on environmental cooperation, trade, crime prevention, military assistance, transportation, taxes, civil aviation, and claims.

Afghanistan is second in numbers of agreements in the dataset, with 86. The Afghanistan agreements include 70 strategic objective grant agreements or amendments to prior strategic objective grant agreements, which are foreign assistance agreements completed through USAID. As the largest recipient of foreign aid by the United States during this time, the pattern of agreements with Afghanistan makes sense. The remaining 16 agreements with Afghanistan include several important debt reduction agreements, two military assistance agreements, two military cooperation agreements, two civil aviation agreements, a communications agreement, two narcotics agreements, the very important "enduring strategic partnership agreement" signed in 2012, and the Bilateral Security Agreement of 2014. The "enduring strategic partnership agreement" encompasses a very significant security pact, in addition to diplomatic relations and economic and military assistance. To signify its significance, it is one of only a few agreements in the dataset signed by the president. The Bilateral Security Agreement was also a very significant agreement. I discuss both agreements in depth below.

The next two most common agreement partners include two key East Asian allies, Japan, with 85 agreements, and South Korea, with 69 agreements. The agreements with Japan include 44 (52 percent) security agreements, including all the varieties of security agreements mentioned above. There are also 29 agreements on science and technology, five transportation agreements and three trade agreements. For South Korea, 46 (67 percent) of the agreements are security agreements and 17 are science and technology agreements. The high number of security agreements are indicative of the significant military alliance between the United States, Japan, and South Korea.

The United Kingdom (UK) and Russia are tied for fourth in the number of agreements in the dataset, with 68 each. The vast majority (79 percent) of agreements with the UK are security agreements, with a few economic, sovereignty, and scientific exchange agreements. The security agreements with the UK mostly involve military cooperation and weapons development, which is indicative of the close military partnership between the United States and the UK. In the case of Russia, half of the agreements are security agreements, and all but two of these relate to arms control, nonproliferation, or nuclear safety. These security agreements mostly involve follow on implementing agreements to ratified arms control conventions. Thus, the security agreements differ from those signed with key allies (e.g., Japan, South Korea, and the UK), which tend to focus on military cooperation and weapons development. The remaining agreements with Russia include 17 research and scientific agreements, 13 specific trade agreements, two transportation agreements, an important agreement facilitating direct secure communications between the two nuclear powers, and a visa agreement.

Mexico (63), Australia (62), Colombia (60), China (50), and Italy (50) round out the top-ten agreement partners. The types of agreements signed with Mexico are indicative of the important trade relationship between the United States and its southern neighbor, as well as the lengthy border shared between the two countries. More than one-third (37 percent) of the agreements are coded as economic, and include trade, transportation, and communications agreements. Agreements with Mexico also include 14 sovereignty agreements, which primarily focus on cooperation along the border. Most (73 percent) of the agreements signed with Australia are security agreements, largely focused on military cooperation and weapons development. Australia and the United States, together, are party to several additional multilateral agreements focused on military cooperation. Half of the agreements with Colombia are economic, including 15 USAID agreements, ten transportation agreements, and five trade agreements. The 13 security agreements with Colombia include eight military assistance agreements, which is the highest number of military assistance agreements in the dataset with a particular state and reflects the US commitment to combating drug cartels in Colombia. Most (78 percent) of the agreements signed with China involve scientific and educational exchanges. The dataset also includes five economic and five security agreements with China. Four of the security agreements relate to nuclear safety and arms control. As is the case with other NATO allies, a majority (54 percent) of the agreements with Italy are security agreements, and these primarily involve military cooperation and weapons development. There are 19 scientific and educational exchange agreements with Italy.

Another way to splice the dataset is to look at the agreement topics by region. Some clear patterns emerge. The United States signed a large share of agreements with Western Europe and East Asia. Outside of those two large regions, the agreement partners are relatively spread out across the globe. Regarding the topics by region, a majority (59.2 percent) of the agreements signed with European states are security agreements. The most significant of these security agreements include ballistic missile basing agreements with the Czech Republic, Poland, and Romania, and agreements having to do with WMD proliferation and nuclear safety in several former Soviet states, including Russia and Ukraine. Outside of Europe, security agreements are most common in Central Asia and Central America. In the case of Central Asia, 47 of the 60 agreements (78 percent) are security agreements, including a dozen agreements dealing specifically with cooperation with the US war in Afghanistan and more than two dozen agreements dealing with arms proliferation and nuclear safety. Most agreements with Central American countries are security agreements (73.8 percent), and most of those are SOFAs (79.4 percent). As mentioned above, the number of SOFAs with Panama inflates these numbers, but SOFAs are also common with Honduras and Guatemala.

Economic agreements follow expected patterns given the recipients of US foreign assistance, since the bulk of these agreements are USAID agreements. For instance, Afghanistan and Pakistan were two of the top three recipients of US foreign aid during this period. Economic agreements, of which the largest portion are aid agreements, make up 82 percent of all executive agreements signed with South Asian states, including 75 aid agreements with Afghanistan and 31 with Pakistan. African and Middle Eastern states also receive a large share of US foreign assistance and therefore economic agreements make up a significant share (49.1 percent) of all agreements completed with states in these regions, and most of these agreements are aid agreements. While a large share of economic agreements in the Americas include aid agreements to developing states including Colombia, Peru, Haiti, Dominican Republic, El Salvador and Costa Rica, trade agreements and other types of economic agreements are also common, including the important trade promotion agreement with Peru signed in 2006.

Cultural, educational, and scientific exchange agreements are most common with developed states, including Western European states (in particular, Italy, Germany, and Sweden) and East Asian states (in particular, China, Japan, South Korea, and Indonesia). Given the proximity of states in the Americas, a much larger share of agreements signed with states in the Western hemisphere fit into the legal and sovereignty categories than for the rest of the globe. One general exception to this finding is that legal agreements are more common in Europe than for other parts of the world outside of the Americas. The Obama administration prioritized completing anti-crime agreements with European states.

Executive Branch Agencies

In Table 5.2, I catalog the executive agreements by executive branch agency for agencies that signed at least 1 percent of the agreements in the dataset. While the DOS completed more executive agreements than any other agency, I find that 20 separate departments or independent agencies completed executive agreements during the period. The DOS completed 43.4 percent of all executive agreements, followed by the Department of Defense (DOD), which completed about one-quarter (24.2 percent) of all agreements. DOS personnel sign a wide range of agreements, including foreign assistance and other economic agreements; military cooperation and other forms of security agreements; and cultural, educational, and scientific exchange agreements. The DOS also completes most legal and sovereignty agreements.

TABLE 5.2 Executive agreements by agency (2005–2020)

Agency completing agreement	*Security*	*Economic*	*Cultural, educ., & science*	*Legal/ sovereignty*	*Total*
Dept. of State	464 35.1%	339 25.6%	285 21.5%	235 17.8%	1,323 43.4%
Dept. of Defense	721 98.0%	4 0.5%	9 1.2%	2 0.3%	736 24.2%
USAID	2 0.6%	317 97.5%	6 1.8%	0	325 10.7%
Nuclear Regulatory Comm.	125 100%	0	0	0	125 4.1%
NASA	0	0	83 100%	0	83 2.7%
US Trade Representative	0	77 100%	0	0	77 2.5%
Dept. of Transportation/ FAA	0	76 100%	0	0	76 2.5%
Dept. of Energy	49 72.1%	0	19 27.9%	0	68 2.2%
Dept. of Interior	0	0	47 100%	0	47 1.5%
Millennium Challenge Corp.	0	41 100%	0	0	41 1.3%
Dept. of Treasury	0	40 100%	0	0	40 1.3%
Dept. of Justice	0	2 6.3%	0	30 93.4%	32 1.1%
Other*	0	20 27.8%	34 47.2%	18 25.0%	72 2.4%
Total	1,361	916	483	285	3,045

**Note*: Other agencies that signed executive agreements included the Department of Homeland Security, Department of Health and Human Services, the Environmental Protection Agency, the Federal Communications Commission, the Department of Agriculture, and the White House.

Unsurprisingly, the focus of the DOD is security agreements. All but 15 of the 736 DOD agreements are security agreements. Most of the security agreements completed by the DOD are routine military exchanges; weapon research and development; nonproliferation assistance; and military cooperation agreements that fit well within the scope of the president's Article II powers as commander-in-chief. The more significant security agreements, including all SOFAs and most basing agreements, cooperation related to the war in Afghanistan, ballistic missile agreements, military assistance agreements, and the more significant versions of nonproliferation agreements are completed by the DOS, rather than the DOD. Such a bifurcation suggests that the most significant agreements are likely to be completed by the DOS, not other executive branch agencies.[17]

Another clear pattern is that while the DOS completes a wide variety of agreements, the other agencies largely relegate their executive agreement activity to a specific type of international agreement, much like what we see with the DOD. The best example of this, other than the DOD, includes agreements completed by USAID, of which there are 325 in the dataset. The USAID agreements are largely implementing agreements for aid packages enacted by congressional foreign aid statutes. However, DOS personnel typically complete debt reduction agreements, a form of foreign assistance that is more significant than the "strategic partnership" aid agreements completed by USAID. All the agreements completed by the Department of Transportation (DOT), including the Federal Aviation Administration (FAA), include air transport agreements, civil aviation agreements, and agreements related to transportation safety. The DOT or the FAA signs most transportation agreements. While the Nuclear Regulatory Commission (NRC) completed most of the agreements related to nuclear safety, the Department of Energy and the DOS completed the remaining such agreements. Agreements completed by NASA and the Department of Interior all involved cooperation in the science and technology fields. The agreements completed by the Department of Justice (DOJ) include primarily crime prevention agreements, including 26 significant agreements on "enhancing cooperation in preventing and combatting serious crime," several of which were signed by Attorney General Eric Holder.

As has been discussed in prior research on executive agreements, most of these international agreements involve routine matters that rarely reach the attention of the White House or cabinet secretaries. Such is the case for both treaties and executive agreements, though treaties do tend to involve more significant issues, on average, and require the White House to transmit the agreement to the Senate accompanied by a transmittal document signed by the president. The DOS employs the Circular 175 process (C-175), as described in Hathaway, *et al.* (2020) for classifying agreements as executive agreements or treaties. The analysis here suggests that agreements completed by the DOS, on average, tend to be more significant and of a less routine nature than agreements completed by other executive branch agencies. Other than the aforementioned "combatting serious crime" agreements and trade agreements completed by the US Trade Representative, a significant majority of agreements signed by officials in agencies other than the DOS are mundane implementation agreements or amendments to existing agreements.

Discussion

The analysis of the executive agreement dataset leads to four conclusions. First, recent presidents have completed numerous very important bilateral agreements as executive agreements rather than as treaties. When contrasted with the paltry number of treaties completed by President Obama and President Trump, this is an important conclusion; diplomacy during the twenty-first century has taken a decidedly unilateral turn.[18] In accordance with legal scholarship, I find that recent presidents regularly make international law with little input from Congress (Bradley and Goldsmith 2018).

Second, a significant percentage of recent executive agreements appear to stem directly from Article II of the Constitution, in particular the president's power as commander-in-chief. Nearly half (44.7 percent) of the executive agreements in the dataset are security agreements, which is unsurprising given the war on terror and the broad range of existing security pacts to which the United States is committed. However, many of the security agreements relate to new agreements focused on nonproliferation, ballistic missile basing agreements, military assistance, and the US military presence in Afghanistan and Iraq. Such agreements represent major security commitments. The degree to which recent presidents were simply executing their function as commander-in-chief or committing the nation to extended security arrangements is unclear. While most of the security agreements may fit the former description, several clearly went beyond the president simply executing his executive function.

Third, the more mundane diplomatic activities represented by most executive agreements continued apace. While Obama and Trump were unable to ratify more than a handful of mutual legal assistance, extradition, investment, and tax treaties, they regularly finalized agreements in these domains as executive agreements. This suggests that recent presidents continued to implement diplomacy in these areas, but largely avoided doing so through treaties. These run-of-the-mill treaties were common throughout the modern era, including during the G.W. Bush presidency, and constitute most of the treaties in the treaty dataset analyzed in Chapter 3. This was not the case, however, during Obama and Trump's presidencies, as was clearly shown in Chapter 2. The paucity of even mundane treaties suggests two possibilities. First and least likely, is that the Obama and Trump administrations did not complete these mundane, but critical, international agreements because they were no longer necessary.[19] Second and more likely, is that recent administrations strategically decided against finalizing many of these sorts of agreements as treaties, instead completing them as executive agreements.[20]

Finally, as Kaye (2013) argues, recent presidents implement US diplomacy using "stealth multilateralism." This can occur in a number of ways, including the president signing multilateral international agreements with little intention of submitting the agreement to the Senate for ratification, but still participating in the multilateral organization or at least abiding by guidelines set forth in the agreement;[21] or, by submitting the agreement to the Senate, with the intention of behaving as if the agreement had been ratified whether or not the Senate approved the agreement;[22] or, by completing the multilateral agreement as an executive agreement, rather than as a treaty, and thus binding the United States to international law without involving Congress—what I have focused on here. Each of these approaches, of course, cuts Congress out of the process.

The Iraq and Afghanistan Agreements

The wars in Afghanistan and Iraq represent two significant foreign policy endeavors of the early twenty-first century that roiled US politics. Both wars were authorized by Congress via formal authorizations to use military force in 2001 and 2002. However, presidents used unilaterally completed executive agreements to formally commit the United States to the security of both Iraq and Afghanistan for many years beyond what was originally considered likely when Congress originally authorized force. President George W. Bush was able to extend the involvement of US forces in Iraq beyond his presidency when he completed two executive agreements with Iraq in November 2008.[23] President Obama extended the US commitment to the security of Afghanistan beyond his presidency when he signed the "enduring strategic partnership agreement" with Afghanistan in 2012 and the more encompassing Bilateral Security Agreement with Afghanistan in 2014.

The Bush administration claimed that the two 2008 agreements with Iraq merely constituted a SOFA which he could complete on his own authority as commander-in-chief. However, several legal scholars and members of the Senate disagreed, as, in combination, the two agreements with Iraq committed US combat forces in that country for three years past the 2008 UN-mandated deadline for withdrawal and included other security and support commitments.[24] Ten months prior to Bush completing the agreements, during a 2008 Democratic presidential debate on January 21, Senator Hillary Clinton (D-NY), stated, "We need legislation in a hurry, which says, 'No, Mr. Bush . . . You cannot bind our country without coming to the United States Congress.' This is a treaty . . . that would have to be presented and approved." Senator Clinton's remarks are illustrative of the opinions of Democrats on the Bush administration's 2008 move to complete the agreements with Iraq as sole executive agreements. Clinton, of course, shared the stage with Senators Biden and Obama, who both agreed with her.[25] Democrats also had public opinion on their side, as the US public had grown wearisome of the Iraq War and wanted it to end.[26]

These Democrats' opinion on the president's authority to unilaterally make security commitments to Iraq took an about-face once they were making the decisions, however. The Obama administration tried to extend the US force presence in Iraq beyond the December 31, 2011, deadline brokered by Bush in 2008 (Parker and Salman 2011),[27] but the negotiations failed in early fall 2011 (Arango and Schmidt 2011; Gordon 2012). The agreement was scuttled due to internal Iraqi politics and a lack of direct White House involvement in pushing the deal. Even so, it was clear at the time that the Obama administration had no intension of submitting the agreement to the Senate as a treaty or to Congress for bicameral approval. They believed the 2002 authorization to use military force in Iraq, which Congress passed prior to Bush's invasion of Iraq, provided all the necessary legal authority to commit the United States to Iraqi security. The Obama administration began the US withdrawal from Iraq once it was clear that a new agreement was not in the cards. With the rise of ISIS following the US departure from Iraq, US troops were sent back. The inability to complete a binding international agreement with Iraq in 2011 did not foreclose the return of US troops. As of the time of this writing (early 2022), US troops remain in Iraq (Phillips 2021). It should be noted that the United States does not have any current treaties in force with Iraq and none of the executive agreements with Iraq in the dataset examined in this chapter required congressional approval.

The enduring strategic partnership agreement with Afghanistan signed by Obama in 2012 is a very broad international agreement which structured the US–Afghanistan relationship. The agreement included a SOFA regarding US military stationed in Afghanistan, continued US military and economic aid, and structured the security relationship between Afghanistan and US forces combating Al Qaida and the Taliban on Afghan territory.[28]

A more encompassing and lengthier agreement with Afghanistan, called the Bilateral Security Agreement, was finalized in November 2013. The deal allowed for the continued presence of US forces in Afghanistan after 2014. President Obama indicated that about 10,000 US troops would remain in Afghanistan through 2016, dropping to about half that number afterwards. The Loya Jirga, Afghanistan's national legislature, gave its approval to the agreement and Afghan President Ashraf Ghani ratified it on September 30, 2014. Despite its significance, Obama did not submit the agreement to Congress for approval (Craig and DeYoung 2013; DeYoung 2014; Shanker and Nordland 2013). Article 26 of the agreement includes the following language:

> This Agreement shall enter into force on January 1, 2015, after the Parties notify one another through diplomatic channels of the completion of their respective internal legal requirements necessary for the entry into force of this Agreement. It shall remain in force until the end of 2024 and beyond, unless terminated pursuant to paragraph 4 of this Article.[29]

In late 2014, President Obama finalized the agreement as a sole executive agreement. Thus, the administration's interpretation of Article 26 is that the agreement, which committed the United States to Afghanistan's security for a decade, could be completed on his sole authority as president. It is telling that the Afghan legislature had more input on the agreement than the US Congress.

The Obama administration brokered dozens of bilateral executive agreements dealing with the war in Afghanistan and expanded the US troop presence in that country, yet the United States did not have a bilateral treaty with Afghanistan in force during this period,[30] nor have any treaties been signed and submitted to the Senate for approval. Clearly, President Obama made solemn security commitments to Afghanistan without input or participation by Congress. The US public had turned against the war by the time Obama was extending US commitments (Good 2011).

Under the auspices of the Bilateral Security Agreement, after considering a withdrawal, President Trump expanded the US troop presence in 2017. The new strategy included increasing the US presence to roughly 15,000 troops and continued training and advising of Afghan forces in their war against the Taliban insurgency (Ewing and Nayler 2017). However, on February 29, 2020, President Trump effectively abrogated the Bilateral Security Agreement with Afghanistan when he signed the "peace agreement" with the Taliban to pull US troops from Afghanistan within 14 months (Welna and Dwyer 2020), a deal the Taliban almost immediately violated with its continued support of Al Qaida (Riedel 2020). The agreement formed the framework for Presidents Biden's withdrawal of US forces from Afghanistan during the summer of 2021, thus ending the United States' longest war after nearly 20 years.

Trade Agreements

The regulation of international commerce is a signature power of the US Congress. During the twentieth century, Congress delegated a significant amount of this authority to the executive so that presidents could negotiate trade deals, largely with the goal of expanding trade (O'Halloran 1993). However, the delegation of trade authority to the president included significant checks by the Congress in that presidents were typically required to get their trade deals approved via statute. Thus, presidents would bring their trade deals to Congress, seeking bicameral approval as congressional-executive agreements (Ackerman and Golove 1995). Over time, obtaining congressional approval became the norm when completing these sorts of agreements (Krutz and Peake 2009). This norm, however, has come under threat by recent presidents, as they have sought to both expand and restrict international trade through unilateral actions, without involving Congress.

The expansion of trade agreements was an important component of President Obama's foreign policy agenda. Acting jointly with Republicans in Congress, Obama successfully completed several bilateral trade agreements as congressional-executive agreements, including accords with South Korea and Colombia. He also negotiated broader multilateral agreements, like the Trans-Pacific Partnership (TPP), but President Trump decided to withdraw from the TPP early in 2017, thus it was never submitted to Congress for approval. Trump focused on revising existing trade agreements as part of his "America First" foreign policy. He had a strong preference for bilateral trade agreements and routinely attacked existing trade agreements as "bad deals."

Despite limited precedence for doing so, both President Obama and President Trump acted unilaterally on trade, at times in the face of congressional opposition. For example, the Obama administration considered treating the Anti-Counterfeiting Trade Agreement (ACTA) as a sole executive agreement after signing the pact in October 2011. Numerous legal scholars argued that this was problematic because the agreement dealt with a subject matter that is clearly within the realm of Congress's enumerated powers, specifically copyright protections, and that prior agreements in this area were submitted to the Senate as treaties (Goldsmith and Lessig 2010; Hathaway and Kapczynski 2011; Ramsey 2017, 285). Hathaway and Kapczynski (2011, 4) conclude that "the possibility that such legal commitments could be made by the President without the input, much less the approval, of Congress . . . raises serious questions about the potential of these agreements to undermine democratic lawmaking." They argue that such an action could weaken the "strength and durability" of international commitments, as Congress might enact future legislation that violates US commitments under international law.

The Obama administration later claimed its action on ACTA was an *ex ante* congressional-executive agreement rather than a sole executive agreement; however, their reliance on existing law was quite dubious (Harrington 2016). The DOS's Legal Advisor, Harold Koh, argued that the ACTA was fully consistent with existing US law. According to Koh, the president is free to complete an agreement on his own authority if such an agreement is consistent with existing law, which is an incredibly broad and questionable view of the treaty power (Bradley and Goldsmith 2018, 1217). Obama's behavior on ACTA underscores Hathaway's (2009) concern regarding ambiguous claims of preauthorization on the part of Congress. This is particularly troubling given the clear constitutional mandate of Congress on international trade and copyright issues and the fact that existing norms require congressional approval for trade agreements. The argument that the president can complete a binding international agreement on any matter "as long they are consistent with and further the policies evident in a domestic congressional scheme" suggests that presidents are free to commit the United States unilaterally unless Congress has legislated that they cannot (Goldsmith 2016, 14). That is a very broad interpretation of presidential power. The ACTA never went into force, however, as counter-protests in Europe led the European Parliament to reject it. According to the Obama administration's arguments, no such legislative approval was required in the United States.

Similar concerns arose when the Obama administration determined that it could complete the Bali Agreement, a WTO trade facilitation agreement, without approval from Congress. The controversy stems from whether the new agreement, as an amendment to an already congressionally approved agreement (the WTO), could be concluded on the president's sole authority, or whether it required congressional approval as is typically done with such amendments (e.g., China's inclusion in the WTO in 2000). The administration's position was that if a trade agreement does not require changes in US domestic law, as in the case of the Bali Agreement, then the need for congressional approval was unnecessary, i.e., the agreement is self-executing as it does not require implementing legislation

(Ramsey 2017, fn. 165). On its surface, this interpretation does not appear problematic. However, such an interpretation suggests any agreement that modifies an existing agreement could qualify as a sole executive agreement and that binding agreements only require congressional approval if they require implementing legislation, i.e., "if no implementation is required, no Congress" (Ku 2013). The United States deposited its acceptance instrument to the Bali Agreement in 2014 without any action from Congress.

The Obama administration pushed the boundaries of what is considered acceptable by international lawyers in international trade.[31] Obama's focus was to expand free trade, through the initiation of additional trade deals. Trade expansion is a domestically controversial policy and Obama tried several times to circumvent any opposition to his efforts that might arise in Congress, including from his own party. President Trump, on the other hand, made his hostility to trade agreements quite apparent, having termed just about every existing trade deal to which the United States is party as "one of the worst deals ever" (Gordon 2018). He threatened to terminate the US–South Korea bilateral trade agreement and US participation in NAFTA, among others.

During the fall of 2017, Trump ramped up his threats to terminate NAFTA, trying to force Mexico and Canada to make significant concessions. Trump clearly believed he could unilaterally terminate the agreement. However, because NAFTA was approved by statute, even if the United States were to withdraw from the agreement, many of its provisions would remain in place because of the statute. The president cannot terminate US laws unilaterally. Plus, Congress could legislate to limit the president's trade authority if they opposed his action or threaten other elements of the president's legislative agenda (Aleem 2017). However, while the legal authority may be unclear, the president could still act, and it is unlikely that Congress or the courts could constrain the president directly. More relevant, however, is that the Congress lacks the wherewithal to constrain the president, as any legislative action would require a veto-proof majority—something quite difficult to obtain in today's political context—and a Republican Congress was unlikely to confront a Republican president over this issue.

Thus, President Trump was able to prosecute his trade war in the face of congressional opposition, including unilaterally leveling tariffs on several key trading partners. While most of Trump's ire focused on China, his tariffs also targeted imports from long-time US allies, including Canada and Germany. Even though many in Congress opposed his actions, there was not much, practically speaking, that they could do to stop him (Peake 2021, 344–5). Of course, the same could be said regarding any congressional effort that might have arisen to block Obama's unilateral actions to promote trade.

Rather than scuttling NAFTA, Trump instead sought to update the agreement with a successor agreement called the US–Mexico–Canada Agreement (USMCA). To force the United States' two largest trading partners to the negotiating table, Trump issued several tariffs on Mexican and Canadian goods. Trump's unilaterally imposed steel and aluminum tariffs on Canada were particularly problematic, given the existing tariff regime governed by NAFTA. In the face of a possible ruinous trade war, Mexico and Canada relented and made some minor concessions to alter NAFTA in the form of the USMCA. Congress approved the agreement in early 2020. Trump also sought new trade deals or revisions on existing trade deals with Japan, China, the UK, and other major trading partners, all without involving Congress. In 2018 Trump used steel and aluminum tariffs as a cudgel to get South Korea to finalize an ongoing renegotiation of its bilateral trade agreement with the United States, which had begun in 2017. He was able to win some concessions to South Korean imports of US autos and foodstuffs. However, the deal was minor enough that the administration determined that it did not require congressional approval and no changes in US statutes were required. The South Korean legislature, however, had to vote to approve the final deal (Tankersley 2018).

Conclusion

During the twentieth century, the rise of executive agreements signaled an important change in how presidents completed most of their binding international agreements. Rather than relying on treaties and the uncertainty they bring with the requirement of Senate approval, presidents used executive agreements to complete a large majority of their agreements. The shift came during the Franklin Roosevelt administration and was completed in the wake of World War Two (Ackerman and Golove 1995). While 94 percent of binding international agreements completed during the second half of the twentieth century were executive agreements, rather than treaties, presidents still regularly employed treaties to complete many of their most significant international commitments. They regularly submitted treaties to the Senate and deployed significant political capital to marshal them through the process, sometimes meeting with lengthy delays and even failure (Krutz and Peake 2009).

As I document in the earlier chapters of this book, partisan polarization, which has grown exponentially during the twenty-first century, has caused recent presidents to avoid the treaty process altogether, as the Senate seems incapable or unwilling to process treaties. As a result, presidents appear to be completing higher shares of their significant international agreements unilaterally rather than involving Congress. The shift began during the George W. Bush presidency, as 96 percent of his agreements were executive agreements. It solidified during the Obama and Trump administrations, as this statistic increased to at least 98 percent, which is likely an underestimate. The shift is a result of the paucity of treaties. Even though modern presidents eschew Article II treaties, they have not stopped signing important binding international agreements. Recent presidents avoided the Congress on executive agreements that, under norms that developed during the twentieth century, presumably require congressional approval. As I document in this chapter, both Bush and Obama committed the United States to significant security arrangements without going through Congress, and both Obama and Trump shifted trade policy, also while avoiding Congress. It is telling that in most of the cases discussed above, the legislatures of treaty partners had to approve each of these agreements, whereas the US Congress did not.

Analysis of the more than 3,000 agreements included in the executive agreement dataset indicates that recent presidents continue to implement US diplomacy without much pause and on a range of important topics. The foreign policy bureaucracy continues to churn out binding international agreements, implementing US diplomacy even with the broken treaty process.

The president's unilateral authority in diplomacy continues to accrue, without much of a response from Congress. While members of Congress have sometimes complained, they have not been able to confront the executive on this issue. This congressional weakness on treaties is largely due to the increasing partisan polarization that has broken the legislative branch. To confront the president, the Congress must legislate and then be able to override the inevitable presidential veto, an insurmountable hurdle when the parties are as polarized as they are today. That said, presidents are not completely free to create international law when existing US law limits their authority. There are limits to their executive agreement powers, though these are not well appreciated in much of the scholarship on international agreements. Again, the problem here may sit with Congress and its unwillingness or inability to serve as a check on presidential unilateralism. Moreover, limits to presidential unilateral authority means the agreements they can complete tend to be weaker and more easily overturned by successors. Pitched partisan fights occurred recently on two vexing problems facing US policymakers: climate change and Iranian efforts to obtain nuclear weapons. President Obama, in the face of concerted Republican opposition, successfully completed two major international agreements dealing with these problems, only to have his accomplishments undone by his successor, President Trump. The two episodes, to which I turn to in the next chapter, highlight the weakness of US commitments when made in this era of partisan polarization, and are indicative of dysfunctional diplomacy.

Notes

1 See Hathaway (2009) and Ramsey (2017) for a discussion of the differences between these types of executive agreements. Ramsey breaks executive agreements down into five categories: congressional-executive agreements with *ex ante* approval, congressional-executive agreements with *ex post* approval, executive agreements with "implicit" congressional approval (however tenuous), sole executive agreements, and nonbinding agreements. The last of Ramsey's categories are better understood as political commitments due to their nonbinding nature, thus they are not executive agreements according to most accounts (Hollis and Newcomber 2009). I address political commitments in Chapter 6.

2 Hathaway (2009, 214) writes, "Even though the [*ex ante* congressional-executive] agreements have been 'approved' by Congress in the narrow legal sense, there is little genuine cooperation between the President and Congress in the process of creating the agreements."

3 *Ex post* congressional-executive agreements come in various forms as outlined in several US statutes, including the Trade Act of 1974; the Omnibus Trade and Competitiveness Act of 1988; the Atomic Energy Act of 1954; and the Fisheries Conservation and Management Act of 1976. See Krutz and Peake (2009, 170–2) and US Senate Committee on Foreign Relations (2001, 236–8). These statutes require some form of congressional approval (or allow for a resolution of disapproval, which is then subject to a presidential veto) for all major trade agreements, nuclear cooperation agreements, and fisheries agreements. This bicameral approval process can also legally substitute for the Senate treaty approval process, should the president decide to go that route, but this is very rare outside of the areas of policy addressed by statute. The best exception to this rule would be the original SALT agreement, which was submitted by President Nixon to Congress for bicameral approval in 1972 (Krutz and Peake 2009, 78).

4 The data that support the findings of this chapter are openly available in the Harvard Dataverse at https://dataverse.harvard.edu/dataverse/jeffreypeake.

5 For a discussion of difficulties in documenting executive agreements, see Harrington (2016), Ramsey (2017), and Hathaway, *et al.* (2020). Through 2013, the DOS provided Case Act reports publicly online (https://2009-2017.state.gov/s/l/treaty/caseact/index.htm), in addition to the TIAS reports of treaty actions available at: www.state.gov/tias/ and https://2009-2017.state.gov/s/l/treaty/tias/index.htm. To complicate matters, the website also reported monthly "treaty actions" through 2012, see: https://2009-2017.state.gov/s/l/treaty/c3428.htm. All three lists include executive agreements, and while many appeared on all three lists, many did not. In 2014, the online Case Act reporting stopped, and only the TIAS and treaty actions lists were available. The treaty actions and TIAS lists also include treaties, so care must be taken not to include those in a dataset of executive agreements. It is important to note none of these lists are complete, and even when combined, do not paint a complete picture. There is no discernable pattern as to why some of the executive agreements are included in one data source, but not the others, other than the fact that the treaty actions list includes some (but not all) agreements not yet in force, whereas the Case Act reporting and TIAS only include agreements in force.

6 The dataset from the Hathaway, *et al.* study is available at: https://dataverse.harvard.edu/dataverse/executiveagreements. It includes agreements from 1989 to January 2017. It should be noted that many of the agreements that were reported on the DOS website were not included in the Hathaway dataset. The reverse is also true. Thanks to these data, hundreds of additional agreements were added to my original dataset, which was based on the website. The two datasets were combined for the study period (2005–20). Duplicate agreements were discarded.

7 Executive agreements were counted during the year in which they were signed (using the last signature for cases where multiple signature dates are listed). For multilateral executive agreements, for which there was only a handful each year, the date of US signature was used.

8 The latest date of signature was used for agreements where multiple dates are listed.

9 The region code is based on Caruson and Farar-Meyers (2007), with some changes to reflect updated geography.

10 This is relatively straightforward. Agreements with international organizations (e.g., the UN, the EU, NATO) are coded as multilateral, as well as agreements with multiple states. Only 5.6 percent of the agreements are multilateral.

11 Here, I adapt the same broad topic codes used in Chapter 3 with one exception. I use the following broad topics: economic, legal, security, and sovereignty agreements. The exception is that of agreements on norms. Only a few of the executive agreements fall clearly within the norms category, and those tend to be environmental cooperation agreements. I added a category to include cultural agreements, educational exchanges, and nonmilitary scientific/research agreements, which do not fit well within any of the treaty categories from Chapter 3. Such agreements are overwhelmingly completed as executive agreements.

12 Each agreement is given a subtopic code based on 23 subtopics, which are more specific than the five broad topic codes. They range from aid and assistance agreements to transportation agreements to military cooperation agreements.

13 I borrow the policy areas used by Caruson and Farar-Myers (2007). There are 14 policy area codes. They range from atomic energy agreements to financial assistance agreements.

14 A range of executive officials representing numerous agencies signs executive agreements. While most of the agreements are signed by a DOS official (most often an embassy official), some are completed by the DOD, DOJ, USAID, NASA, US Trade Representative, etc. In some rare instances, the representative signing the document is a cabinet secretary (e.g., Secretary of State, Attorney General), or even the president or vice president. The DOS is the default agency when it was unclear which agency completed/signed the agreement. In most cases where the DOS is not the agency, it is clear on the front page of the document that the agreement is an agreement between the DOD (or other agency) and the corresponding agency. When it is not obvious from page one of the agreement, the signatures (and their stated official position) are examined, as well as the text therein. Internet searches helped identify some of the signing officials. Unfortunately, their names or titles were sometimes not included, which required coders to read signatures and then conduct searches. When it was not possible to identify the official who signed the document or the text of the document was not included, as is the case for the agreements added from the Hathaway study and Case Act reports, we extrapolated from other similar agreements to identify the agency. If there was not such a discernable and clear pattern, the default was used (DOS).

15 While many of these agreements are specific in nature, more than two dozen are agreements "on enhancing cooperation in preventing and combating serious crime." Such executive agreements are significant tools used by the DOJ in facilitating legal treaties. As an indication of their significance, Obama's Attorney General, Eric Holder, signed several of these agreements.

16 These numbers can be compared to the number of submitted Article II treaties from the treaty dataset in Chapter 3, which covers the 1949 to 2020 period. US presidents submitted to the Senate multiple treaties with all the top-20 executive agreement partners listed above except for Afghanistan. Top treaty partners include Canada (42), Germany (19), Japan (18), Russia (18), the UK (17), and Mexico (16).

17 However, this bifurcation does not appear to be the case for legal and trade agreements. DOJ personnel typically complete the significant "combatting serious crime" agreements. The same is the case for trade agreements—the US Trade Representative

completes new and more significant agreements and personnel in the DOS typically complete amendments to already existing agreements.

18 By unilateral here, I mean in terms of shared power with the Congress. I do not mean that presidents have eschewed working with other states when it comes to diplomatic endeavors.

19 I believe this to be unlikely because when I examine the list of bilateral treaties transmitted to the Senate since 1949, I find numerous tax treaties and amendments to existing tax treaties throughout, at least until 2008. Similar patterns emerge for extradition treaties, and, to a lesser extent, investment treaties and legal assistance treaties. It strains logic to assume that the practical necessity of these agreements disappeared after the Bush presidency. Moreover, DOJ documents indicate that, as of 2015, the United States has mutual legal assistance treaties with 70 countries, which means the United States has no such treaty with most states, so the need for such treaties still exists.

20 The data presented in a recent analysis by Nyarko (2019) support this conclusion.

21 The Bush and Obama administrations did this with the International Criminal Court (ICC) and various climate change agreements, including the Kyoto Protocol. Other examples include partial supporting behavior on the part of the Bush and Obama administrations on issues related to the CTBT and the Mine Ban Treaty (Kaye 2013).

22 When a country signs a treaty, under international law it is expected that it will endeavor to comply with the treaty whether domestic approval occurs or not.

23 I am referring here to two agreements completed on November 17, 2008, which include the Strategic Framework Agreement for a relationship of Friendship and Cooperation and the Agreement on the withdrawal of United States Forces from Iraq and the organization of their activities during their temporary presence in Iraq.

24 Initially, the Bush Administration argued that one of the agreements, referred to as the Strategic Framework Agreement, was a political commitment rather than a binding executive agreement, and that the president could complete that agreement on his own authority as it was not legally binding. They abandoned this line of argument, however, eventually claiming both agreements constituted sole executive agreements (Hollis and Newcomer 2009). I discuss political commitments in Chapter 6.

25 Biden, then chair of the SFRC, came out strongly in opposition to the notion that the president could bind the United States to continued military intervention in Iraq without congressional approval (Abramowitz 2008). Clinton sponsored the Congressional Oversight of Iraq Agreements Act of 2007 (S. 2426), which would have, among other things, expressed "the sense of Congress that any bilateral agreement between the United States and Iraq involving 'commitments or risks affecting the nation as a whole,' including a status of forces agreement (SOFA), that is not a treaty approved by two-thirds of the Senate ... or authorized by legislation does not have the force of law." It would have prohibited the spending of funds for carrying out such an agreement. Senator Obama was a cosponsor of Clinton's bill. In August of 2008, Biden introduced a similar bill (Iraq Security Agreement Act of 2008).

26 For trends in public opinion on the Iraq War, see https://news.gallup.com/poll/1633/iraq.aspx.

27 In the spring of 2011, Secretary of Defense Robert Gates, in a visit to Iraq, signaled that the United States may keep forces past the deadline to facilitate security in Iraq, but doing so required that Iraq make a formal request. During his Senate confirmation hearings in July, Gates's replacement, Leon Panetta, stated that the administration

was ready "to take whatever steps are necessary to protect" progress in Iraq, to include some continued presence of US forces (Radio Free Europe 2011). On August 19, *Stars and Stripes* reported that Panetta had stated that Iraq and US leaders had basically agreed to begin a process of negotiation for a continued US military presence in Iraq past 2011 (Baron 2011).

28 For more on this significant agreement, see https://obamawhitehouse.archives.gov/the-press-office/2012/05/01/fact-sheet-us-afghanistan-strategic-partnership-agreement and Rubin (2012). It was not a mere SOFA, as stated by administration officials in their claims of inherent executive authority.

29 The text of the agreement is located at: https://www.afghanistan-analysts.org/wp-content/uploads/2014/10/BSA-ENGLISH-AFG.pdf.

30 See the Treaties in Force, published at: www.state.gov/treaties-in-force/. There were dozens of executive agreements in force between the United States and Afghanistan during the Obama presidency, however. Similarly, the United States does not have any bilateral treaties in force with Iraq.

31 The Obama administration did not limit its push to agreements on international trade and security. The Obama administration acceded to the Minamata Convention on Mercury unilaterally, without seeking congressional approval, using the same rationale employed for the trade actions mentioned here. The Minamata Convention is an important multilateral agreement governing production, use, and disposal of mercury, a dangerous chemical (Goldsmith 2016).

6

WEAK COMMITMENTS

The Limits of Presidential Unilateralism

While the use of unilateral international agreements is attractive to presidents for a variety of reasons accentuated by partisan polarization, it also has serious drawbacks. Agreements completed on the president's unilateral authority are more easily overturned by successors, making for much less credible international commitments than agreements made with the support of the legislative branch. As shown in Chapter 5, recent presidents have pushed the envelope of executive authority when making diplomatic agreements, clearly violating norms whereby presidents would submit the most consequential and controversial agreements to Congress for approval. However, often their unilateral efforts yielded weak international commitments. This conclusion is demonstrated clearly by two of President Obama's signature foreign policy accomplishments: the 2015 Iran Nuclear Agreement and the 2015 Paris Agreement on Climate Change. The Iran Agreement is a nonbinding political commitment, and the Paris Agreement combines elements of a binding executive agreement with nonbinding language, making for a hybrid agreement (Goldsmith 2016). As a result, the agreements were much weaker than they would have been if the president had sought expanded authority from Congress to complete a binding agreement or had taken the treaty route. Those options were closed to Obama because the Republican-controlled Congress opposed both agreements.

The 2015 Iran Nuclear Agreement and the 2015 Paris Agreement on Climate Change provide relevant and important examples of how partisan polarization and increased presidential unilateralism has led to dysfunctional diplomacy. The Iran Agreement is a very important multilateral agreement that was the culmination of years of negotiation to forestall Iran's acquisition of nuclear weapons. Despite heavy opposition to the agreement in Congress, the Obama administration managed to complete the agreement on the president's own authority, causing

DOI: 10.4324/9781003347422-6

significant controversy domestically and leading several Republican presidential candidates to promise abrogation of the agreement on day one of their presidency. The Paris Agreement was similarly completed unilaterally by Obama, despite clear opposition by the Republican majority in Congress. In each case, the resulting agreements were far less resilient than a treaty or congressionally approved executive agreement would have been. This weakness had profound implications, as President Trump announced in the summer of 2017 that the United States would leave the Paris Agreement and he officially abrogated the Iran Agreement in 2018.

The Iran and Paris agreements, when placed in the broader context of recent president's disuse of treaties and reliance on other forms of international agreements, point to two competing concerns: the need for action on the diplomatic stage to shape international politics versus the need for those actions to withstand challenges to their legitimacy. With the ascendency of President Trump, who was clearly hostile to multilateral agreements, a third concern is also evident: unilateral actions are less resilient, as they are more easily overturned by the president's successor and have more limited "compliance pull" among signatories (Goldsmith 2016, 465). The framers of the Constitution clearly intended for Congress to play a role in the diplomatic process, yet Obama's actions circumvented the legislature, even in instances where members of Congress went on record opposing Obama's policies or his approach. When agreements have broad support in Congress, they are seen as more legitimate and credible (Martin 2000; Milner 1997). Because the Obama administration often circumvented Congress in favor of unilateral action, the resulting agreements were seen as less legitimate and credible. As we saw play out during the Trump presidency, this has important implications for US foreign policy.

In this chapter, I introduce the concept of the political commitment, a third type of international agreement that has yet to be addressed in this book, and briefly discuss their importance in US diplomacy. A discussion of political commitments is relevant, here, because the substance of both of President Obama's signature agreements (Iran and Paris) purposely avoided binding legal language, including, instead, political commitments on behalf of the United States. As a result, they were easily undone by his successor. The distinction underscores their fundamental weakness as diplomatic commitments, as well as the confusion that existed at the time of their completion, an important consideration for separation of powers concerns regarding the president's role as diplomat in chief. Next, I discuss the Iran Nuclear Agreement and the Paris Agreement on Climate Change, in turn. The discussion underscores the inherent difficulty of completing a major international agreement on a controversial issue during the era of partisan polarization.

Political Commitments

Political commitments are international agreements whereby the president makes a commitment to another state or multiple states to undertake a particular action.

Political commitments are neither a treaty nor an executive agreement and are not considered a formal treaty under international law and thus are nonbinding. Hollis and Newcomer (2009, 517) define a political commitment "as a nonlegally binding agreement between two or more nation-states in which the parties intend to establish commitments of an exclusively political or moral nature." The breach of treaties and executive agreements "can generate both political and legal consequences . . . only politics governs the political commitment" (520). Bradley and Goldsmith (2018, 1201) offer the following definition:

> A political commitment is an agreement, usually written, between the President or one of the President's subordinates and a foreign nation or foreign agency. Its defining characteristic is that it imposes no obligation under international law and a nation incurs no state responsibility for its violation. As a result, a successor President is not bound by a previous President's political commitment under either domestic or international law and can thus legally disregard it at will.

Moreover, "political commitments produce expectations of future conduct, whether in terms of a change in behavior from the status quo or a continuation of existing behavior" (Hollis and Newcomer 2009, 522). Thus, not all joint statements or communiques made by the president constitute political commitments.

Hollis and Newcomer (2009, 513) summarize the importance of political commitments to US foreign policy, writing that the:

> instrument functions as an indispensable tool of U.S. foreign relations, one with potentially significant consequences not only for how others treat the United States . . . but also for future executive and congressional conduct. Political commitments can operate on extended timelines, create deep normative expectations, and involve extensive institutional arrangements. Moreover, in the absence of international legal enforcement mechanisms, the international consequences of political commitments mimic those of treaty commitments.

Despite their significance, there is very little debate regarding how political commitments relate to the treaty power and separation of powers issues more broadly. Moreover, there are no legal mechanisms for the transparency and oversight of political commitments, and presidents are free to make them at will, if they do not contradict current law. To be sure, consequential political commitments can generate significant controversy, and they offer the president a way to commit to an international action without involving Congress.

Examples of significant political commitments include the Shanghai Communiqué, which established a new relationship between the People's Republic of China and the United States during the Nixon administration and led to the eventual abrogation of the US security treaty with Taiwan; the Helsinki Accords, which established a forum for human rights and other disputes that was the precursor to the Organization for Security and Cooperation in Europe; and several recent climate change agreements including the 2008 Group of Eight Declaration on the Environment and Climate Change and the 2014 US–China Joint Announcement on Climate Change (Hollis and Newcomer 2009). Another important example is the Budapest Memorandum on Security Assurances, completed by the United States, UK, Russia, and Ukraine in 1994. That agreement provided "security assurances" to Ukraine in exchange for the relinquishment of its nuclear arsenal. Russia violated the agreement in 2014 with its annexation of Crimea and then further did so with its invasion of Ukraine in 2022. There was much debate in 1994 on whether the agreement would be legally binding, and the United States emphasized it was a political commitment rather than a legally binding agreement (Borda 2022).

As described by Bradley and Goldsmith (2018), political commitments are often regulatory in nature, where the president commits to some action on his own legal authority. Presidents can follow up these nonbinding commitments with executive orders and national security directives effectuating the agreement. Thus, political commitments are often used in conjunction with other unilateral presidential powers. The problem is that such commitments are not reported to Congress and lack transparency, so it is often difficult to discern when a nonbinding agreement has been completed (Ramsey 2017).

Moreover, given that political commitments often look like treaties or executive agreements,[1] it can sometimes be unclear during negotiations whether the executive intends to complete a binding international agreement (i.e., a treaty or executive agreement) or a political commitment. Intent to complete an agreement as a political commitment rather than a legally binding agreement is definitive of a nonbinding agreement, though it may not always be evident to the untrained eye (Hollis and Newcomer 2009, 523). There is often confusion between the two once negotiations are completed, even among policymakers, legal scholars, and other signatories since the distinctions are not always clear (Ramsey 2017). This was clearly the case for the Iran Nuclear Agreement and the Paris Agreement on Climate Change. As I describe below, both agreements were wholly or partially completed as political commitments, which allowed the president to skirt congressional approval requirements (Ramsey 2016). Political commitments, because they are nonbinding, are quite fragile and may be abrogated by future presidents with only political rather than legal costs. As discussed below, Trump's behavior on these agreements demonstrates their fragility.

The Iran Nuclear Agreement

The 2015 nuclear agreement with Iran, known officially as the Joint Comprehensive Plan of Action (JCPOA), is a controversial international agreement that pitted the

Republican Congress against President Obama in his efforts to broker a deal with Iran and five other leading powers where Iran would give up its efforts to develop nuclear weapons in exchange for the elimination of certain economic sanctions. The other five signatories include China, Russia, the UK, France, and Germany.[2] The JCPOA, which was signed on July 14, 2015, was the culmination of nine years of diplomatic efforts to forestall the development of a nuclear arsenal by Iran. The United States and its allies enforced a crippling economic sanctions regime that brought the Iranians to the bargaining table (Drezner 2021).

As the agreement took shape, it was clear that in exchange for giving up its nuclear weapons program, the sanctions regime against Iran would need to be substantially reduced. Such action was politically controversial in the United States because congressional Republicans, and some Democrats, had routinely pushed for harsher action against Iran rather than diplomacy. In their view, Iran was not just seeking a nuclear arsenal, but was a terrorist-supporting state bent on the destruction of one of the United States' greatest allies, Israel. That the Israeli government preferred less diplomacy on the issue also made it a litmus test for members of Congress on their support for Israel. President Obama lacked the authority to completely shelf the sanctions against Iran because the sanctions regime was statutory, and Congress was unlikely to budge in providing him additional authority to remove them completely. The president's authority was limited in that he was only legally able to waive certain sanctions every six months.

As the diplomatic efforts moved toward completion in early 2015, 47 Republican senators went on record opposing unilateral action by the president on the pending deal, indicating in their March 2015 "open letter" to Iran that any such agreement, if it were to be legally binding, would need congressional approval and any future president would be free to renege on the deal if such approval was not forthcoming. The letter stated that any agreement "not approved by Congress is a mere executive agreement."[3] While much discussion ensued in the press about executive agreements versus treaties, it turns out that the agreement eventually signed in July was neither a treaty nor an executive agreement, but rather a nonbinding political commitment that relied on the existing congressionally delegated presidential authority to grant sanction waivers (Goldsmith 2016).

The preamble in the agreement stated the following "Iran and [the other parties to the JCPOA] will take the following voluntary measures within the timeframe as detailed in this JCPOA and its Annexes" (quoted in Ramsey 2017, 322). The words "will take" and "voluntary measures" are diplomatic parlance for nonbinding language, and the JCPOA had other indicators of a nonbinding agreement, including no ratification clause and its official name, which suggested reciprocal policy actions rather than the typical name of convention or agreement. On the other hand, specific components of the agreement are indicative of a binding agreement, including the establishment of a dispute resolution mechanism, promises reaching far into the future, and it included very specific information regarding timetables and sanctions relief (Ramsey 2016, 108–9).

The confusion surrounding the JCPOA's legal nature is understandable. The administration initially argued, via the Vice President's office, that the president could complete the agreement on his own authority as an executive agreement. However, the president lacked the authority to eliminate or permanently waive sanctions due to statutes that governed Iranian sanctions. The statutes only authorized the president to temporarily suspend sanctions. Indeed, the president's legal authority to unilaterally complete a binding agreement on sanctions in this case was nonexistent, given existing law (Hollis 2015). The lack of presidential authority to unilaterally make a legally binding commitment, coupled with strong opposition in Congress, threatened to undercut one of Obama's signature foreign policy accomplishments. However, a political commitment, paired with the use of existing presidential authority to temporarily suspend sanctions, offered an opportunity for Obama to fulfill the commitments necessitated by the Iran agreement. Goldsmith (2016, 466) explains:

> The Obama team's imaginative answer to this conundrum was to locate the authority to fulfill the political commitments in independent domestic law authorities that were not designed to effectuate or approve international agreements. With the Iran Deal, Obama pledged in a political commitment to lift U.S. sanctions, and then followed through on that pledge by exercising an independent, pre-existing congressionally conferred authority to waive the sanctions in the national interest.

In short, the president already had the legal authority under the sanctions laws to suspend certain economic sanctions on Iran periodically; thus, additional congressional authorization to do so was not required. The primary weakness of this approach was that, under the law, the waivers had to be issued every six months, meaning Obama's successor could easily abrogate the agreement by refusing to issue the waiver.[4]

The political commitment solution was problematic as it gave credence to the Republican argument that Obama's successor was free to renege on the agreement should they wish to—and many of the Republican candidates for the presidency were stating they would do just that, should they be elected. For example, during his winning campaign for the presidency, Donald Trump indicated his opposition to the JCPOA and signaled that he would tear up the agreement once he was president. After all, if President Obama had the legal authority to waive the sanctions, his successor certainly had the authority to not waive them when the time came to issue the periodic waiver, absent a congressionally authorized legally binding agreement and changes to the statutes governing Iranian sanctions.

Moreover, a political agreement cannot legally bind one party (i.e., the Iranians), and not the others (Hollis 2015). Thus, the nonbinding nature of the agreement meant that it was also nonbinding for the Iranians, and thus, lacked "compliance pull" (Goldsmith 2016, 465). Fixing this latter problem required action at the UN

Security Council, which was required to suspend UN-mandated sanctions on Iran. This occurred soon after the agreement was signed, as the Security Council passed Resolution 2231, endorsing the JCPOA and terminating prior resolutions that subjected Iran to sanctions over its nuclear weapons program.

Realizing that the political commitment approach was problematic, the Obama administration supported congressional efforts to require congressional review of the agreement once it was completed. However, Obama's support was contingent on whether the law required congressional approval for the president to effectuate the agreement. A compromise was forged by Senator Corker (R-TN) and Senator Cardin (D-MD) and passed in May 2015 with a bipartisan vote. The law, entitled the Iran Nuclear Agreement Review Act (INARA, PL 114–17), suspended the president's waiver authority on Iranian sanctions for 60 days while Congress reviewed and debated the agreement, after which time the president could waive sanctions (authority he already had) if Congress failed to enact a joint resolution of disapproval during that time (Raju and Everett 2015). It should be noted, however, that the act did not require a vote of approval—the agreement would go into effect if Congress approved the agreement, *or did nothing*, but could only be stopped if Congress passed the disapproval resolution. The INARA did not authorize the president to complete a legally binding executive agreement with Iran, so even though it effectively involved Congress in the process it did not provide the president any additional authority to make a binding agreement. Thus, the eventual agreement was not a congressionally authorized executive agreement, as some legal scholars argued at the time (Ackerman and Golove 2015, but see Ku 2015).

The joint resolution of disapproval provided for in the INARA was subject to a presidential veto, which undercut any real chance for Congress to successfully block the agreement. While the INARA inserted Congress into the process once the deal was signed, it did so with little real effect, because any joint resolution of disapproval would need to overcome a presidential veto. This had the practical effect of turning the required support necessary for congressional approval of the agreement from two-thirds of the Senate in the case of a treaty or a majority vote of both chambers in the case of an *ex post* congressional-executive agreement to just one-third plus one in just one chamber, the minimum required to sustain a presidential veto. It also provided a patina of legitimacy to the president's authority, as it appeared that Congress was giving its go ahead to the president to sign the deal.

The agreement was signed in July 2015, and the 60-day clock started. Republican opposition to the deal was immediate and strident, with Senator Corker remarking that the administration "had been fleeced" (Welsh 2015). The Republican-controlled House of Representatives acted quickly to disapprove the deal, voting to take away the president's authority to waive sanctions until January 2017. However, action to confront the president stalled in the Senate, as a Democratic filibuster killed the Republican effort to enact a resolution of disapproval, which the president would have vetoed, and the president was able to fulfill his political commitment to suspend US sanctions. Taylor (2019) reports that the Republicans benefited from the ineffectiveness of INARA in stopping the agreement. They understood that passage of the disapproval resolution was unlikely, and a veto was forthcoming if it did pass. It gave Republicans an election issue on which they could pummel Democrats, while at the same time allowing the president to complete his diplomatic agreement. In the end, they would not be blamed for killing the agreement, something on which many Republicans were ambivalent.

Obama was in a weak position domestically. He lacked the authority to sign a legally binding agreement and there was no way Republicans in Congress would approve a binding agreement or give him the authority to complete one. Thus, he had to resort to a method that has led many to question the legitimacy of his actions. While legal, Obama's approach was politically unpopular. Moreover, given the significance of the agreement and its subject area, these legitimacy concerns were justified, as "it represented an aggressive use of the president's independent authority over nonbinding agreements" (Ramsey 2017, 323). In effect, as Goldsmith (2016) argues, Obama creatively used existing statutory authority not intended to authorize international agreements to implement an international agreement contrary to the wishes of Congress. Also, Members of Congress were still confused as to whether the agreement was a legally binding agreement or a political commitment, as evidenced by the fact that the State Department (DOS) had to clarify as late as September 2015 that the agreement was not legally binding, i.e., that it was a political commitment.[5]

The case of the Iran Nuclear Agreement suggests that even when congressional majorities oppose presidential action on international agreements, the president may be able to act despite this opposition. This is especially the case when statutes provide for greater presidential authority through delegation (i.e., waiver authority in the case of sanctions), as is the case with so much of the president's authority in foreign policy, generally, and in making international agreements, especially (Krutz and Peake 2009).[6] To be sure, joint action by the branches in the form of a treaty or congressionally authorized executive agreement has more legitimacy and is binding under international law, thus binding future presidents, but the political context, in the words of Secretary Kerry, made receiving congressional approval of such agreements "physically impossible." The case also illustrates that the polarized politics Kerry lamented makes it equally difficult for the Congress to guard its own foreign policy prerogatives via the legislative process, especially regarding delegated authority, given the president's veto power. In the end, President Obama was able to act, and Congress was left to react, with little real effect.

The weakness of the nonbinding nature of the agreement is clearly demonstrated by President Trump's abrogation of the JCPOA, announced on May 8, 2018. At the behest of his national security advisors, President Trump issued the sanctions waivers twice before finally refusing to do so a third time. Calling the

Iran agreement "one of the worst and most one-sided transactions the United States has ever entered into," Trump announced the termination of US participation in the JCPOA and the reimposition of the suspended sanctions on Iran. The White House claimed that Iran was in breach of the agreement, but the UN and the DOS had indicated numerous times that Iran had not violated the JCPOA prior to Trump's decision (Da Vinha 2019).

Abrogation of the agreement, absent Iranian violations, caused serious political problems with other agreement participants. For example, even though the United States reimposed sanctions following Trump's decision, the other parties to the agreement tried to continue to keep their commitments, making US sanctions less effective overall. To combat this problem, US sanctions included secondary sanctions, i.e., sanctions on firms in other states that trade with Iran. Initially, the administration provided waivers to these secondary sanctions, but one year after leaving the deal, they were imposed as well. This action further threatened the deal, as the other signatories' firms had to decide whether Iranian oil and the Iranian market was worth being cut out of the much larger US market, and, as a result, Iranian oil exports plummeted, and Iran's economy suffered significantly (Bartlett and Ophel 2021; Drezner 2021).

Iran responded by announcing it would no longer be bound by the agreement if other states were in breach. This included the provocative move of enriching uranium beyond levels allowed in the agreement. During the summer of 2019, tensions in the Persian Gulf region significantly increased, leading to some claims that the United States and Iran were on the brink of war, as the United States committed thousands of additional troops and military assets to the region, including strategic bombers, air defense systems, and a carrier strike group. The Iranians downed a US unarmed drone, and President Trump considered a military strike on Iranian facilities, but called off the strike shortly before it was to commence (Wright 2019). The Iranians continued their uranium enrichment program, in violation of the agreement, substantially reducing the "break-out time" necessary to enrich enough uranium to develop a nuclear weapon, even in the face of crippling economic sanctions (De Luce 2022).

Trump's threats to leave the deal throughout 2017 and his eventual abrogation in 2018 highlight the fragility of the Iranian Nuclear Agreement. If Obama had been free to negotiate a binding agreement or if he had negotiated a binding agreement and received congressional approval, Trump's legal authority to abrogate the agreement would be limited, as the agreement would have significantly greater domestic legitimacy and codification in US law. To leave the agreement, the president would need to follow whatever process was put into place for exiting the agreement. That said, presidents appear to have the constitutional authority to unilaterally terminate duly ratified treaties and executive agreements, as President Bush did with his announcement of his intention to leave the Anti-Ballistic Missile (ABM) Treaty in 2001.[7] It is very likely that Trump could have left the agreement, whether it was binding or not, just as he left other duly ratified treaties during his term in office.

President Biden made reviving the Iran Nuclear Agreement an important foreign policy priority in 2021, but reviving the old deal, or forging a new deal has proven difficult. During negotiations, Iran's new president appointed a hardliner to represent Iran at the negotiations in Vienna, significantly diminishing prospects toward the end of 2021. Trump's abrogation of the JCPOA in 2018 has significantly complicated matters, as the Iranians, who are now closer than ever to a nuclear weapon due to the agreement's collapse, look for assurances that future presidents cannot back out of the eventual agreement. In other words, they are now explicitly seeking a binding agreement rather than a political commitment (Lynch 2021), which would require a new agreement altogether or substantive revisions to the JCPOA. Of course, given existing law, a binding agreement (i.e., an executive agreement or treaty) would require congressional action, either a two-thirds vote in the Senate—an impossibility—or a majority vote in both chambers of Congress. Biden's prospects for bicameral approval in Congress are greater than Obama's were in 2015, given Democrats controlled both chambers of Congress in 2022. However, Democrats had historically slim majorities and enough Democrats were opposed to the JCPOA previously that even that path proved problematic.

While Biden could rejoin the JCPOA unilaterally and execute the agreement by signing the periodic sanctions waivers just as Obama did, future presidents would not be bound by his commitment. Republican Senators made this plainly clear when 33 of them signed a letter in early 2022, reminiscent of their March 2015 letter, indicating that a new Republican president would tear up the agreement in January 2025 (Jakes 2022). In their letter, they claimed that rejoining the JCPOA or any similar agreement should require a treaty, but such a requirement would doom the agreement (De Luce 2022). In April 2022, talks on reviving the JCPOA came to a standstill and in early May, a majority of the Senate, including 16 Democrats, passed a nonbinding resolution indicating they wanted a broader agreement than what the Iranians had indicated they are willing to sign (Desiderio 2022; Liechtenstein and Toosi 2022). Prospects for a revival of the JCPOA are indeed grim at the time of this writing. This begs the following question: why would the Iranians sign on to such a fragile deal, only to have it broken again following the next presidential election? Meanwhile, as negotiations inch along, and with the Biden administration distracted by the Russian invasion of Ukraine, Iran continues to reduce its breakout time to produce a nuclear weapon, making a direct military confrontation with Iran more likely. Such an eventuality would be a disaster for US foreign policy.

The Paris Agreement on Climate Change

One of Obama's most significant foreign policy legacies was the advancement of the climate change agenda via the negotiation and completion of the Paris Agreement on Climate Change, which was perhaps "the most important multilateral agreement of the 21st century" up to that time (Patrick 2019, 252). The Paris Agreement was completed in December 2015 and has been signed by 195 countries. It provides another important example where the Obama administration completed a major international agreement despite significant opposition by the majority party in Congress. Accounts of the negotiations of the accord suggest that US domestic politics structured negotiations of the agreement in late 2015. Republican opposition to the agreement was well known and it was understood that any legally binding agreement that required congressional approval, i.e., a treaty or an *ex post* congressional-executive agreement, would go nowhere in Congress. As a result, US negotiators pushed for a deal built on a hybrid model mixing legally binding language from the 1992 UN Framework on Climate Change (UNFCC), a ratified treaty, with nonbinding voluntary pledges for reductions on carbon emissions. The procedural requirements in the Paris Agreement were legally binding and constitute an executive agreement; however, the substantive components regarding nationally determined emission reduction commitments were voluntary and signify a political commitment.

The binding and nonbinding nature of the agreement make for a constitutionally dubious product according to some legal scholars. For instance, Ramsey (2016) points out that the structure of the agreement has all the characteristics of a binding agreement, including ratification procedures, signature, procedures for withdrawal, and much of the language is binding and commits the signatories to a general goal of reducing emissions well into the future. The specified goals and emissions levels are nonbinding, but that does not make the agreement nonbinding with respect to international law, as it takes on the basic character of a treaty as defined in the Vienna Convention on the Law of Treaties (Bodansky 2016).

The basic understanding that a legally binding climate treaty was politically impossible, given the political realities in the United States, significantly challenged negotiations in Paris (Busby 2016; Goldenberg 2015). After all, while the Kyoto Protocol, the precursor to the Paris Agreement, was signed by the Clinton administration, it was not submitted to the Senate due to clear Republican opposition, and President Bush subsequently unsigned the treaty. The language in Kyoto regarding national commitments on emissions was binding, and thus required Senate approval as a treaty. Using nonbinding language regarding the nationally determined commitments in the Paris Agreement was focused largely on skirting requirements for domestic ratification in the United States. As expected, Republicans in the Senate were opposed to Obama's move on the Paris Agreement, indicating that the president was making promises he could not keep and that any such agreement required Senate approval as a treaty, where it would undoubtedly die from neglect (Demerjian and Mufson 2015). Republicans argued that the lack of legally binding language regarding the carbon emissions levels did not mean the agreement was not a treaty under domestic law, as previous treaties also included some nonbinding language. The president ignored these Republican complaints and ratified the agreement on his own authority.

While some legal scholars are certain that the Paris Agreement constitutes a political commitment (e.g., Goldsmith 2016), my reading of contemporary accounts indicates that there was much confusion regarding the actual nature of the Paris Agreement upon its completion (Busby 2016). Often skeptics will point to parts of the agreement and state it should be an Article II treaty under domestic law, requiring Senate consent. Kind of like the adage, "if it looks like a duck and quacks like a duck, it's a duck," but replacing duck with treaty. Others will state that it is not a treaty, but a mere executive agreement, as if an executive agreement is nonbinding on future presidents. Executive agreements are binding under international law. They are the same as a treaty, after all. That international law does not distinguish between treaties and executive agreements certainly complicates the issue. Thus, the confusion does not just lie in whether the agreement is a treaty or executive agreement, but whether the agreement is binding under international law—is it a treaty/executive agreement or a political commitment? As in the Iran Agreement case, this is the distinction that matters, and, as Ramsey (2016) and Bodansky (2016) argue, the Paris Agreement is clearly binding under international law as it includes much binding language. Taylor (2019), who served on the Senate Foreign Relations staff during this period, also refers to the Paris Agreement as a binding executive agreement, with voluntary nationally determined carbon emissions goals.

Goldsmith (2016) argues that the Paris Agreement was like the Iranian Nuclear Agreement in that the commitments made dealing with carbon emission targets were nonbinding, and that the president could implement these commitments domestically under existing legal authority through the Clean Air Act and other existing laws. However, the Paris Agreement is significantly more complicated because of its hybrid nature. Goldsmith (2016, 466) argues that the agreement is "a binding international obligation, elements of which the president could probably commit the nation to pursuant to a 1992 framework treaty" already consented to by the Senate. The 1992 UNFCC obligated parties to various reporting and other requirements, so including legally binding language in the Paris Agreement meant that the president could complete the agreement as an executive agreement pursuant to an approved treaty, but the nonbinding language on carbon targets would thus not require additional approval by Congress because they constituted a political commitment and no change in US law was required to implement them. If that language were legally binding, i.e., if the language legally obligated states to fulfill their nationally determined commitments, then congressional approval would be required.

As negotiations neared completion, whether the Paris Agreement was binding international law, and its character under US law became a cause for concern for diplomats, too. US negotiators, including Secretary of State John Kerry, emphasized the voluntary nature of the nationally determined commitments, stating that the Paris Agreement is "definitely not going to be a treaty," noting that there were "not going to be legally binding reduction targets like Kyoto." Kerry's focus was at home—he was fending off the Republican arguments that the agreement would need to be submitted to the Senate for consent. However, his statement caused backlash from European counterparts, who stated that the final agreement would be a legally binding agreement, no matter its title, and US diplomats had to clarify that the agreement would legally bind states to a process, but the emissions commitments would constitute political commitments and be voluntary in nature (Demirjian and Mufson 2015).

During the 2016 presidential campaign, Trump made his hostility to the Paris agreement quite clear, and more broadly questioned the wisdom of action to curb climate change, as he believed the economic costs were too great and that the science was dubious. During the campaign, he referred to climate change as a Chinese manufactured hoax (Worland 2019). That hostility carried over to his presidency, as Trump appointed climate change skeptics to key environmental positions in the executive branch, including the administrator at the EPA, Scott Pruitt. Against the advice of some of his closest advisors (Da Vinha 2019), on June 1, 2017, Trump announced in a Rose Garden address his decision to withdraw from the Paris agreement. Trump stated that his decision to leave the agreement represented "a reassertion of America's sovereignty" (Patrick 2019, 252).

Because the agreement is a hybrid one—partially binding and partially nonbinding—the United States was not free to leave the agreement under the agreement's binding terms until November 4, 2020. In a twist of fate, this was just one day after Election Day 2020, an election Trump lost to Joe Biden, a supporter of the Paris Agreement. In fact, signatories were not authorized to give notice of departure until November 4, 2019, so the Trump administration's official announcement, which came in 2017, was more than two years premature. Moreover, the parts of the agreement that Trump opposed included the voluntary greenhouse emissions standards, due to their economic effects. Trump could have voided these or unilaterally reduced US commitments, without withdrawing from the agreement (Meyer 2017). Additionally, because the United States was still party to the agreement until November 2020, it continued to send a delegation to the governing body under its legal obligations. However, the US delegation did not have much standing to provide input on changes to other states' commitments, given its premature announcement of departure.

In a way, Trump's unilateral announcement on the Paris agreement was meaningless, other than that it handicapped US efforts to negotiate a "better deal," something the president stated he wanted to do. The practical effect was that it ceded US leadership on international efforts to slow climate change, clearly stated the administration's abandonment of climate change mitigation efforts, and was a serious setback in the global effort.[8] Also, in terms of presidential authority, it was not legally controversial, as discussed above, since presidents have long had the authority to terminate duly ratified treaties through the process outlined in the treaty, let alone executive agreements, and no one questioned the president's authority to leave the agreement. The case, however, lays plain the weakness of the Paris Agreement, due to the nonbinding nature of the commitments on emissions and the ambiguity regarding its other binding provisions. The broken domestic politics on treaties appear to have contributed to the nonbinding nature of the agreement, as discussed above, which led to a very fragile deal.

On January 20, 2021, in one of his first presidential actions, President Biden signed the necessary paperwork to rejoin the Paris Agreement, and immediately set out to reverse many of the regulatory rollbacks from the Trump administration (McGrath 2021; Rott 2021). One effort to catalog Trump's deregulatory efforts and Biden's regulatory efforts, indicates that 57 percent of Trump's rules related to climate change mitigation had been reversed by Biden during the administration's first 100 days, and that the effort was ongoing (Barnosky, *et al.* 2021).[9] President Biden led a large US delegation to the UN climate change meetings in November 2021 in Glasgow, where he recommitted the United States to ambitious emissions goals and made new political commitments to assist developing countries to meet their climate goals (Naylor 2021). Biden's show of force in Glasgow signaled a significant change in terms of US leadership on climate change, but the president's ability to meet those commitments given political difficulties at home was met with some skepticism by diplomats from other countries (Linskey, *et al.* 2021).

The on-again, off-again commitments to international efforts at tackling climate change underscores the weakness of US leadership, made worse by the polarized domestic political environment. Why should the rest of the world follow the US lead on climate change when the next administration might decommit the United States from Paris or any future agreements? The history of US behavior on climate agreements underscores this concern. Democratic presidents have made broad promises on climate change before, only to be undercut by their Republican successors (Levitz 2021). Additionally, whatever commitments President Biden makes abroad on climate change are mitigated by domestic politics. While the administration can act unilaterally to mitigate climate change by issuing new rules and regulations, broader action requires congressional approval of additional spending. Moreover, Biden's unilateral regulatory actions can be easily reversed by the next president (Nilsen and Ward 2021).

Conclusion

The cases analyzed in this chapter demonstrate the weakness of international commitments made by presidents when they lack congressional support, particularly on controversial issues like Iran's nuclear weapons development and climate change. The weakness is especially highlighted in an era of partisan polarization, where the next president of a different political party is very likely to reverse agreements that their partisans view as unwise, weak, or illegitimate. The two cases also highlight the significant confusion that results from the multiple means available to presidents to complete international commitments, including treaties and executive agreements, as well as political commitments. While the first two categories of agreements are legally binding international commitments, the third is not, even though such agreements may take on the characteristics of binding agreements. The lack of transparency and clarity in US law regarding the different categories only muddies the waters. It is not my intention to provide clarity on this largely legal matter, but rather to highlight the lack of clarity to demonstrate why this may be an important political problem for presidents as they seek to execute US diplomacy and for members of Congress looking to hold the president accountable on international agreements.

What is a president to do when faced with a vexing international problem that can only be solved through multilateral action when whatever agreements they make at the negotiating table are likely to be nonstarters at home due to partisan politics? President Obama's largely negative experience on treaties taught him that relying on congressional approval for important international agreements was a fool's errand, as doing so meant no international agreement would be completed. Goldsmith (2016, 456) explains that "in this context, the Obama team made singular innovations by cobbling together tools that significantly expanded the President's power to make international agreements without Congress' consent, and sometimes in the face of clear congressional opposition." The Iran and Paris agreements would not have happened without US leadership at the negotiating table and the only way to secure the deals on behalf of the United States was to cobble together existing tools of the presidency: political commitments and broad statutory delegations of authority. Goldsmith (2016, 467) concludes that Obama used "old tools" to form a "powerful new form of international agreement" for the United States. This is a significant broadening of executive power vis-à-vis the Congress regarding international agreements, and Congress is impotent to respond directly due to the president's veto power.

While President Obama was able to act unilaterally on the Iran and Paris agreements, irrespective of congressional wishes, the innovation suffers from significant weaknesses when compared to other forms of international agreements. Most obvious is that any future president can easily leave the agreement, as we saw President Trump do in each case. Trump's behavior has led to additional concerns from parties to the agreements once the United States rejoined the Paris Agreement and has tried to revive the JCPOA during Biden's presidency. Treaty partners now doubt the ability of President Biden to create lasting commitments, understanding that the next Republican president might abrogate the agreement. Consider a world where the US president completes a major arms control agreement, and it is an open question as to whether the next president will live up to the agreement. That is effectively the world we live in today and provides a stark demonstration of dysfunctional diplomacy.

Notes

1 For example, written political commitments may contain an article devoted to exiting the agreement or to dispute resolution.

2 For further background and technical issues on the Iranian Nuclear Agreement, see Katzman and Kerr (2016).

3 For text of the letter, see www.bbhub.io/assets/sites/2/150309-Cotton-Open-Letter-to-Iranian-Leaders.pdf. The language used by Senator Cotton (R-AR), stating that the agreement would be a "mere executive agreement," is confusing, because an executive agreement is just like a treaty, in that it is binding under international law. It is likely that the senator meant "political commitment" rather than executive agreement, but the confusion is unsurprising, as numerous scholars and even members of the administration referred to the agreement as an executive agreement that did not require congressional approval. There is also the common refrain that executive agreements are somehow nonbinding (i.e., they are just "gentlemen's agreements"), which is fallacious, given the category of political commitments discussed above.

4 The approach is also constitutionally suspect, as the president's action upended the statutory regime regarding Iranian sanctions without affirmative congressional action (see Estreicher and Menashi 2017).

5 For example, there was an exchange of letters between Representative Pompeo (R-KS) and the DOS, indicating the degree to which Members of Congress were confused as to the nature of the agreement (Weybrecht 2015).

6 Delegated authority on sanctions and international agreements is just one example of congressional delegation to the executive of important legislative functions. President Trump's actions in the wake of congressional opposition on the imposition of new tariffs, his continued support of Saudi Arabia in the Yemeni civil war, and national emergencies (with respect to the border wall) all stem from previously delegated authority to the president. In several cases, Congress passed joint resolutions of disapproval regarding Trump's actions, only to have Trump's vetoes of those resolutions sustained (Peake 2021).

7 However, as Bradley and Goldsmith (2018) argue, the constitutional authority to terminate a congressionally ratified international agreement is untested, as the federal court cases involving the ABM treaty, and President Carter's actions regarding a security treaty with Taiwan, did not address the actual legal question, since they were dismissed as nonjusticiable political questions. If we go off past practice, any domestic legal challenge to Trump's leaving the agreement—if it were a binding agreement—would likely be dismissed. Since the agreement is merely a political commitment, however, there is no legal question as to whether Trump or a future president could leave the agreement on their own. A binding agreement, if it had included changes in US statutes on Iranian sanctions, may have limited Trump's actions legally, as he cannot alter US law unilaterally, unless the statute included such a delegation of authority to the president.

8 What was meaningful, however, were the Trump administration's efforts to rollback regulations designed to mitigate climate change. McGrath (2021), citing the Sabin Center for Climate Change Law at Columbia University, reports there were "175 rollback actions taken by the Trump administration to eliminate federal climate mitigation and adaptation measures." A listing of the rollbacks is available at: https://climate.law.columbia.edu/climate-deregulation-tracker.

9 A separate analysis conducted at Columbia University confirms the substantial number of deregulatory rollbacks. The list is available at: https://climate.law.columbia.edu/content/climate-reregulation-tracker.

7
CONCLUSIONS

Dysfunctional diplomacy is a serious problem for the United States. As a global leader, the United States must be able to complete binding international agreements that can withstand the next presidential election. As a democracy, its most important agreements must have domestic support and the legitimacy that comes with legislative approval. As a major beneficiary of an ordered world, the United States must be able to participate fully in the development of international law. Finally, as the world's largest economy, the United States must be able to forge trade agreements. The United States must fully participate with other leading states to confront the most vexing problems facing the world today, including climate change, pandemics, arms proliferation, and human rights degradation. The vast and growing commitment problem stemming from dysfunctional diplomacy that I describe in this book does not bode well in terms of effectively confronting these daunting problems.

I started this book quoting Secretary of State John Kerry's observation during congressional testimony on the Iran Nuclear Accord that "you can't pass a treaty anymore." For the most part, Kerry's observation was spot on. Last century, presidents would submit dozens of treaties during a two-year Senate, while also completing most of their international agreements unilaterally as executive agreements. On average, presidents from 1949 to 2008 submitted 32 treaties per two-year Congress. Since 2008, that average is just under eight, and President Biden submitted just two treaties through April 2022. While delays were common and some high-profile failures occurred prior to 2009, the Senate usually considered the president's treaties and passage rates were relatively high, averaging 77 percent. Simply put, Presidents Obama, Trump, and Biden rarely opted to complete their international agreements as Article II treaties, relying almost entirely on unilateral mechanisms to complete their international agreements. On the rare occasion

DOI: 10.4324/9781003347422-7

when Obama or Trump submitted a treaty, their treaties were routinely ignored by the Senate and their success rates on treaties are the lowest among modern presidents, at 36 percent.

The trend in the disuse of treaties that President Obama began continued with President Trump and President Biden, and the Senate continues to shirk its advice and consent role. Agreement partners are fully aware of the difficulty presidents face in securing approval of treaties, and it has made it harder for US diplomats to close deals, as agreement partners wonder if any eventual deal will outlast the current president. For example, renegotiation of the Iran Nuclear Accord in 2022 proved difficult for Biden, as the Iranians demanded an agreement that would last beyond his presidency. At the time of this writing, ongoing negotiations do not look promising. Of course, US domestic politics are not the entirety of the problem, as shifts in the geopolitical context (e.g., Russia's invasion of Ukraine and increasing oil prices) makes dealmaking more difficult (Adghirni and Tirone 2022).

Thus, the recent politics of international agreements presents a couple of puzzles worth solving. First, why have recent presidents turned away from treaties? It could be that presidents have done so because they can—they have unilateral options available to complete international agreements. Such an answer is intuitively simple. However, unilateral options are not new, as presidents throughout the modern era had them in their tool chests. What changed in the political context that might have led to this shift in presidential behavior? Second, why has the process broken down so significantly in the Senate that the institution appears unable to process treaties, including the more routine bilateral treaties on mundane topics such as taxes and extradition? Clearly, the two questions are linked, as a broken Senate process provides further incentives for presidential unilateralism.

The domestic politics of international agreements have changed considerably over the past 20 years. As I document in this book, partisan polarization is largely to blame for this significant shift. The statistical analyses clearly indicate that, as polarization increases, presidents use fewer treaties and treaties they submit to the Senate take longer to process. The recent Senate has been setting new records for partisan polarization each year. The case studies confirm these statistical results, and demonstrate that the problem is especially potent for major multilateral treaties that address significant issues including the law of the sea, human rights, the environment, and arms control. As a result of this broken process, and because presidents have unilateral options, recent presidents have relied overwhelmingly on executive agreements and nonbinding political commitments, often with the intent of skirting the Senate. The unilateral commitments, however, are weaker and easily overturned by successors, as we saw during Trump's presidency.

Conservative Republicans have long been suspicious of treaty making. As a result, the United States has a checkered history in participating in the multilateral institutions treaties often create. Those suspicions have held even greater weight recently as the two parties have grown more ideologically polarized, and globalization becomes a bugaboo for the far right. Supermajority requirements in the Senate embolden conservative Republicans to oppose a range of international agreements, including mostly symbolic human rights treaties to hugely important arms control agreements. Such opposition was especially potent during the Obama administration, as Republicans routinely killed treaties or forestalled action on languishing treaties. Until the ascendency of President Trump, perhaps the greatest critic of the United States' participation in international law, Republican presidents largely resisted partisan efforts to reject treaties. Trump's Republican predecessors had treaty records of significant accomplishment on topics Republicans now routinely reject, including arms control, human rights, and environmental treaties. A different Republican president might approach international treaty making differently than Trump, but that is an unlikely prospect given the stranglehold the far right appears to have on the party. If Trump were to run again and win in 2024, the situation will only worsen.

Indeed, this is a grim situation. A host of international problems confront the world, and its most powerful state is handicapped by dysfunctional politics that have shattered any domestic consensus on how to address these problems. Presidents seeking solutions are left with half-measures available in existing statutes. For example, the president can periodically waive economic sanctions in exchange for the Iranians giving up on efforts to develop nuclear weapons, but they cannot remove them entirely, and the next president can simply refuse to issue the waiver, abrogating the deal. Presidents can commit internationally to using their existing executive regulatory authority via the EPA to limit carbon emissions to halt climate change, but the next president can easily reverse those regulatory actions. In both cases, a fully ratified treaty addressing the problem would make for a much stronger commitment and international law, but domestic politics and the high bar for ratification in the United States preclude Senate approval. We saw these dynamics play out with the Iran Nuclear Agreement and the Paris Climate Accord.

The president is in a stronger position to legally commit the United States to the security of a failed state for years to come, without seeking the approval of Congress. Presidents Bush and Obama made these commitments to Iraq and Afghanistan unilaterally, with little input from Congress, where many opposed the presidents' actions. Yet there was little Congress could do about it, as confronting the executive's unilateralism required legislation. The legislature is handicapped considerably by partisan polarization, and confronting the president requires bipartisan supermajorities to overcome the eventual veto. We saw this play out with President Trump, who successfully vetoed numerous congressional attempts to rein him in through congressional resolutions of disapproval on topics related to international agreements, including military action in Iran, US participation in Yemen, and arms sales to Arab states (Peake 2021).

While congressional impotence in checking the president is particularly clear on security agreements where the president's plenary executive powers are greatest, we have seen it manifest in recent years on several other issues, as well. Last century,

Congress delegated a tremendous amount of power to the executive, including powers that are clearly situated in Article I of the Constitution. Trade policy is perhaps the best example of this in foreign policy, yet significant congressional delegations exist on other foreign policy issues in which international agreements play a role. When Congress enacted statutes delegating authority to the executive, it often included checks on the president, requiring congressional approval in the case of significant agreements on arms transfers, nuclear cooperation, fisheries, military bases, and trade (Krutz and Peake 2009). Such direct checks were weakened considerably when legislative vetoes were deemed unconstitutional by the Supreme Court in 1983 (*INS v. Chadha* [462 US 919], see Hathaway, *et al.* 2020, 633–4). Resolutions of approval, which constituted legislative vetoes, were then amended to require resolutions of disapproval, which could be vetoed by the president. Prior to President Obama, presidents took these constraints seriously. In the more recent era of partisan polarization, however, presidents have looked for ways to skirt these requirements, committing the United States unilaterally to agreements on trade, arms control, and climate change.

As I document in my prior book on treaty politics, past presidents were often hemmed in by institutional politics when considering how to complete their international agreements (Krutz and Peake 2009). Their unilateral proclivities were often checked by the legislature and the president's own desire to maintain unilateral tools for the sake of efficiency. The burgeoning literature on presidential unilateralism has largely found that presidents tend to do what "they can get away with" (Howell 2003, 187). If Congress was willing and able to check the president, then the president was less likely to push the boundaries of unilateral action. Those checks appear to be disabled altogether today by partisan polarization, even when the other party controls the Congress and especially during unified government. President Obama completed major agreements unilaterally, even though most of Congress opposed his actions. President Trump started a trade war, demanding the renegotiation of major trade agreements, even though his own party in Congress opposed his actions. Weak congressional checks on the president require presidents to abide by basic norms of separation of powers, i.e., to be willing to consider requirements for congressional support when completing international agreements. Such norms seem quaint during the current era of partisan polarization, as partisans in Congress oppose the president's actions due to politics and presidents seek ways to skirt the legislature to avoid these partisan fights.

The domestic politics of international agreements are fundamentally broken, and demonstrate the costs of partisan polarization and presidential unilateralism. With a broken Senate, presidents are emboldened to act unilaterally, as the Congress is typically unable or unwilling to check the unilateral impulses of the executive. This situation has profound implications for US participation in international law, and more broadly, diplomacy. When US presidents act unilaterally, they often do so without domestic support—thus US participation in international law is less legitimate democratically. Unilateral actions also make for awfully weak commitments, and a weaker international legal regime, and US diplomats, as a result, have less influence when negotiating international law. This became quite apparent with President Trump's behavior, as he routinely undermined prior commitments made by the United States with brash rhetoric, often delivered by Twitter.

The undermining of basic norms, first by Obama and followed up by Trump, could have lasting impact on US participation in international law, and implies a significantly weaker international legal regime and US leadership of that regime, well into the future. The United States has failed to ratify numerous multilateral conventions that have been ratified by all but just a handful of states. It stands alone as the only country in the world not to have ratified the UN biodiversity convention, an incredibly important environmental treaty, or the Convention on the Rights of the Child. In addition, it remains outside the major conventions dealing with disability rights and women's rights, as well as the international bodies governing the trade of pesticides and hazardous chemicals, and UN bans on land mines and cluster munitions. The list is quite long, and, as a result, the United States cedes both its leadership and moral authority on these issues.

Mea Culpa

I have not always been so down on the politics of international agreements. My first book on the topic was largely upbeat. In *Treaty Politics and the Rise of Executive Agreements* (Krutz and Peake 2009), Glen Krutz and I argued that the rise in executive agreements we observed during the twentieth century largely resulted from a need for efficiency as the United States dealt with its expanding leadership role. While the politics of treaties were often partisan affairs involving rough-and-tumble politics, and presidents sometimes struggled to get treaties through the Senate due to the supermajority requirement, we were largely sanguine in our conclusions. The empirical record of the twentieth century suggested that such politics were part and parcel of a system of separation of powers that set up an "invitation to struggle" over the direction of US foreign policy (Corwin 1984).

While the rise of executive agreements during the twentieth century provided an opportunity for presidents to skirt the Senate treaty process, presidents, for the most part, did not abuse their power, but rather worked with Congress to protect it. When leaders in Congress complained or acted to rein in the president, presidents typically complied. In other words, the system seemed to function well. While commitment problems existed during the twentieth century, they were not as clear and obvious as we see today, and presidents still used Article II treaties to complete many of their most significant agreements. We discounted as alarmists those political scientists who pointed to executive agreements as part and parcel of the imperial presidency (e.g., Crenson and Ginsberg 2007). But the alarmists had valid concerns, and should not have been dismissed. If the institutional process that we described in *Treaty Politics* ever broke down, which it clearly has since we wrote the book, presidents could act unilaterally in direct opposition to most of the Congress. We set aside those concerns because they were not evident in the empirical record at the time. Now the concerns are validated by the recent record, and the results for separation of powers and US foreign policy are alarming.

A reassessment of the argument in *Treaty Politics* is required. The argument centered on the importance of institutional norms that developed over time, governing the separation of powers and the processing of international agreements. "Norms are standards of appropriate behavior and are an integral part of international and domestic politics and policies" (Panke and Petersohn 2017, 574). There is a vast literature on norms in international relations, much of it focusing on the role played by the United States, the only global hegemon, in policing appropriate behavior by states and upholding the liberal international order it helped build after World War Two. The United States' commitment problem certainly stresses these international norms. On the domestic politics side, for a separation of powers system to work effectively, the norms of "mutual tolerance" and "forbearance" are essential. Levitsky and Ziblatt (2018) write, "Two basic norms have preserved America's checks and balances in ways we have come to take for granted: mutual toleration, or the understanding that competing parties accept one another as legitimate rivals, and forbearance, or the idea that politicians should exercise restraint in deploying their institutional prerogatives." These norms have eroded over time, particularly since the end of the Cold War and the concomitant acceleration of partisan polarization. This erosion has proven disastrous for treaty politics.

Many of the criticisms of President Trump's foreign policies, for example, focus on how his policies and diplomatic style violated these international and institutional norms (e.g., Cohen 2019; Farrow 2018; Peake 2021). After all, President Trump's "America First" approach to foreign policy presented a direct challenge to the historical leadership role played by the United States. The Constitution established a singular executive, provisioning the presidency with significant authority in the creation and conduct of foreign and national security policy. To constrain the executive, the framers also set up an elaborate system of shared powers and checks and balances, so that other institutions, most notably the Congress, could check this singular executive.

Over time, however, the constitutional guardrails on presidential authority, particularly in foreign policy, have eroded, as Congress has delegated substantial additional authority to the executive. This is a broad trend in foreign policy, including in war powers, trade, agreement making, and even spending authority (Binder, Goldgeier, and Saunders 2020; Fisher 2000; Rudalevige 2005). The courts largely stayed on the sidelines during constitutional conflicts between the elected branches, particularly in foreign policy, and, when they did intervene, they typically sided with the executive (Fisher 2017). The constitutional checks on the executive are further weakened by extreme partisanship (Fallows 2017; Goldgeier and Saunders 2018; Schulz 2017). The trends documented in this book demonstrate that the problem extends to the politics of international agreements, which has led to dysfunctional diplomacy. While President Trump may have laid bare the problem, many of the trends documented in this book were initiated by President Obama.

The implications of the breakdown of norms and dysfunctional politics are serious. First and foremost, this is no way for a superpower to act. The United States is weaker because it is not able to fully participate in international law. As a result, it loses the moral high ground on a host of daunting global issues. Moreover, its commitments are weak because they are more likely to change following the next presidential election. The on-again, off-again behavior by US presidents on international commitments is not sustainable. Second, the trends noted here represent an erosion of democratic constraints on executive authority, given the lack of accountability provided by legislative participation in the process. Third, the constitutional process simply does not work. The treaty clause, with its supermajority requirement in the Senate, has proven to be unworkable under conditions of partisan polarization. Such was the case for several decades following the Civil War, another period of heightened partisan polarization. It is certainly the case now. These last two points are related. If the process in the Senate worked as it should, recent presidents might be more inclined to work with Congress on their international agreements.

Finally, we should question the wisdom of the framers in requiring a supermajority in the Senate to approve treaties. Given the equal representation afforded states of vastly different populations in the Senate, it is the "most malapportioned legislature in the world" (Lee and Oppenheimer 1999, 2). Thus, a minority of 34 senators representing less than 10 percent of the population can block a popular treaty (Dahl 2003; Hathaway 2008, 1310). The arithmetic carries over to the veto, as well, such that a similar minority can sustain a president's veto of a congressional effort to check his or her unilateral action. As Levinson (2006, 110) maintains, the treaty approval clause "is just one more assignment of a veto power to what may on occasion be the one-third-plus-one of senators representing a tiny fraction of the American polity." The supermajority requirement also caters to the political extremes (Hathaway 2008, 1310), which is exacerbated by increased partisan polarization, and explains why the United States sits outside of many of the world's most significant multilateral conventions.

Prospects for Change

How might functional politics in US diplomacy be restored? Going back to the process that worked somewhat effectively last century is unlikely to solve the problems identified in this book. While the use of treaties for many significant agreements was certainly better than what we see today—the complete absence of treaties or congressional input in favor of presidential unilateralism—the treaty clause still caused significant strain on the system and is partly why presidents came to rely so heavily on unilateral methods to complete their international agreements (Krutz and Peake 2009). The process relied too heavily on separation of powers norms of mutual tolerance and forbearance, which are notably absent in today's polarized politics. Reliance on such norms is a fool's errand, given the state of US politics today, and as demonstrated time and again during the Trump presidency (Peake 2021).

To address this question, we first should have some idea of how an effective process ought to work. In most democracies, executives are given the authority to negotiate treaties, but those agreements usually require simple legislative approval via the standard parliamentary process. In his review of constitutional provisions on treaty ratification, Mendez (2017, 91) found that "the overwhelming majority of constitutional systems require legislative approval of at least certain important, and often widely defined, categories of treaties," and that the typical process follows the standard legislative rules for legislation. Only three other constitutions include a single-chamber supermajority requirement for treaty ratification like the United States, including Micronesia, Philippines, and Iraq. Hathaway (2008) found similar results in her analysis of the treaty clauses in 183 constitutions that existed in 2007.[1] Clearly defining which types of treaties require legislative approval and which do not would be a great place to start in fixing the process in the United States. Mendez (2017) identifies a global trend in greater legislative control over treaty ratification, which in practice is precisely the opposite of what has occurred in the United States, given the dysfunction and presidential unilateralism described in this book.

The United States already has a bicameral approval process in place for some congressional-executive agreements which require statutory approval. While this represents less than 1 percent of executive agreements completed in the last two decades (Hathaway 2009), it is a process that could be more widely adopted for significant agreements. Trade agreements, for example, often require legislation to approve them given the fact that the agreements require changes in US law. Numerous important examples exist where presidents codified international law on a range of topics through the simpler legislative process, rather than the treaty process. The United States joined important international organizations through this process following World War Two, including the International Monetary Fund and the International Bank for Reconstruction and Development in the wake of the Bretton Woods Agreement; and several UN organizations, including the World Health Organization and the UN Educational, Scientific, and Cultural Organization (Hathaway 2008, 1300). This was a period of major change in international law, and while the United States signed and ratified several key treaties, numerous major agreements were ratified through the regular legislative process as well.

The bicameral approval process also affords a role for the House of Representatives. Only simple majorities in both chambers are required to approve the agreements, rather than the two-thirds required in the malapportioned Senate through the treaty clause. Thus, the process satisfies concerns related to democratic legitimacy (Levinson 2006, 111). One fix, then, as suggested by Hathaway (2008), is to use this process for almost all significant international agreements. While amending the Constitution to ditch the treaty clause is probably a nonstarter, given the power it affords smaller states and the unattainable ratification requirement of three-fourths of states, clear precedents exist for presidents to submit for bicameral approval pretty much any international agreement they would ordinarily submit as a treaty. Congress could legislate on the matter, requiring bicameral approval for new executive agreements in specific categories or for agreements that might ordinarily follow the Article II process.

The trick here would be determining which agreements should require legislative approval. It would be implausible to require all the hundreds of executive agreements completed annually to receive congressional approval. One starting place might be to focus on issues clearly covered by Article I of the Constitution, i.e., those powers that are clearly in the realm of Congress and the federal government. Today, presidents unilaterally complete a host of binding international agreements on matters that sit squarely in the realm of Article I. Congress should seek to reverse this trend and require bicameral approval for more of the important agreements that stem from Article I powers.

The Article II treaty process could be reserved for agreements that influence state laws, including tax and extradition treaties, thus addressing federalism concerns. Solemn security commitments, including new alliances (e.g., adding new members to NATO), might also be included, given their obvious importance and far-reaching significance, as well as other forms of agreements that were typical at the time of the Constitutional Convention. After all, when the treaty clause was written in 1787, treaties were typically limited to alliances, peace treaties, and treaties delineating boundaries. Since that time, however, "treaty making has come to encompass practically all areas in which national governments regulate" (Mendez 2017, 86–7). The Article II treaty process could be reserved for this narrower set of agreements. Finally, sole executive agreements could remain an option for agreements that are clearly within the realm of the president's Article II powers. Congress would need to play a significant oversight role, however, to ensure that sole executive agreements were limited to the president's plenary powers and did not violate existing statutes. Whatever process is worked out, it should emphasize congressional involvement to restore shared power. Not all agreements would require congressional approval. In fact, most so-called congressional-executive agreements could receive preauthorization in statute, but those statutes and the transparency surrounding agreement classification must improve for Congress to play its constitutionally prescribed role.

Even if the approval process were to remain largely unchanged, there are other less obtrusive changes that would improve the situation. Congressional participation in the process, even if it is indirect, requires an effective transparency regime.

Congress cannot, and has not, participated effectively in international agreements, largely owing to the failed transparency regime governing executive agreements. As Hathaway, *et al.* (2020) clearly demonstrate in their careful study of Case Act reporting documents over a nearly 30-year period, the current transparency regime simply does not work:

> The overall picture that emerges is one of dysfunction and non-accountability: there is reason to believe that the executive branch's reporting to Congress has been incomplete; the entire process is opaque to everyone involved, including executive branch officials and congressional staffers; and Congress is failing in its oversight role.
>
> *635*

The State Department (DOS) routinely fails to uphold statutory requirements to publish most executive agreements on its website and to report all executive agreements to Congress within 60 days of their entry into force. Moreover, the legal authority to complete agreements, also required in reports to Congress, is often tenuous or is based on vague references to Article II.[2] Late reporting has been a consistent problem since the Case Act and its various amendments were enacted in the 1970s.[3]

A new transparency regime would effectively facilitate congressional involvement and oversight into the international lawmaking process. Hathaway, *et al.* (2020) make two relatively modest suggestions to improve the situation and bring executive behavior more in line with the spirit of current legal requirements. First, all executive agreements should be centrally collected in a similar manner that the federal government collects new regulations in the *Federal Register* and then published in searchable digital media placed on the internet.[4] Much like regulations, executive agreements have the force of law, and it is unconscionable that legislators and the public cannot know what that law is due to an ineffective transparency regime. Moreover, full transparency is the necessary first requirement for the public and Congress to be able to hold the executive accountable for unilateral action on executive agreements. This will allow the public and interested civil society groups to alert Congress when there are concerns, facilitating congressional oversight. Second, Hathaway, *et al.* (2020) recommend that when publishing executive agreements, the government should be required to clearly cite the legal authority underpinning the agreement. The specific statute should be cited, and if the agreement is based entirely on the president's Article II powers, that should be clearly stated. Only then can the legal bases for executive agreements be properly assessed.

Another problem related to transparency is the confusion surrounding whether presidents intend to complete a treaty, a binding executive agreement, or a political commitment when negotiating significant international agreements. Such decisions by the president should be crystal clear from the start, widely reported in the press, and shared with Congress. If the executive intends to complete a binding international agreement, it should be required to report that intention to Congress. Even in the case of political commitments, which are a plenary power of the president, there ought to be a formal reporting mechanism, at least for the most significant agreements. Only then can Congress effectively participate in the process through oversight. While secrecy may be required in some cases, there are mechanisms already in place for the executive to share top-secret information with certain committees in Congress. The partisanship evident in the case of the Iran Nuclear Agreement could have been mitigated by transparency, as it might have precluded Republican senators from writing open letters to Iran demonstrating their ignorance as to the legally binding nature of executive agreements, when the president's intention all along was to complete a political commitment.

At the least, transparency on existing political commitments should be improved, as the current transparency regime on international agreements excludes them. Excluding political commitments from required reporting may provide incentives for the executive to complete nonbinding agreements to skirt transparency requirements and accountability, thus one fix would be to require the publication of significant or important political commitments once they are made, much like what is required for executive agreements (Hathaway, *et al.* 2020, 709).

Another important change, which would require significantly more effort, would be limiting delegations of executive authority on international agreements. While delegation is an important component of US government, when presidents abuse their powers because Congress is unable or unwilling to check them due to partisan polarization, the system breaks down. Many of the statutory delegations dealing with foreign policy were passed during the Cold War, when the United States was unified domestically in confronting the Soviet threat. With the end of the Cold War consensus, are such broad delegations of authority necessary? This is doubtful, and if Congress were able to effectively legislate on the matter, they probably would do so. That legislative vetoes are unconstitutional, in the wake of *INS v. Chadha* (1983), is a serious barrier to fixing this problem, as they would make for an obvious solution. Resolutions of disapproval, the current state of the art for legislative involvement, are unworkable, as the resulting presidential vetoes are easily sustained. In effect, they turn the Constitution's treaty clause on its head, such that just one-third plus one of the House or the Senate is needed to allow a president's agreement to go into effect. Moreover, presidents are likely to veto any new laws which limit their delegated authority, so passage would require large bipartisan majorities. Reversing past delegations of authority is probably implausible; however, Congress should tread carefully when considering any new delegations of authority in this realm, as they cannot rely on presidents to limit their own authority. As has already been stated, executive forbearance provides only cold comfort these days.

Enacting these changes would be daunting under ordinary circumstances. In our current situation of partisan polarization, the prospects for doing so are indeed dim. Broad bipartisan majorities would be required. If those are unattainable, and I would submit that they are, a president willing to sign laws limiting executive authority would be necessary. Perhaps a president, well steeped in the politics of the Senate, would understand the importance of congressional participation in the international agreement process. A president who had previously served as chair of the Senate Foreign Relations Committee (SFRC) might also be inclined to fix the broken system of treaty politics, as they are likely to understand the problem given their familiarity with it. The current moment, with President Biden, who previously chaired the SFRC, might be the lynchpin to seeing some improvements in the process. Such reform, however, would require Congress to take the initiative, as it is unlikely to come from the president. If there are enough members of Congress looking out for the institution's power—an important part of maintaining separation of powers—then perhaps members of Congress might seek reform.

After all, as Madison explained in *Federalist 51*:

> the great security against a gradual concentration of the several powers in the same department, consists in giving to those who administer each department the necessary constitutional means and personal motives to resist encroachments of the others . . . Ambition must be made to counteract ambition. The interest of the man must be connected with the constitutional rights of the place.

To fix the United States' dysfunctional diplomacy, Congress needs to authoritatively protect its rightful place in the process, as too much power has accrued to the executive. Congress has the means to do so, but the question is whether members of the institution are motivated to check the president's aggrandizement of their powers. In this polarized era, partisan ambitions obliterate the connections legislators have to the institution of Congress and, thus, their motivations to protect their role in the policymaking process, at least so far as international agreements go.

Concluding Thoughts

It is paradoxical that presidential unilateralism leads to weaker US diplomacy. Presumably, a powerful president free to conclude binding international agreements on their own, without intrusion by the Congress, has greater leeway to commit the United States to major obligations well into the future. At least that is how it looks at first glance. A more comprehensive examination of the process and politics of international agreements in recent years, accounting for both domestic and international politics, suggests that the opposite situation obtains. Instead, partisan polarization, which has led to dysfunction in the treaty process, has left presidents unable to legally bind the United States to major international agreements, making the US commitment problem even worse than it was last century. Dysfunctional diplomacy presents a major problem for the United States as it confronts major global problems.

Even in the wake of President Trump's electoral victory in 2016, partly attributable to his bold "America First" foreign policy agenda, the US public appears to prefer multilateralism and international engagement to solve major problems. Such an approach clearly fits with President Biden's approach to foreign policy. Numerous surveys indicate public opposition to isolationism and strong preferences for global engagement. But the public is also put off by unilateralism, both in terms of the United States acting alone and presidents acting without legislative support (Patrick 2019, 257). While the partisan polarization that infects Congress these days also impacts public opinion on foreign policy, with a growing divide between the parties among the public, there remains significant public consensus that the United States must engage with world partners to address major problems (Balz and Clement 2020; Smeltz, *et al.* 2020). Americans still largely support multilateralism, despite the voices of a vocal minority. The United States cannot solve the world's problems alone, whether those problems include the proliferation of weapons of mass destruction, the degradation of the environment, or stopping the next pandemic. Engaging with the world requires the United States to be able to forge lasting international agreements, something it has been unable to do for the last fifteen or so years.

Notes

1 Hathaway (2008) also found that the United States is one of only a handful of states that elevate treaties approved by only one chamber in a bicameral legislature to the same status as domestic law; the other states are Mexico and Tajikistan. Most states in her analysis require the same procedure for treaty approval as they do for domestic legislation.

2 Hathaway, *et al.* (2020), 637) find that less than 50 percent of the more than 5,000 cover memos they examined cite existing legal authority that expressly authorizes the executive to complete legally binding agreements. About one-fifth of these citations are arguably baseless.

3 In their article, Hathaway, *et al.* (2020), clearly lay out how the agreement classification process works in the DOS, referred to as the C-175 process. The article is an excellent source of information on what is a very opaque process.

4 While the *Federal Register* requirement for regulations requires their publication prior to going into effect, Hathaway, *et al.* (2020) indicate that Congress, in the case of most executive agreements, has been satisfied with reporting after an agreement is in force. For the sake of efficiency, they propose to keep after-the-fact reporting requirement for executive agreements intact, except in cases where Congress deems prior reporting is necessary, as it has done for agreements in several areas, including fisheries, nuclear cooperation agreements, and arms transfers.

REFERENCES

Abramowitz, Michael. 2008. "Democrats Attack Iraq Security Proposal." *Washington Post*, January 24: A09.

Ackerman, Bruce A., and David Golove. 1995. *Is NAFTA Constitutional?* Cambridge, MA: Harvard University Press.

Ackerman, Bruce A., and David Golove. 2015. "Can the Next President Repudiate Obama's Iran Agreement?" *The Atlantic*, September 10. www.theatlantic.com/politics/archive/2015/09/can-the-next-president-repudiate-obamas-iran-agreement/404587/, accessed March 24, 2022.

Adghirni, Samy, and Jonathan Tirone. 2022. "Biden's Hopes for an Iran Deal Fade Just When the World Needs Oil Most." *Bloomberg News*, May 12. www.bloomberg.com/news/articles/2022-05-12/iran-nuclear-talks-fizzle-just-when-markets-need-oil-the-most, accessed May 18, 2022.

Adler, David Gray. 2004. "The Law: Termination of the ABM Treaty and the Political Question Doctrine: Judicial Succor for Presidential Power." *Presidential Studies Quarterly* 34 (March): 154–66.

Aleem, Zeeshan. 2017. "We Asked Six Experts If Congress Could Stop Trump from Eliminating NAFTA." *Vox*, October 26. www.vox.com/policy-and-politics/2017/10/26/16505508/nafta-congress-block-trump-withdraw-trade-power, accessed June 18, 2021.

Almond, Roncevert Ganon. 2017. "U.S. Ratification of the Law of the Sea Convention: Measuring the raison d'état in the Trump era." *The Diplomat*, May 24, 2017. https://thediplomat.com/2017/05/u-s-ratification-of-the-law-of-the-sea-convention/, accessed January 26, 2022.

Alston, Philip. 1990. "U.S. Ratification of the Covenant on Economic, Social and Cultural Rights: The Need for an Entirely New Strategy." *American Journal of International Law* 84 (2): 365–93.

American Bar Association. 2022. "Convention on the Rights of Persons with Disabilities." American Bar Association website. www.americanbar.org/advocacy/governmental_legislative_work/priorities_policy/promoting_international_rule_law/conventionontherightsofpersonswithdisabilities/, accessed January 30, 2022.

Angelo, Mary Jane, Rebecca Bratspies, David Hunter, John Knox, Noah Sachs, and Sandra Zellmer. 2012. "Reclaiming Global Environmental Leadership: Why the United States Should Ratify Ten Pending Environmental Treaties." Center for Progressive Reform, White Paper #1201.

Arango, Tim, and Michael S. Schmidt. 2011. "Despite Difficult Talks, U.S. and Iraq Had Expected Some American Troops to Stay." *New York Times*, October 21. www.nytimes.com/2011/10/22/world/middleeast/united-states-and-iraq-had-not-expected-troops-would-have-to-leave.html, accessed February 21, 2022.

Arms Control Association. 2020. "Comprehensive Test Ban Treaty at a Glance." Fact Sheets and Briefs. www.armscontrol.org/factsheets/test-ban-treaty-at-a-glance, accessed February 13, 2022.

Auerswald, David, and Forrest Maltzman. 2003. "Policymaking through Advice and Consent: Treaty Consideration in the United States Senate." *Journal of Politics* 65 (November): 1097–1110.

Baker, Ross K. 2015. *Is Bipartisanship Dead? A Report from the Senate*. Boulder, CO: Paradigm.

Baldez, Lisa. 2014. *Defying Convention: US Resistance to the UN Treaty on Women's Rights*. New York: Cambridge University Press.

Balz, Dan, and Scott Clement. 2020. "Poll: Sharp Partisan Differences Now Exist on Foreign Policy, Views of American Exceptionalism." *Washington Post*, September 17. www.washingtonpost.com/politics/poll-foreign-policy-trump-democrats/2020/09/16/8e2d903e-f836-11ea-be57-d00bb9bc632d_story.html, accessed May 23, 2022.

Barnosky, Clara, Jane Sadler, Richard Yates, and Zachary Zimmerman. 2021. *Reversing Trump Environmental Rollbacks: A 100 Day Analysis on the Biden Administration's Reversals*. Berkeley Law School research report. www.law.berkeley.edu/wp-content/uploads/2021/05/Trump-Rollbacks-Report.pdf, accessed March 27, 2022.

Baron, Kevin. 2011. "Panetta: Iraq Has Agreed to Negotiate Extended U.S. Presence." *Stars and Stripes*, August 19. www.stripes.com/news/panetta-iraq-has-agreed-to-negotiate-extended-u-s-presence-1.152633, accessed February 21, 2022.

Bartlett, Jason, and Megan Ophel. 2021. "Sanctions by the Numbers: U.S. Secondary Sanctions." Center for New American Security, August 26. www.cnas.org/publications/reports/sanctions-by-the-numbers-u-s-secondary-sanctions, accessed March 24, 2022.

Behsudi, Adam. 2016. "Obama Puts Congress on Notice: TPP Is Coming." *Politico*, August 12. www.politico.com/story/2016/08/obama-congress-trade-warning-226952, accessed June 17, 2021.

Bellinger, John B., III. 2012. "Obama's Weakness on Treaties." *New York Times*, December 18. www.nytimes.com/2012/12/19/opinion/obamas-weakness-on-treaties.html, accessed May 4, 2022.

Bellinger, John B., III. 2019. "The Trump Administration's Approach to International Law and Courts: Are We Seeing a Turn for the Worse?" *Case Western Reserve Journal of International Law* 51 (7): 7–27.

Bennett, D. Scott, and Allan C. Stam III. 1996. "The Duration of Interstate Wars, 1816–1985." *American Political Science Review* 90 (2): 239–57.

Binder, Sarah, James Goldgeier, and Elizabeth N. Saunders. 2020. "The Imperial Presidency Is Alive and Well." *Foreign Affairs*, January 21. www.foreignaffairs.com/articles/2020-01-21/imperial-presidency-alive-and-well, accessed May 19, 2022.

Blanchfield, Luisa. 2015a. "The U.N. Convention on the Elimination of All Forms of Discrimination Against Women: Issues in the U.S. Ratification Debate." Congressional Research Service, CRS Report R40750. https://crsreports.congress.gov/product/pdf/R/R40750/26, accessed January 31, 2022.

Blanchfield, Luisa. 2015b. "The United Nations Convention on the Rights of the Child." Congressional Research Service, CRS Report R40484. https://crsreports.congress.gov/product/pdf/R/R40484/25, accessed January 30, 2022.

Blanchfield, Luisa and Cynthia Brown. 2015. "The United Nations Convention on the Rights of Persons with Disabilities: Issues in the U.S. Ratification Debate." Congressional Research Service, CRS Report R42749. https://fas.org/sgp/crs/misc/R42749.pdf, accessed January 30, 2022.

Bodansky, Daniel. 2016. "The Legal Character of the Paris Agreement." *Review of European, Comparative, and International Environmental Law* (2): 142–50.

Böller, Florian. 2022. "Brakeman or Booster: Presidents, Ideological Polarization, Reciprocity, and the Politics of US Arms Control." *International Politics* 59: 725–48.

Boockmann, Bernhard. 2006. "Partisan Politics and Treaty Ratification: The Acceptance of International Labour Organisation Conventions by Industrialized Democracies, 1960–1996." *European Journal of Political Research* 45: 153–80.

Borda, Aldo Z. 2022. "Ukraine War: What Is the Budapest Memorandum and Why Has Russia's Invasion Torn It Up?" *The Conversation*, March 2. https://theconversation.com/ukraine-war-what-is-the-budapest-memorandum-and-why-has-russias-invasion-torn-it-up-178184, accessed March 27, 2022.

Bradley, Curtis A., and Jack L. Goldsmith. 2018. "Presidential Control over International Law." *Harvard Law Review* 131 (5): 1203–97.

Brett, James T. 2021. "United States Could Be a Leader on Behalf of People with Disabilities Around the World." *Boston Globe*, November 22. www.bostonglobe.com/2021/11/22/opinion/united-states-can-be-leader-behalf-people-with-disabilities-around-world/, accessed February 11, 2022.

Brown, Chad P., and Douglas A. Irwin. 2018. "What Might a Trump Withdrawal from the World Trade Organization Mean for US Tariffs?" Policy Brief for the Peterson Institute for International Economics. www.piie.com/system/files/documents/pb18-23.pdf, accessed June 18, 2021.

Burns, William J. 2020. "Polarized Politics Has Infected American Diplomacy." *The Atlantic*, June 6. www.theatlantic.com/ideas/archive/2020/06/polarized-politics-has-infected-american-diplomacy/612778/, accessed May 9, 2022.

Busby, Josh. 2016. "The Paris Agreement: When Is a Treaty Not a Treaty?" *Duck of Minerva*, April 21. www.duckofminerva.com/2016/04/the-paris-agreement-when-is-a-treaty-not-a-treaty.html, accessed March 25, 2022.

Cadei, Emily. 2010a. "For GOP, a Cold War Is Not Hawk Enough." *CQ Weekly*, May 17, p. 1191.

Cadei, Emily. 2010b. "Ratification of New START Approved." *CQ Weekly*, December 27, p. 2943.

Canfil, Justin Key. 2020. "Trump's Nuclear Test Would Risk Everything to Gain Nothing." *War on the Rocks*, July 8. https://warontherocks.com/2020/07/trumps-nuclear-test-would-risk-everything-to-gain-nothing/, accessed February 13, 2020.

Cardin, Ben. 2016. "The South China Sea Is the Reason the United States Must Ratify UNCLOS." *Foreign Policy*, July 13. https://foreignpolicy.com/2016/07/13/the-south-china-sea-is-the-reason-the-united-states-must-ratify-unclos/, accessed January 26, 2022.

Caruson, Kiki, and Victoria A. Farrar-Myers. 2007. "Promoting the President's Foreign Policy Agenda: Presidential Use of Executive Agreements as Policy Vehicles." *Political Research Quarterly* 40 (December): 631–44.

Center for Arms Control and Non-Proliferation. 2011. "What Could Possibly be Wrong with Ratifying Nuclear Weapons Free Zones? Senator Kyl?" June 13. https://armscontrolcenter.org/what-could-possibly-be-wrong-with-ratifying-nuclear-weapons-free-zones-sen-kyl/, accessed February 13, 2022.

Cleves, Mario, William Gould, Roberto G. Gutierrez, and Yulia V. Marchenko. 2010. *An Introduction to Survival Analysis Using Stata*, 3rd ed. College Station, TX: Stata Press.

Cohen, Eliot A. 2019. "America's Long Goodbye: The Real Crisis of the Trump Era." *Foreign Affairs*, January/February. www.foreignaffairs.com/articles/united-states/long-term-disaster-trump-foreign-policy, accessed May 19, 2022.

Colin, Sebastian. 2016. "China, the US, and the Law of the Sea." *China Perspectives* 2: 57–62. https://doi.org/10.4000/chinaperspectives.6994, accessed May 4, 2022.

Congressional Research Service. 2013. "Persistent Organic Pollutants (POPs): Factsheet on Three International Agreements." CRS Report: RS22379, October 23.

Conrad, Courtenay R., and Emily Ritter. 2017. "A Trump Moratorium on International Treaties Could Roll Back Human Rights—Here at Home." Monkey Cage Blog, *Washington Post*, March 1. www.washingtonpost.com/news/monkey-cage/wp/2017/03/01/a-trump-moratorium-on-international-treaties-could-roll-back-human-rights-here-at-home/, accessed May 4, 2022.

Corwin, Edward S. 1984. *The President: Office and Powers, 1787–1984*. 5th ed. New York: New York University Press.

Cox, Ramsey. 2013. "Advocates Bash Corker's Opposition to Disability Treaty." *The Hill*, December 23. https://thehill.com/blogs/floor-action/senate/193910-advocates-bash-corkers-opposition-to-disability-treaty, accessed January 30, 2022.

Cox, Ramsey, and Julian Pecquet. 2012. "Senate Rejects United Nations Treaty for Disabled Rights in a 61–38 Vote." *The Hill*, December 4. https://thehill.com/policy/international/270831-senate-rejects-un-treaty-for-disabled-rights-in-vote, accessed January 28, 2022.

Craig, Tim, and Karen DeYoung. 2013. "Karzai Intends to Press Showdown with Obama over Security Pact, Aide Says." *Washington Post*, November 23. www.washingtonpost.com/world/asia_pacific/karzai-doesnt-trust-us-intends-to-press-showdown-with-obama-aide-says/2013/11/23/f32e9b08-546f-11e3-9ee6-2580086d8254_story.html, accessed May 4, 2022.

Crenson, Matthew, and Benjamin Ginsberg. 2007. *Presidential Power: Unchecked and Unbalanced*. New York: Norton.

Cronin, Patrick M., and Melodie Ha. 2018. "Toward a New Maritime Strategy in the South China Sea." *The Diplomat*, June 22. https://thediplomat.com/2018/06/toward-a-new-maritime-strategy-in-the-south-china-sea/, accessed January 26, 2022.

Da Vinha, Luis. 2019. "Competition, Conflict, and Conformity: Foreign Policy Making in the First Year of the Trump Presidency." *Presidential Studies Quarterly* 49 (2): 280–309.

Dahl, Robert A. 1950. *Congress and Foreign Policy*. New York: Harcourt Brace and Co.

Dahl, Robert A. 2003. *How Democratic Is the American Constitution?* 2nd ed. New Haven, CT: Yale University Press.

Dangerfield, Royden J. 1933. *In Defense of the Senate: A Study in Treaty Making*. Norman, OK: University of Oklahoma Press.

Darmawan, Aristyo Rizka. 2021. "The USA and UNCLOS: Time to Ratify." *Fulcrum*, February 22. https://fulcrum.sg/the-usa-and-unclos-time-to-ratify/, accessed January 26, 2022.

De Luce, Dan. 2022. "Biden Is Betting Republican Senators Lack Votes to Derail Revival of Iran Nuclear Deal." March 2, 2022. www.nbcnews.com/investigations/biden-betting-republican-senators-lack-votes-derail-revival-iran-nucle-rcna18174, accessed March 24, 2022.

Deibel, Terry L. 2002. "The Death of a Treaty." *Foreign Affairs* 81 (5): 142–61.

DeLaet, C. James, and James M. Scott. 2006. "Treaty-Making and Partisan Politics: Arms Control and the U.S. Senate, 1960–2001." *Foreign Policy Analysis* 2 (2): 177–200.

Demerjian, Karoun, and Steven Mufson. 2015. "Trick or Treaty? The Legal Question Hanging over the Paris Climate Change Conference," *Washington Post*, November 30. www.washingtonpost.com/news/powerpost/wp/2015/11/30/trick-or-treaty-the-legal-question-hanging-over-the-paris-climate-change-conference/, accessed March 25, 2022.

Desiderio, Andrew. 2022. "Congress Fires Its First Warning Shot on Biden's Iran Deal." *Politico*, May 5. www.politico.com/news/2022/05/05/congress-warning-biden-iran-deal-00030448, accessed May 13, 2022.

Dewar, Helen, and Kevin Sullivan. 1997. "Senate Republicans Call Kyoto Pact Dead." *Washington Post* December 11, A37. www.washingtonpost.com/wp-srv/inatl/longterm/climate/stories/clim121197b.htm, accessed February 11, 2022.

DeYoung, Karen. 2014. "Obama to Leave 9,800 U.S. Troops in Afghanistan," *Washington Post*, May 27. www.washingtonpost.com/world/national-security/obama-to-leave-9800-us-troops-in-afghanistan-senior-official-says/2014/05/27/57f37e72-e5b2-11e3-a86b-362fd5443d19_story.html, accessed May 4, 2022.

DeYoung, Karen, and Philip Rucker. 2017. "Trump Lays Groundwork to Change U.S. Role in the World." *Washington Post*, January 26. www.washingtonpost.com/world/national-security/trump-lays-groundwork-to-change-us-role-in-the-world/2017/01/26/812998e6-e404-11e6-a547-5fb9411d332c_story.html, accessed May 4, 2022.

Diab, Joseph. 1992. "United States Ratification of the American Convention on Human Rights." *Duke Journal of Comparative and International Law* 2 (2): 323–43.

Drezner, Daniel W. 2021. "The United States of Sanctions: The Use and Abuse of Economic Coercion." *Foreign Affairs* (September/October). www.foreignaffairs.com/articles/united-states/2021-08-24/united-states-sanctions, accessed March 31, 2022.

Dwyer, Colin. 2020. "Trump Administration Loosens Obama-Era Restrictions on Land Mine Use." *NPR*, January 21. www.npr.org/2020/01/31/801632498/trump-administration-loosens-obama-era-restrictions-on-land-mine-use, accessed February 12, 2022.

Englehart, Neil A., and Melissa K. Miller. 2014. "The CEDAW Effect: International Law's Impact on Women's Rights." *Journal of Human Rights* 13 (1): 22–47.

Eshbaugh-Soha, Matthew, and Jeffrey S. Peake. 2011. *Breaking through the Noise: Presidential Leadership, Public Opinion and the News Media*, Stanford, CA: Stanford University Press.

Estreicher, Samuel, and Steven Menashi. 2017. "Taking *Steel Seizure* Seriously: The Iran Nuclear Agreement and Separation of Powers." *Fordham Law Review* 86: 1199–1250.

Ewing, Philip, and Brian Naylor. 2017. "'We Are Not Nation Building Again,' Trump Says While Unveiling Afghanistan Strategy." *NPR*, August 21. www.npr.org/2017/08/21/545044232/trump-expected-to-order-4-000-more-troops-to-afghanistan, accessed February 21, 2022.

Fallows, James. 2017. "The Broken Check and Balance." *The Atlantic*, October 31. www.theatlantic.com/politics/archive/2017/10/republicans-in-congress-youve-got-another-chance/544466/, accessed May 19, 2022.

Farrow, Ronan. 2018. *War on Peace: The End of Diplomacy and the Decline of American Influence*. New York: Norton.

Finn, Peter. 2013. "NRA Opposed U.N. Arms Treaty." *Washington Post*, March 16. www.washingtonpost.com/world/national-security/us-nra-square-off-over-small-arms-treaty/2013/03/16/ae495dae-8d76-11e2-b63f-f53fb9f2fcb4_story.html, accessed February 13, 2022.

Fisher, Louis. 1985. *Constitutional Conflicts between Congress and the President*. Princeton, NJ: Princeton University Press.

Fisher, Louis. 2000. *Congressional Abdication on War and Spending*. College Station, TX: Texas A&M University Press.

Fisher, Louis. 2001. "Historical Background and Growth in International Agreements." Chapter 2 in U.S. Senate Committee on Foreign Relations, *Treaties and Other International Agreements: The Role of the United States Senate*, 106th Cong., 2d sess. Committee Print.

Fisher, Louis. 2017. *Supreme Court Expansion of Presidential Power: Unconstitutional Leanings*. Lawrence, KS: University Press of Kansas.

Fleming, Denna Frank. 1930. *Treaty Veto of the Senate*. New York: Putnam's.

Franck, Thomas M., and Edward Weisband. 1979. *Foreign Policy by Congress*. New York: Oxford University Press.

Friedrichs, Gordan M. 2022. "Conceptualizing the Effects of Polarization for US Foreign Policy Behavior in International Negotiations: Revisiting the Two-Level Game." *International Studies Review* 24 (1). https://doi.org/10.1093/isr/viac010.

Galbraith, Jean. 2019. "President Trump 'Unsigns,' Arms Trade Treaty After Requesting Its Return from the Senate." *American Journal of International Law* 113 (4): 813–17.

Glennon, Michael J. 1990. *Constitutional Diplomacy*. Princeton, NJ: Princeton University Press.

Goldenberg, Suzanne. 2015. "How US Negotiators Ensured Landmark Paris Climate Deal Was Republican-Proof." *The Guardian*, December 13. www.theguardian.com/us-news/2015/dec/13/climate-change-paris-deal-cop21-obama-administration-congress-republicans-environment, accessed March 25, 2022.

Goldgeier, James, and Elizabeth N. Saunders. 2018. "The Unconstrained Presidency: Checks and Balances Eroded Long before Trump." *Foreign Affairs*, September/October. www.foreignaffairs.com/articles/2018-08-13/unconstrained-presidency, accessed May 19, 2022.

Goldsmith, Jack. 2016. "The Contributions of the Obama Administration to the Practice and Theory of International Law." *Harvard International Law Journal* 57 (2): 455–73.

Goldsmith, Jack, and Lawrence Lessig. 2010. "Anti-Counterfeiting Agreement Raises Constitutional Concerns." *Washington Post*, March 26, A23.

Good, Chris. 2011. "When and Why Did Americans Turn Against the War in Afghanistan?" *The Atlantic*, June 22. www.theatlantic.com/politics/archive/2011/06/when-and-why-did-americans-turn-against-the-war-in-afghanistan/240880/, accessed February 23, 2022.

Gordon, Michael R. 2012. "In U.S. Exit from Iraq, Failed Efforts and Challenges." *New York Times*, September 22. www.nytimes.com/2012/09/23/world/middleeast/failed-efforts-of-americas-last-months-in-iraq.html?ref=statusofforcesagreement&_r=0, accessed February 21, 2022.

Gordon, Phillip H. 2018. "The Worst Deals Ever." *Foreign Affairs*, August 23. www.foreignaffairs.com/articles/2018-08-23/worst-deals-ever, accessed June 17, 2021.

Gostin, Lawrence O., Harold H. Koh, Michelle Williams, Margaret A. Hamburg, Georges Benjamin, William H. Foege, *et al.* 2020. "US Withdrawal from WHO Is Unlawful and Threatens Global and US Health and Security." *The Lancet* 396 (August 1): 293–5.

Groves, Steven. 2021. "Key Treaties that Threaten American Sovereignty, Which the Senate Must Oppose During the Biden Presidency." Heritage Foundation, January 28, Issue Brief No. 6045.

Haas, Richard. 2020. "Trump's Foreign Policy Doctrine? The Withdrawal Doctrine." *Washington Post*, May 27. www.washingtonpost.com/opinions/2020/05/27/trumps-foreign-policy-doctrine-withdrawal-doctrine/, accessed June 18, 2021.

Harrington, Ryan. 2016. "Understanding the 'Other' International Agreements." *Law Library Journal* 108: 343–60.

Hathaway, Oona A. 2008. "Treaties' End: The Past, Present and Future of International Lawmaking in the United States." *Yale Law Journal* 117 (7): 1236–1372.

Hathaway, Oona A. 2009. "Presidential Power over International Law: Restoring the Balance." *Yale Law Journal* 140: 210–12.

Hathaway, Oona A. 2020. "Reengaging on Treaties and Other International Agreements (Part 1): Donald Trump's Rejection of International Law." *Just Security*, October 2. www.justsecurity.org/72656/reengaging-on-treaties-and-other-international-agreements-part-i-president-donald-trumps-rejection-of-international-law/, accessed May 25, 2022.

Hathaway, Oona A., Curtis A. Bradley, and Jack L. Goldsmith. 2020. "The Failed Transparency Regime for Executive Agreements." *Harvard Law Review* 134 (2): 629–725.

Hathaway, Oona A., Curtis A. Bradley, and Jack L. Goldsmith. 2021. Executive Agreements Database. *Harvard Dataverse*, V1. https://dataverse.harvard.edu/dataverse/executiveagreements.

Hathaway, Oona A., and Amy Kapczynski. 2011. "Going It Alone: The Anti-Counterfeiting Trade Agreement as a Sole Executive Agreement." *Insights* 15 (23).

Hersman, Rebecca K. C. 2000. *Friends and Foes: How Congress and the President Really Make Foreign Policy*. Washington, DC: Brookings Institution.

Hollis, Duncan B. 2015. "Dealing with Iran: A Primer on the President's Options for a Nuclear Agreement." OpinioJuris, March 11. http://opiniojuris.org/2015/03/11/dealing-with-iran-a-primer-on-the-presidents-options-for-a-nuclear-agreement/, accessed March 24, 2022.

Hollis, Duncan B., and Joshua J. Newcomer. 2009. "'Political' Commitments and the Constitution." *Virginia Journal of International Law* 49 (3): 507–84.

Holt, W. Stull. 1933. *Treaties Defeated in the Senate*. Baltimore: Johns Hopkins University Press.

Homan, Patrick. 2016. *Getting to 67: The Post-Cold War Politics of Arms Control Treaty Ratification*. New York: Routledge.

Howell, William G. 2003. *Power without Persuasion: The Politics of Direct Presidential Action*. Princeton, NJ: Princeton University Press.

Howell, William G. 2005. "Unilateral Powers: A Brief Overview." *Presidential Studies Quarterly* 35 (3): 417–39.

Howell, William G., and Jon C. Pevehouse. 2007. *While Dangers Gather: Congressional Checks on Presidential War Powers*. Princeton, NJ: Princeton University Press.

Hudson, John, and Paul Sonne. 2020a. "Trump Administration Discussed Conducting First U.S. Nuclear Test in Decades." *Washington Post*, May 20. www.washingtonpost.com/national-security/trump-administration-discussed-conducting-first-us-nuclear-test-in-decades/2020/05/22/a805c904-9c5b-11ea-b60c-3be060a4f8e1_story.html, accessed February 13, 2022.

Hudson, John, and Paul Sonne. 2020b. "Trump Administration to Withdraw from Open Skies Treaty in a Further Erosion of Arms Control Pacts with Russia." *Washington Post*.

www.washingtonpost.com/national-security/2020/05/21/882d460a-9b68-11ea-b60c-3be060a4f8e1_story.html, accessed February 13, 2022.

Hudzik, Elizabeth M. 2010. "A Treaty on Thin Ice: Debunking the Arguments Against U.S. Ratification of the U.N. Convention on the Law of the Sea in a Time of Global Climate Crisis." *Washington University Global Studies Law Review* 9 (2): 353–70.

Jakes, Lara. 2022. "Iran Nuclear Deal Inches toward Revival, But Faces Critics in U.S." *New York Times,* February 17. www.nytimes.com/2022/02/17/us/politics/iran-nuclear-deal-biden.html, accessed March 24, 2022.

Jenkins, Bonnie Denise. 2021. "Remarks to the Conference on Facilitating the Entry into Force of the Comprehensive Nuclear Test Ban Treaty." U.S. Department of State. www.state.gov/remarks-to-the-conference-on-facilitating-the-entry-into-force-of-the-comprehensive-nuclear-test-ban-treaty/, accessed February 12, 2022.

Jett, Dennis. 2014. "Republicans are Blocking Ratification of Even the Most Reasonable International Treaties." *New Republic,* December 26. https://newrepublic.com/article/120646/ratification-arms-trade-treaty-others-blocked-republicans, accessed February 13, 2022.

Johnson, Loch K. 1984. *The Making of International Agreements: Congress Confronts the Executive.* New York: New York University Press.

Johnson, Robert David. 2006. *Congress and the Cold War.* New York: Cambridge University Press.

Jones, Benji. 2021. "Why the US Won't Join the Single Most Important Treaty to Protect Nature." *Vox,* May 20. www.vox.com/22434172/us-cbd-treaty-biological-diversity-nature-conservation, accessed February 12, 2022.

Jones, Christopher M., and Kevin P. Marsh. 2014. "The Odyssey of the Comprehensive Nuclear-Test-Ban Treaty." *Nonproliferation Review* 21 (2): 207–27.

Kanter, Arlene S. 2019. "Let's Try Again: Why the United States Should Ratify the United Nations Convention on the Rights of People with Disabilities." *Touro Law Review* 35: 301–43.

Katzman, Kenneth, and Paul K. Kerr. 2016. Iran Nuclear Agreement. CRS Report, R43333.

Kaufman, Natalie Hevener. 1990. *Human Rights Treaties and the Senate: A History of Opposition.* Chapel Hill: University of North Carolina Press.

Kaye, David. 2013. "Stealth Multilateralism." *Foreign Affairs* 92 (5): 113–24.

Keaten, Jamey. 2021. "Biden's US Revives Support for WHO, Reversing Trump Retreat." Associated Press, January 21. https://apnews.com/article/us-who-support-006ed181e016afa55d4cea30af236227, accessed June 18, 2021.

Kelley, Judith, and Jon Pevehouse. 2015 "An Opportunity Cost Theory of US Treaty Behavior." *International Studies Quarterly* 59 (3): 531–43.

Krepon, Michael, and Dan Caldwell, eds. 1991. *The Politics of Arms Control Treaty Ratification.* New York: St. Martin's.

Kreps, Sarah E., Elizabeth N. Saunders, and Kenneth A. Schultz. 2018. "The Ratification Premium: Hawks, Doves, and Arms Control." *World Politics* 70 (4): 479–514.

Krutz, Glen S., and Jeffrey S. Peake. 2006. "The Changing Nature of Presidential Policymaking on International Agreements." *Presidential Studies Quarterly* 36 (September): 391–409.

Krutz, Glen S., and Jeffrey S. Peake. 2009. *Treaty Politics and the Rise of Executive Agreements: International Commitments in a System of Shared Powers.* Ann Arbor, MI: University of Michigan Press.

Ku, Julian. 2013. "Does the US Congress Have to Approve the New WTO Agreement?" Opiniojuris Blog, September 12. http://opiniojuris.org/2013/12/09/u-s-congress-approve-new-wto-agreement-apparently/, accessed February 21, 2022.

Kupchan, Charles A., and Peter L. Trubowitz. 2007. "Dead Center: The Demise of Liberal Internationalism in the United States." *International Security* 32 (2): 7–44.

Lantis, Jeffrey S. 2009. *The Life and Death of International Treaties*. New York: Oxford University Press.

LeBlanc, Lawrence J. 1991. *The United States and the Genocide Convention*. Durham, NC: Duke University Press.

Lee, Frances. 2009. *Beyond Ideology: Politics, Principles and Partisanship in the U.S. Senate*. Chicago: University of Chicago Press.

Lee, Frances. 2015. "How Party Polarization Affects Governance." *Annual Review of Political Science* 18: 261–81.

Lee, Frances E., and Bruce I. Oppenheimer. 1999. *Sizing up the Senate: The Unequal Consequences of Equal Representation*. Chicago, IL: University of Chicago Press.

Levinson, Sanford. 2006. *Our Undemocratic Constitution*. New York: Oxford University Press.

Levitsky, Steven, and Daniel Ziblatt. 2018. "This Is How Democracies Die." *The Guardian*, January 21. www.theguardian.com/us-news/commentisfree/2018/jan/21/this-is-how-democracies-die, accessed May 19, 2022.

Levitz, Eric. 2021. "Why the World Can't Trust America on Climate." *New York Magazine*, April 22. https://nymag.com/intelligencer/2021/04/why-the-world-cant-trust-biden-on-climate-change.html, accessed March 27, 2022.

Lewis, Hope. 2009. "'New Human Rights: U.S. Ambivalence toward the International Economic and Social Rights Framework." Chapter 5 in *Bringing Human Rights Home*, ed. Cynthia Soohoo, Catherine Albisa, and Martha F. Davis. Philadelphia: University of Pennsylvania Press.

Lewis, Jeffrey B., Keith Poole, Howard Rosenthal, Adam Boche, Aaron Rudkin, and Luke Sonnet. 2022. *Voteview: Congressional Roll-Call Votes Database*. https://votev iew.com/.

Liechtenstein, Stephanie, and Nahal Toosi. 2022. "Iran Nuclear Talks Freeze Amid Terrorist Label Spat—Even with Deal on the Table." *Politico*, April 28. www.politico.eu/arti cle/iran-nuclear-talks-freeze-amid-terrorist-label-spat-even-with-deal-on-the-table/, accessed May 13, 2022.

Lindsay, James M. 1994. *Congress and the Politics of U.S. Foreign Policy*. Baltimore: Johns Hopkins University Press.

Linskey, Annie, Brady Dennis, and Maxine Joselow. 2021. "Biden Apologizes for Trump-Era Absence on Climate, Pitching a Robust Agenda that Is On Shaky Ground at Home." *Washington Post*, November 1. www.washingtonpost.com/climate-environment/2021/11/01/cop26-biden-glasgow-america/, accessed March 27, 2022.

Long, J. Scott, and Jeremy Freese. 2006. *Regression Models for Categorical Dependent Variables Using Stata*. 2nd ed. College Station, TX: STATA Press.

Lynch, Colum. 2021. "A Last-Ditch Effort to Save the Iran Deal." *Foreign Policy*, December 28. https://foreignpolicy.com/2021/12/28/iran-nuclear-deal-jcpoa-vienna-capabilities-biden/, accessed March 24, 2022.

McGrath, Matt. 2021. "US Rejoins Paris Accord: Biden's First Act Sets Tone for Ambitious Approach." *BBC News*, February 19. www.bbc.com/news/science-environment-55732 386, accessed March 27, 2022.

MacNaughton, Gillian, and Mariah McGill. 2012. "Economic and Social Rights in the United States: Implementation without Ratification." *Northeastern University Law Journal* 4 (2): 365–406.

Mann, Thomas E., and Norman J. Ornstein. 2012. *It's Even Worse than It Looks*. New York: Basic Books.

Margolis, Lawrence. 1986. *Executive Agreements and Presidential Power in Foreign Policy*. New York: Praeger.

Martin, Lisa L. 2000. *Democratic Commitments: Legislatures and International Cooperation*. Princeton, NJ: Princeton University Press.

Martin, Lisa L. 2005. "The President and International Commitments: Treaties as Signaling Devices." *Presidential Studies Quarterly* 35 (September): 440–65.

Mauldin, William. 2016. "Administration Officials Give up on Pacific Trade Deal." *Wall Street Journal*, November 11. www.wsj.com/articles/obama-administration-gives-up-on-pacific-trade-deal-1478895824, accessed June 17, 2021.

Mehchu, Ndjuoh. 2021. "No Child Left Behind? An Interest-Conversion Roadmap to the U.S. Ratification of the Convention on the Rights of the Child." *NYU Annual Survey of American Law* 76 (1): 1–32.

Mendez, Mario. 2017. "Constitutional Review of Treaties: Lessons for Comparative Constitutional Design and Practice." *International Journal of Constitutional Law* 15 (1): 84–109.

Meyer, Robinson. 2017. "Trump and the Paris Agreement: What Just Happened?" *The Atlantic*, August 4. www.theatlantic.com/science/archive/2017/08/trump-and-the-paris-agreement-what-just-happened/536040/, accessed March 25, 2022.

Milkis, Sidney M., and Michael Nelson. 1999. *The American Presidency: Origins and Development, 1776–1998*. Washington, DC: CQ Press.

Milner, Helen V. 1997. *Interests, Institutions, and Information: Domestic Politics and International Relations*. Princeton, NJ: Princeton University Press.

Morales, Margaret. 2014. "The Stockholm Convention." Duke University Superfund Research Center, August 12. https://sites.nicholas.duke.edu/superfund/the-stockholm-convention/.

Moravcsik, Andrew. 2005. "The Paradox of U.S. Human Rights Policy." Chapter 6 in *American Exceptionalism and Human Rights*, ed. Michael Ignatieff. Princeton, NJ: Princeton University Press.

Myrick, Rachel. 2021. "America Is Back, but for How Long? Political Polarization and the End of U.S. Credibility." *Foreign Affairs*, June 14. www.foreignaffairs.com/print/node/1127556, accessed May 4, 2022.

Mui, Ylan Q. 2017. "Withdrawal from Trans-Pacific Partnership Shifts U.S. Role in World Economy." *Washington Post*, January 23. www.washingtonpost.com/business/economy/withdrawal-from-trans-pacific-partnership-shifts-us-role-in-world-economy/2017/01/23/05720df6-e1a6-11e6-a453-19ec4b3d09ba_story.html, accessed June 17, 2021.

Naylor, Brian. 2021. "Biden Announces Plan in Glasgow to Help Poorer Countries with Climate Change." NPR, November 1. www.npr.org/2021/11/01/1050999296/biden-will-announce-a-plan-in-glasgow-to-help-poorer-countries-with-climate-chan, accessed March 27, 2022.

Nevitt, Mark. 2021. "China, Climate Change, Credibility: Why It's (Finally) Time for the US to Join the Law of the Sea Convention," *Just Security*, September 23. www.justsecurity.org/78335/china-climate-change-credibility-why-its-finally-time-for-the-us-to-join-the-law-of-the-sea-convention/, accessed January 27, 2022.

Nilsen, Ella, and Alex Ward. 2021. "Biden Wants to Convince the World America Can Be Trusted on Climate Change." *Vox*, April 21. www.vox.com/22395564/climate-change-biden-summit-world-pitch, accessed March 27, 2022.

Nyarko, Julian. 2019. "Giving the Treaty a Purpose: Comparable Durability of Treaties and Executive Agreements." *American Journal of International Law* 113 (1): 54–89.

O'Halloran, Sharyn. 1993. "Congress and Foreign Trade." Chapter 10 in *Congress Resurgent: Foreign and Defense Policy on Capitol Hill*, ed. Randall B. Ripley and James M. Lindsay, Ann Arbor, MI: University of Michigan Press.

Olabuenaga, Pablo Arocha. 2019. "Why the Arms Trade Treaty Matters—and Why It Matters that the US Is Walking Away." *Just Security*, May 8. www.justsecurity.org/63968/why-the-arms-trade-treaty-matters-and-why-it-matters-that-the-us-is-walking-away/, accessed February 13, 2022.

Panke, Diana, and Ulrich Petersohn. 2017. "President Donald J. Trump: An Agent of Norm Death." *International Journal* 72 (4): 572–79.

Parker, Ned, and Raheem Salman. 2011. "Iraq, U.S. to Discuss Extended Stay for Troops." *LA Times.com*, August 3. www.latimes.com/news/nationworld/world/la-fg-iraq-us-20110803,0,3545876.story, accessed February 21, 2022.

Patrick, Stewart. 2019. *The Sovereignty Wars: Reconciling America with the World*. Washington, DC: Brookings Institution.

Peake, Jeffrey S. 2016. "Agenda-Setting Dynamics and Differences Across Issues: Agenda Setting on the Economy and Foreign Policy," Chapter 17 in *Handbook of Public Policy Agenda Setting*, ed. Nikolaos Zahariadis. Cheltenham, UK: Edward Elgar.

Peake, Jeffrey S. 2017. "The Domestic Politics of U.S. Treaty Ratification: Bilateral Treaties from 1949–2012." *Foreign Policy Analysis* 13 (4): 832–53.

Peake, Jeffrey S. 2018. "Obama, Unilateral Diplomacy, and Iran: Treaties, Executive Agreements, and Political Commitments," Chapter 8 in *Presidential Leadership and National Security: The Obama Legacy*, ed. Richard S. Conley. Abingdon, UK: Routledge.

Peake, Jeffrey S. 2021. "Trump's Unorthodox Foreign Policy," Chapter 14 in *The Unorthodox Presidency of Donald J. Trump*, ed. Paul E. Rutledge and Chapman Rackaway. Lawrence, KS: University Press of Kansas.

Peake, Jeffrey S., and Glen S. Krutz. 2014. "President Barack Obama, Partisanship, and the Politics of International Agreements." *2014 Annuaire Français des Relations*, for English version: http://papers.ssrn.com/sol3/papers.cfm?abstract_id=2587806.

Peake, Jeffrey S., Glen S. Krutz, and Tyler Hughes. 2012. "President Obama, the Senate and the Polarized Politics of Treaty-Making." *Social Science Quarterly* 93 (5): 1295–1315.

Phillips, Dave. 2021. "U.S. Troops are Still Deploying to Iraq Even as Afghanistan War Ends." *New York Times*, September 21. www.nytimes.com/2021/09/20/us/troops-deploy-iraq.html, accessed February 21, 2022.

Pifer, Steven. 2021. "Saving the Open Skies Treaty." Brookings Institution, January 27. www.brookings.edu/blog/order-from-chaos/2021/01/27/saving-the-open-skies-treaty/, accessed February 13, 2022.

Powell, Catherine. 2012. "The Senate's Failure to Ratify the U.N. Disabilities Treaty Is a Shame." *New York Times*, December 7. www.nytimes.com/roomfordebate/2012/12/06/have-treaties-gone-out-of-style/the-senates-failure-to-ratify-the-un-disability-treaty-is-a-shame, accessed January 28, 2022.

Prins, Brandon C., and Bryan W. Marshall. 2009. "Senate Influence or Presidential Unilateralism? An Examination of Treaties and Executive Agreements from Theodore Roosevelt and George W. Bush." *Conflict Management and Peace Science* 26 (2): 191–208.

Putnam, Robert D. 1988. "Diplomacy and Domestic Politics: The Logic of Two-Level Games." *International Organization* 42 (3): 427–60.

Radio Free Europe. 2011. "U.S. Troops Look Set to Stay in Iraq Beyond 2011." June 10. www.rferl.org/content/iraq_us_troops_will_stay_after_years_end/24231366.html, accessed February 21, 2022.

Raju, Manu, and Burgess Everett. 2015. "How Cardin and Corker Clinched the Iran Deal." *Politico*, April 14. www.politico.com/story/2015/04/ben-cardin-bob-corker-iran-deal-116979, accessed March 24, 2022.

Ramsey, Michael D. 2016. "Evading the Treaty Power? The Constitutionality of Nonbinding Agreements." *Florida International University Law Review* 11 (2): 371–87.

Ramsey, Michael D. 2017. "The Treaty and Its Rivals." Chapter 7 in *Supreme Law of the Land? Debating the Contemporary Effects of Treaties within the United States Legal System*, ed. Gregory H. Fox, Paul R. Dubinsky, and Brad R. Roth. New York: Cambridge University Press.

Riedel, Bruce. 2020. "The U.N. Exposes the Limits of the Trump Peace Plan with the Taliban." Brookings Institution. www.brookings.edu/blog/order-from-chaos/2020/06/08/the-u-n-exposes-the-limits-of-the-trump-peace-plan-with-the-taliban/, accessed February 21, 2022.

Roberts, Dan. 2015. "John Kerry Warns Congress: Back Iran Nuclear Deal or Face Dire Consequences." *The Guardian*, July 28. www.theguardian.com/world/2015/jul/28/john-kerry-iran-nuclear-deal-congress-hearing, accessed June 14, 2021.

Rogin, Josh. 2010a. "White House Moving Ahead on New START with or without Kyle." *The Cable*, November 19, 2010. https://foreignpolicy.com/2010/11/19/white-house-moving-ahead-on-new-start-with-or-without-jon-kyl/, accessed June 14, 2021.

Rogin, Josh. 2010b. "New START Headed toward Ratification as GOP Support Grows." *The Cable*, December 20. https://foreignpolicy.com/2010/12/20/new-start-headed-toward-ratification-as-gop-support-grows/, accessed June 14, 2021.

Rogin, Josh. 2017. "The Trump Administration Cancels a Plan to Curtail the Use of Cluster Bombs." *Washington Post*, November 30. www.washingtonpost.com/news/josh-rogin/wp/2017/11/30/the-trump-administration-cancels-a-plan-to-curtail-the-use-of-cluster-bombs/, accessed May 4, 2022.

Rott, Nathan. 2021. "Biden Moves to Have U.S. Rejoin Climate Accord." *NPR*, January 20. www.npr.org/sections/inauguration-day-live-updates/2021/01/20/958923821/biden-moves-to-have-u-s-rejoin-climate-accord, accessed March 27, 2022.

Rubin, Alissa J. 2012. "With Pact, U.S. Agrees to Help Afghans for Years to Come." *New York Times*, April 22. www.nytimes.com/2012/04/23/world/asia/us-and-afghanistan-reach-partnership-agreement.html, accessed February 21, 2022.

Rudalevige, Andrew. 2005. *The New Imperial Presidency: Renewing Presidential Power after Watergate*. Ann Arbor, MI: University of Michigan Press.

Saunders, Sarah, and Mariah Meek. 2021. "America Can Lead Again in Global Conservation." *The Hill*, January 8. https://thehill.com/opinion/energy-environment/533139america-can-lead-again-in-global-conservation, accessed February 11, 2022.

Schlesinger, Arthur M., Jr. 1973. *The Imperial Presidency*. Boston: Houghton Mifflin.

Schor, Elana. 2010. "Obama Admin Steps up Pressure to Ratify Treaties on Toxics." *New York Times*, September 24. https://archive.nytimes.com/www.nytimes.com/gwire/2010/09/24/24greenwire-obama-admin-steps-up-pressure-to-ratify-treati-73636.html, accessed February 12, 2022.

Schultz, Kenneth A. 2017. "Perils of Polarization for U.S. Foreign Policy." *Washington Quarterly* 40 (4): 7–28.

Seligman, Lara and Robbie Gramer. 2019. "What Does the Demise of the INF Treaty Mean for Nuclear Arms Control?" *Foreign Policy*, August 2. https://foreignpolicy.com/2019/08/02/what-does-the-demise-of-the-i-n-f-treaty-mean-for-nuclear-arms-control-intermediate-nuclear-forces-new-start-strategic-arms-limitation-nonproliferation-trump-russia-arms-control-explained/, accessed February 13, 2022.

Setear, John K. 2002. "The President's Rational Choice of a Treaty's Preratification Pathway: Article II, Congressional-Executive Agreement, or Executive Agreement?" *Journal of Legal Studies* 31 (January): S5–S39.

Shanker, Thom, and Rod Nordland. 2013. "Pact May Extend U.S. Troops' Stay in Afghanistan." *New York Times*, November 20. www.nytimes.com/2013/11/21/world/asia/afghan-pact-kerry-apology-.html, accessed May 4, 2022.

Shanker, Thom, and David E. Sanger. 2001. "White House Wants to Bury Pact Banning Tests of Nuclear Arms." *New York Times*, July 7, A1. www.nytimes.com/2001/07/07/world/white-house-wants-to-bury-pact-banning-tests-of-nuclear-arms.html, accessed May 4, 2022.

Shaver, Lea. 2010. "The Inter-American Human Rights System." *Washington University Global Studies Law Review* 9 (4): 639–76.

Shull, Steven A. 2006. *Policy by Other Means: Alternative Adoption by Presidents*. College Station, TX: Texas A&M University Press.

Simmons, Beth A. 2009. *Mobilizing for Human Rights: International Law in Domestic Politics*. New York: Cambridge University Press.

Smeltz, Dina, Ivo Daalder, Karl Friedhoff, Craig Kafura, and Brendan Helm. 2020. "Divided We Stand: Democrats and Republicans Diverge on U.S. Foreign Policy." Chicago Council on Global Affairs, September 17. www.thechicagocouncil.org/research/public-opinion-survey/2020-chicago-council-survey, accessed May 23, 2022.

Spiro, Peter J. 2001. "Treaties, Executive Agreements, and Constitutional Method." *Texas Law Review* 79 (April): 961–1035.

Starks, Tim. 2010. "Treaty Sparks Concern Over Stockpile." *CQ Weekly*, April 19, p. 965.

Starks, Tim, and Frank Oliveri. 2010. "No Quick Action on Arms Accord." *CQ Weekly*, April 19, p. 964.

Stewart, David P. 2017. "Recent Trends in U.S. Treaty Implementation." Chapter 6 in *Supreme Law of the Land? Debating the Contemporary Effects of Treaties within the United States Legal System*, ed. Gregory H. Fox, Paul R. Dubinsky, and Brad R. Roth. New York: Cambridge University Press.

Stohl, Rachel. 2019. "Trump Unsigns the Arms Trade Treaty: How Did We Get Here?" *War on the Rocks*, May 3. https://warontherocks.com/2019/05/trump-unsigns-the-arms-trade-treaty-how-did-we-get-here/, accessed May 4, 2022.

Sullivan, Scott. 2017. "Treaties and the Trump Administration's Failure to Understand the Human Rights of National Security." *Just Security*. www.justsecurity.org/37825/dangerous-thinking-draft-order-multilateral-treaties-trump-administrations-failure-understand-human-rights-national-security/, accessed June 14, 2021.

Tananbaum, Duane. 1988. *The Bricker Amendment Controversy*. Ithaca, NY: Cornell University Press.

Tankersley, Jim. 2018. "Trump Signs Revised Korean Trade Deal." *New York Times*, September 24. www.nytimes.com/2018/09/24/us/politics/south-korea-trump-trade-deal.html, accessed February 21, 2022.

Taylor, Margaret L. 2019. "Senate Treatment of Select International Agreements, 2013–2018." *AJIL Unbound* 113 (1): 184–8.

Trubowitz, Peter, and Peter Harris. 2019. "The End of the American Century? Slow Erosion of the Domestic Sources of Usable Power." *International Affairs* 95 (3): 619–39.

Trubowitz, Peter, and Nicole Mellow. 2011. "Foreign Policy, Bipartisanship, and the Paradox of Post-September 11 America." *International Politics* 48: 164–87.

U.S. Senate Committee on Foreign Relations. 2001. *Treaties and Other International Agreements: The Role of the United States Senate*. 106th Cong., 2d sess. Committee Print.

Wallner, James I. 2020. *The Death of Deliberation: Gridlock and the Politics of Effort in the United States Senate*. Lanham, MD: Lexington Books.

Walt, Stephen M. 2019. "America's Polarization Is a Foreign Policy Problem, Too." *Foreign Policy*, March 11. https://foreignpolicy.com/2019/03/11/americas-polarization-is-a-,foreign-policy-problem-too/, accessed May 9, 2022.

Welna, David, and Colin Dwyer. 2020. "U.S. Signs Peace Deal with Taliban After Nearly 2 Decades of War in Afghanistan." *NPR*, February 29. www.npr.org/2020/02/29/810537586/u-s-signs-peace-deal-with-taliban-after-nearly-2-decades-of-war-in-afghanistan, accessed February 21, 2022.

Welsh, Teresa. 2015. "Corker to Kerry: 'You've been Fleeced' on Iran Deal." *U.S. News and World Report*, July 23. www.usnews.com/news/articles/2015/07/23/corker-to-kerry-youve-been-fleeced-on-iran-deal, accessed March 24, 2022.

Weybrecht, Matthew. 2015. "State Department Affirms That Iran Deal Is Only Political Commitment." Lawfare, November 28. www.lawfareblog.com/state-department-affirms-iran-deal-only-political-commitment, accessed March 25, 2022.

Whitlock, Craig, and Glenn Kessler. 2010. "Senators: Sign Treaty to Ban Land Mines." *Democrat-Gazette*, May 9. www.nwaonline.com/news/2010/may/09/senators-sign-treaty-ban-land-mines-20100509/, accessed February 13, 2022.

Wong, Kristina, and Sean Lengell. 2012. "DeMint: The Law of Sea Treaty Now Dead." *Washington Times*, July 16. www.washingtontimes.com/news/2012/jul/16/demint-says-law-sea-treaty-now-dead/, accessed January 26, 2022.

Worland, Justin. 2019. "Donald Trump Called Climate Change a Hoax. Now He's Awkwardly Boasting about Fighting It." *Time*, July 8. https://time.com/5622374/donald-trump-climate-change-hoax-event/, accessed May 15, 2022.

Wright, Austin. 2012. "Law of the Sea Treaty Sinks in the Senate." *Politico*, July 16. www.politico.com/story/2012/07/law-of-the-sea-treaty-sinks-in-senate-078568, accessed January 27, 2022.

Wright, Robin. 2019. "What Will Follow Trump's Canceled Strike on Iran?" *New Yorker*, June 21. www.newyorker.com/magazine/2019/07/01/what-will-follow-trumps-cancelled-strike-on-iran, accessed March 24, 2022.

Yen, Jerry H. 2013. "Persistent Organic Pollutants (POPs): Fact Sheet on Three International Agreements." Congressional Research Service, CRS Report RS22379. https://crsreports.congress.gov/product/pdf/RS/RS22379/22, accessed May 10, 2022.

INDEX

Note: Page numbers in *italics* indicate figures and in **bold** indicate tables on the corresponding pages.

For Product Safety Concerns and Information please contact our EU
representative GPSR@taylorandfrancis.com
Taylor & Francis Verlag GmbH, Kaufingerstraße 24, 80331 München, Germany

www.ingramcontent.com/pod-product-compliance
Ingram Content Group UK Ltd.
Pitfield, Milton Keynes, MK11 3LW, UK
UKHW022355190926
475702UK00015B/2307

9780367429775